YOUNG THUGS

YOUNG THUGS

Inside the Dangerous World of Canadian Street Gangs

MICHAEL C. CHETTLEBURGH

HarperCollins*PublishersLtd*

Young Thugs
© 2007 by Michael C. Chettleburgh. All rights reserved.

Published by HarperCollins Publishers Ltd

First Edition

No part of this book may be used or reproduced in any manner whatsoever without the prior written permission of the publisher, except in the case of brief quotations embodied in reviews.

HarperCollins books may be purchased for educational, business, or sales promotional use through our Special Markets Department.

HarperCollins Publishers Ltd
2 Bloor Street East, 20th Floor
Toronto, Ontario, Canada
M4W 1A8

www.harpercollins.ca

Street-gang distribution map (page 23) reprinted with permission from CISC (Criminal Intelligence Service Canada), originally published in CISC's *2006 Annual Report on Organized Crime in Canada.*

Library and Archives Canada Cataloguing in Publication

Chettleburgh, Michael C.
Young thugs: inside the dangerous world of Canadian street gangs / Michael C. Chettleburgh.

ISBN-13: 978-0-00-200839-6
ISBN-10: 0-00-200839-4

1. Gangs—Canada. 2. Juvenile delinquents—Canada. I. Title.

HV6439.C3C43 2007 364.106'60971 C2007-900621-3

HC 9 8 7 6 5 4 3 2 1

Printed and bound in the United States
Set in Minion
Design by Sharon Kish

For Robin and Chelsea

CONTENTS

FOREWORD

Young Thugs: Inside the Dangerous World of Canadian Street Gangs provides a comprehensive portrait of the emerging Canadian street-gang problem. Broad in scope and containing poignant stories of the outcome of gang activity, *Young Thugs* is both descriptive (highlighting the extent of street gangs in Canada and the lure of the gang for young people) and prescriptive (setting out an intelligent approach that we should all embrace to stem what appears to be a problem on the rise). If you care about keeping your children safe from gangs, you should take the time to read this book.

As a thirty-one-year police veteran and as someone who has spent his entire career dealing with gangs and the resulting epidemic in the world's street-gang capital, Los Angeles, I can say without hesitation that this book is a timely one. Over the past five years I have had the pleasure of travelling to many cities in Canada to share my street-gang insights with police agencies, community groups, parents and others. Because gang rivalries are increasingly rearing their ugly head, I know that anxiety about street gangs is high, hence the demand for my expertise. With the greatest respect intended to my many Canadian friends, however, the challenge is that most Canadians really don't know a lot about the street-gang organism. In writing *Young Thugs,* Michael Chettleburgh, whom I have gotten to know well during my time in Canada, has made a significant contribution to helping others understand gangs at a time when Canada needs it most.

One of the key strengths of *Young Thugs* is its honest and intelligent appraisal of what is driving some youth to street gangs. Blaming the United States, the media or lazy youth is the easy way out, and Chettleburgh does not fall victim to these convenient and simplistic excuses. Rather, he demonstrates, as I have confirmed over the decades, that street gangs are a product of Canada's doing—root causes such as poverty, insufficient parenting, racism, flawed government decisions, and many more. Understanding street gangs and their lure to young people is important, but more so is recognizing what a country like Canada can do to slow their growth and prevent youth from joining in the first place. It is in this respect that *Young Thugs* shows its greatest merit. Chettleburgh argues that a balanced approach is necessary to prevent the growth of gangs, and he is absolutely correct. Heavy-handed police suppression alone will not solve the street-gang problem, nor will other "get tough" sanctions of the criminal justice system. For proof you need only look at the worsening gang situation in my country, one that shows no signs of abatement. Prevention, early intervention, effective parenting and real opportunities for young people hold the key, and Chettleburgh's insights in this regard distinguish *Young Thugs* as some of the best thinking on street gangs in North America.

Despite his no-nonsense critique of the status quo and recent government moves on the issue of street gangs, Chettleburgh remains optimistic. In this respect his book, while dealing with a serious subject indeed, offers us many rays of hope. As he eloquently suggests, what Canada suffers from is not a problem with street gangs, but one of people's lack of willingness to act. So perhaps the problem with gangs is not so intractable, because Canadians—and people from every other country, for that matter—have the power to change the way they act and address, in an intelligent fashion, the causes of street gangsterism.

Young Thugs is a passionate analysis of the Canadian street-gang situation, and it's no wonder, as Chettleburgh is one of the country's most enthusiastic advocates of youth-crime prevention. What distinguishes him from others who have written on this topic, and what makes this book so unique, is that he is neither cop, academic nor government policymaker. Chettleburgh's work in the area of gangs has taken him to all of these domains, however, and his diversity of experience is reflected in *Young Thugs,* a practical and objective treatment of the street-gang issue. *Young Thugs* informs, and should inspire you too to take concrete action against street gangs. After all, our children deserve, and now require, nothing less.

Tony "Pac-Man" Moreno, author of *Lessons from a Gang Cop* and
31-year veteran officer with the Los Angeles Police Department

INTRODUCTION

How the Murder of Two Innocent Teenagers Sparked a War on Street Gangs

Anyone who has taken an adult training program of any kind knows that in virtually every class a skeptic will surface to challenge either the expertise of the trainer or the content of the program, or sometimes both. In January 2003 I helped the Ottawa Police Service (OPS) obtain a small grant from the Ontario Solicitor General's office, under their Proceeds of Crime Funding Initiative, to develop and implement a street-gang training program for front-line patrol officers and other specialized OPS personnel.

At that time, memories of the violent 1995 murder of seventeen-year-old Sylvain Leduc at the hands of the Ace Crew street gang were still fresh in Ottawa's collective consciousness, and a troubling rise in gang activity was evident on the street. Since I had been acting as a consultant to the OPS since 1995 on various youth-crime-prevention projects, including a major one that sought in part to address gang issues, my expertise in youth crime and street gangs was welcome on a small planning committee that became known as Project Gang Training. Joining me were Detective Sergeant Patrick Lowell, twenty-eight-year veteran Detective Sergeant Ken Doyle of the Major Crimes unit, and the force's tireless youth intervention coordinator, a civilian member of the service, Louise Logue. Funds in hand, we set about designing a one-day program that would sensitize OPS members to the characteristics of street gangs and gang communication and give them tips on informant development, court preparation and officer safety, among other things.

Knowing that cops as trainees are generally a suspicious lot, inclined to trust only other police personnel who are more experienced or battle-ready, we decided to hire as program leader the world's foremost street-gang expert, Tony Moreno of the Los Angeles Police Department, who led the LAPD's career criminal–gangs unit. Hiring Moreno as a trainer was like hiring Wayne Gretzky in the prime of his career to teach young NHL hockey players in the early stages of theirs. So deep is Tony's knowledge about street gangs and gang psychology that there is simply no one better to learn from. Moreno had worked gangs for twenty-eight years in the most gang-infested areas of Los Angeles: South Central, Hollingbeck, Rampart, Watts, 18th Street, Compton. He toiled sixty-plus-hour weeks in a city with tens of thousands of street-gang members, a city where violence was the number-one cause of death for people under thirty-five. He was known as "Pac-Man" Moreno, a nickname bestowed upon him by South Central gangsters; his reputation and yellow police car inspired the character played by Sean Penn in the movie *Colors.*

The program was designed and training groups were assembled over two months, each consisting of thirty to forty officers, most of them with three to eight years of service experience. After establishing his impressive credentials, Moreno prefaced each discussion by saying that the most dangerous young gangster in L.A. was no different from the most dangerous young gangster in Ottawa—both were equally capable of extreme violence and harm. The difference, he stated, was only in the number of gangsters in each city. Moreno then delivered an engaging and fact-filled six-hour program, complete with disturbing anecdotes and stunning visual props: gang-violence footage, pictures of local gang tattoos and graffiti, prison intake X-rays of gangsters' anal cavities showing concealed hunting knives and other contraband. His presentation was supported by a lecture from the OPS's two-person gang unit describing the local scene and active gangs like the Ledbury Banff Crips, West Side Boys and Greely Crew Xtreme. The program was then capped by Lowell's grisly narrative of the murder of Leduc (more on this in Chapter 2), which was meant to reiterate the point that there were indeed street gangs in the nation's capital, that they were dangerous, and that front-line officers needed to be prepared.

We asked attendees to comment on the quality of the content, the presenter's knowledge and the value of the material for their role as front-line officers. The response to the program, as measured by more than 250 evaluation forms, was excellent across every dimension. However, every time the program was offered, a skeptic would emerge and try to undermine the goodwill we had established. He (it was always a male) was the one who sat at the back of the room, arms folded over his chest, frequently peering at his watch, the supplied notepaper in front of him devoid of a solitary nugget of the information that had been shared during the day. He was the cop who—never raising his hand according to standard classroom protocol—tendered every comment with a dismissive "Yeah, but . . ." in a direct challenge to the experts in front of him. Since I was the paid program consultant, these same individuals sought me out afterwards to give me their two cents' worth. Ottawa wasn't Los Angeles, they insisted. The Ace Crew murder, while serious, wasn't anything more than an isolated incident that was not emblematic of a gang problem in the city. Young people were simply not as dangerous as adults, and there was no evidence that street gangs were a national issue. Accusing me of sensationalizing a nonexistent problem for my own profit, they suggested that the money could have been better spent on advanced patrol training or ammunition for the ever-popular shooting range.

These critiques were disturbing, especially coming from cops who worked the streets of Canada's fourth-largest city, several of whom had been around when Leduc was brutalized. I knew, as did my fellow training program organizers, that this was not an isolated problem. The Ace Crew case demonstrated the violence of which street gangs were capable, and we knew of other, no less disturbing cases elsewhere in the country, such as the 1995 gangland-style murder of thirteen-year-old "Beeper" Spence in Winnipeg at the hands of Aboriginal street-gang members. The signs that portended a growing Canadian street-gang problem were evident: continued inner-city decay; changing demographics; cuts to community programs and recreation opportunities for youth; increased demand for and availability of emerging street drugs such as crack cocaine, ecstasy and methamphetamine; a new Youth Criminal Justice Act that prevented police from making formal charges except for serious offences; massive court backlogs; flawed deportation processes; and lack of political leadership on the issue, among other things.

It was perhaps during those confrontations with the skeptics that the seed for this book was planted. If front-line cops in a major Canadian police service could be relatively ignorant and skeptical about the existence of a street-gang problem, then surely our politicians and government policymakers would be even more so. And if this was the case, then everyday Canadians would be all but completely innocent of knowledge about street gangs. Without the engagement of ordinary citizens, I surmised, our country's response to street gangs would remain passive, and Canadians, especially young ones, would therefore be in some danger. Fascinated as I was by the complexities of the street-gang phenomenon, which has existed for centuries, and as the parent of a four-year-old daughter who might someday be exposed to street gangs in some way, I knew I needed to invest much more of my time in the issue and, through the written word, attempt to reach a much broader audience.

To sound the clarion call about gangs, I knew I needed to examine gang crimes, since they demonstrate the psychology of gangs and their youthful combatants in stark contrast to non-gang-involved youngsters. But for me to truly make a case for a call to action on gangs, good data was required, the absence of which was striking. Unlike our American neighbours, who had studied youth gangsters for more than two decades, by 2002 the Canadian government had done little to examine the issue. In 1993 the Solicitor General of Canada produced the report *Youth Gangs on Youth Gangs*, a perfunctory look at involvement in gangs through the eyes of youth. Later, in 1994, the Solicitor General of Canada and Justice Canada sponsored a national conference on youth violence and gangs, hosted by the Federation of Canadian Municipalities, which produced the report *Youth Violence and Youth Gangs: Responding to Community Concerns.*

Five years later, in 1999, the Solicitor General of Canada convened the much-ballyhooed National Forum on Youth Gangs, a two-day series of discussions moderated by Chief Pierre Sangollo of the Sainte-Julie, Quebec, Police Service. Recognizing that the problem of street gangs was not new, the forum's organizers nonetheless admitted that "not a great deal" of Canadian research had been done on the issue. With only 120 participants, including police service members, researchers, government personnel and 16 representatives of various youth groups, the forum resulted in only a handful of anemic recommendations. There was no call for more information, and no call for more practical research to quantify and qualify a problem that everyone recognized as existing, but of which none knew the exact dimensions.

With the successful Project Gang Training behind me, I approached the office of the Solicitor General of Canada in late 2002 and pitched the idea of conducting the first-ever national survey of police agencies on the issue of youth gangs. The purpose of the proposed survey was to assess the extent and characteristics of the youth-gang problem in communities throughout Canada, as reported by law enforcement agencies. With good data, I argued, the government could obtain a baseline upon which to measure changes over time in the level of youth-gang activity reported by police, and would thus enhance their ability to develop effective prevention and suppression strategies. The Solicitor General agreed and commissioned me to implement the 2002 Canadian Police Survey on Youth Gangs, which was sent out in February 2003 to 349 police chiefs and RCMP detachment commanders across the country.

At first I was concerned that police chiefs might face a dilemma with the survey. On the one hand, admitting to a youth-gang problem in their jurisdiction would give credence to their constant pleas for more resources for front-line police. On the other hand, what police chief would want to admit to a contentious crime problem—young "gangbangers"—on his or her watch? But my fears were unfounded, and the response to the survey was overwhelming. More than 264 agencies completed the survey, a response rate of 76 percent. Of the respondents, 63 police services indicated that youth gangs were indeed active in their jurisdiction in 2002, with the earliest years of onset being 1975 and 1979 in Surrey and Vancouver, British Columbia, respectively. Together, in all 63 jurisdictions—in large gang hot spots such as Toronto, Montreal, Ottawa and Vancouver, and in small cities such as Petrolia, Tisdale, Moose Jaw, Tofino, Amherst and points in between—an estimated 434 active youth gangs were reported, encompassing more than 7,000 members under the age of twenty-one. Surprisingly, on a per capita basis Saskatchewan had the highest concentration in the country—1.34 gang members per 1,000 people—more than four times the concentration in Ontario (0.29 per 1,000).

Depending on your point of view, a group of seven thousand criminals in a country of more than thirty million people may not impress. If someone told you that seven thousand home services contractors in Canada deal only in cash to evade taxes, you might be only mildly surprised. However, if someone told you that seven thousand suspected al Qaeda terrorists or Paul Bernardo–like sexual predators are among us, that would grab your attention. But what about those seven thousand youth-gang members? In 2002, with so little public awareness of youth gangs beyond the Leduc and Spence murders, the number alone failed to give perspective.

The additional survey findings, however, gave a context for that number. Of the seven thousand estimated youth-gang members, about half were under the age of eighteen. Nationally, 6 percent of youth-gang members were thought to be young females. Demolishing the stereotype of black-only gangsters, respondents reported that youth gangs were ethnically diverse, with the largest proportion of gang members being African-Canadian (25 percent), followed closely by First Nations members (21 percent) and Caucasians (18 percent), among other groups. Moreover, the findings suggested that not only were gang members diverse, so too were their gangs. More than a third of youth gangs comprised members from two or more racial or ethnic groups, again challenging long-held stereotypes of youth gangs as being organized along ethnic lines.

This "hybrid" gang composition versus the stereotypical inner-city gang was one thing, but what about their activities? Here, a troubling picture emerged. Nationally, 72 percent of gang members were thought to be involved in assaults, followed by drug trafficking (69 percent), break and enter (68 percent), vandalism (64 percent) and intimidation/extortion (56 percent). The police respondents indicated that youth-gang members were involved in more than a third of street sales of marijuana and almost a fifth of sales of crack cocaine. Perhaps most disturbingly, almost half of the respondents believed that the youth gangs had established relationships with organized crime syndicates, including Asian and outlaw motorcycle groups. Youth gangs standing together with mentors and business partners in organized crime gave mass to that abstract seven thousand.

Armed with what I believed was striking and important data—certainly sufficient to mobilize government and community leaders to address a material problem—I submitted my final report to the Solicitor General's office in December 2003. After my findings were reviewed by the policy advisors, I was told that a report would be produced and released, via a national press conference, sometime in the spring of 2004. Pleased that the information would receive the attention it deserved, I went about other projects, including editing and publishing Tony Moreno's acclaimed book, *Lessons from a Gang Cop.*

By April 2004, however, I had learned that the promises of a government policy official can be readily trumped by the department's communications people, whose job it is to "manage issues" in the manner most favourable to the sitting minister (at the time, Solicitor General Wayne

Easter). Following standard procedure, government publications are sent to the communications department for review before being officially approved for release. Immediately upon their receipt of the gang report, the backpedalling began. What business did I have asking questions about the ethnic composition of gangs? How could this be considered a national survey when only police agencies were invited to participate? While the questions were ostensibly meant to undermine my credibility and attack the survey methodology, one department official, on condition of anonymity, confirmed my suspicion: the questions were a Trojan horse disguising the day's political agenda.

The late winter and early spring of 2004 were a tumultuous time in Canadian politics. As Canada's twenty-first prime minister, Paul Martin opened his first session of Parliament on February 2, 2004. He needed a new mandate to affirm his newly acquired authority, and talk of a spring election hung in the Ottawa air. Unfortunately for Martin, eight days into the new parliamentary session, Auditor General Sheila Fraser released her annual report, the contents of which launched the Liberal "sponsorship scandal." What was initially seen to be an easy romp for Martin and his party into a fourth straight majority government was a hotly contested affair from the moment the governor general dissolved the House of Commons on May 23.

The real objections to the national gang survey then became apparent. I was told that the department's communication officials were concerned about the impact of the resulting data if it were released prior to the June 28 election. The results could reflect poorly on the Liberal government, since it had been in power for the past eleven years, a period in which the youth gang problem had been allowed to grow. Others were concerned that the report would lead to demands for money by Toronto's black activists and western Canadian Aboriginal leaders, who had been dealing with violent gangs for years. Apparently to avoid any "I told you so" grousing during an election campaign, the gang survey report was put on the back burner.

On June 3, 2004, Allan Wood, a reporter for the *National Post* who had managed to obtain a copy of the report, ran a story on the front page titled "Youth Gang 'Epidemic' Predicted." Its secondary heading read, "Almost half of gang members linked to organized crime, federal report says." With the cat out of the bag, I awaited a reaction, not sure of what to expect. But except for one or two letters to the editor in the *Post,* the response was negligible.

This lack of public interest and debate on the subject after the report's release was edifying. It seemed that, unless people were affected in some way by street-gang crime, it was considered an "elsewhere" problem. To be sure, residents of Toronto's Jane–Finch, Ottawa's Banff and Ledbury, and Vancouver's Main and Hastings areas knew they had street gangs, but residents of those cities who steered clear of the "troubled" neighbourhoods remained largely ignorant of how dangerous the gangs were, and the creeping growth of their brutality.

But things changed forever in 2005, the "year of the gun" in Toronto, and street gangs were thrust into public consciousness as never before. The city had seventy-eight homicides in 2005, just ten short of the record high of 1991. The fact that a majority of the victims (fifty-two) died by gunfire drove the issue of gangs to the very top of Toronto's dog-eared complaints list, which includes commuting times, crumbling roads, increasing property taxes, aggressive panhandlers and urban decay, among others. When Toronto-centric media conglomerates began to pay attention, the gangs issue engendered an official "public outcry" for the first time. Despite similar dramatic gunplay in other Canadian cities that same year—including Vancouver, Winnipeg and Montreal—Toronto became "ground zero" for street gangs.

The manner in which the street-gang issue morphed into a public crisis, and the response of our political leaders, deserves special analysis. From January 1 to November 17, 2005, forty-seven people were killed by gunfire in Toronto. Throughout the year, community leaders pressed the municipal, provincial and federal governments to join them in dealing with the spiralling gang issue. However, their prescriptions were sometimes at odds with one another, a situation not helped by the inability of the black community, intimidated by gangs, to help themselves by stepping forward as witnesses to dozens of crimes. The forty-seven murders produced no outcry, nor were they enough to make government officials descend upon Toronto, money and legislative changes in hand, to pledge a get-tough approach to gangs. More than one grizzled major-crimes or gang-unit cop has whispered to me over the years, with typical gruff directness, "As long as gangsters are shooting other gangsters, no one is gonna give a fuck."

Malcolm Gladwell, in his thought-provoking book *The Tipping Point*, defines that social phenomenon as the moment of critical mass. I contend that the brazen murder of Amon Beckles on November 18, 2005—Toronto's forty-eighth gun death of the year—was our country's tipping point for street gangs. Beckles, just eighteen years old, was at Toronto West Seventh-Day Adventist Church in Etobicoke to attend the funeral of a friend, seventeen-year-old Jamal Michael Hemmings, who had been shot in a gang-related incident. As Beckles was taking a cigarette break outside, three or more men, one brandishing a semi-automatic weapon, opened fire on him, and he died soon afterwards.

The murder of Beckles, who police said had been a potential material witness to the gun slaying of Hemmings, rattled Toronto and galvanized politicians through its sheer audacity. Clichéd phrases—"Toronto has lost its innocence" and "Toronto the good is now Toronto the bad"—made the rounds, as if hollow words were sufficient to describe the depths to which the street gangs had descended. Fingers pointed everywhere, looking for the cause of Toronto's street-gang problem. Looking at one symptom rather than the whole disease, Mayor David Miller suggested the U.S. was exporting its problem of violence to the streets of Toronto. Others blamed Canada's immigration policies that allowed Jamaicans into our country, along with their alleged propensity for violence. Rexdale rapper Jelleestone, who had made a CD called *The Hood Is Here,* stated on CBC Radio that gangs were caused by none other than Brian Mulroney.

Eight days after Beckles's murder, Paul Martin's minority government fell and the thirty-ninth general election campaign began. So did the race for the hearts and minds of Canadians, especially Torontonians, who were concerned about gangs. Currying favour in vote-rich, Liberal-friendly Toronto, Paul Martin promised a ban on handguns if re-elected. Money was promised to police services for more front-line officers to deal with gangs, and to provincial court systems for more Crown attorneys to process a growing backlog of cases. New proposals were floated by the Left, the Right and all points between on the political spectrum for tougher mandatory minimum sentences for gun crimes. Stephen Harper, soon to become our twenty-second prime minister, unveiled a $100-million-a-year crime package that included provisions for youth as young as fourteen to be tried as adults for serious crimes. Martin countered by proposing tougher border patrol initiatives to stem the tide of smuggled guns. Largely as an afterthought urged by social scientists and left-leaning community activists, these get-tough suppression proposals were augmented by talk of soon-to-be-financed early intervention and prevention measures to address the root causes of gang involvement.

Long on proposed initiatives but short on concrete plans, Canada's shock-and-awe war on street gangs was thus announced; more ordinance was to be deployed against the issue than in the past twenty years combined. But escalating political pronouncements cannot be equated with public outcry. That would finally come when, on October 10 and December 26, 2005, respectively, seventeen-year-old Philippe Haiart of Winnipeg and fifteen-year-old Jane Creba of Toronto were caught in the crossfire of gang disputes and died on downtown city streets. Two gang-related homicides of innocent teenagers did what dozens before across the country could not do: rally public engagement in the fight against street gangs.

:::

We live in a culture of fear in which we compound our worries beyond reason. If cancer or mad cow disease doesn't kill you, then the avian flu pandemic (always just around the corner) will. If you don't die in a fiery jetliner crash at the hands of terrorists, then you will surely die of a massive heart attack because of your impending morbid obesity.

This book is designed not to scare, but rather to inform. It would be easy, and highly manipulative, to play to people's fears about marauding gangsters shooting innocent Canadians on busy city streets, notwithstanding the reality of the tragic Haiart and Creba deaths. On the issue of street gangs I could become a purveyor of fear. Playing to people's insecurities to drive my own agenda, I could publicly declare that street gangs are an epidemic and young gangsters a cancerous scourge, imploring governments to take every possible action to suppress and incarcerate them. But vending fear is not what I am about, nor is it the purpose of this book. Yes, street gangs have demonstrated time and time again that they can be dangerous organisms and that their members display an appalling proclivity to do harm. The gang-related murders of Leduc, Spence, Haiart and Creba, to name only a few, make us recoil in indignation, but these deaths, however wanton and tragic, do not an epidemic make.

Our country is at an important crossroads with street gangs and their young members. Now that fragile public and political awareness finally exists, the moves we make during the next ten years will be crucial to avoiding what could easily become a street-gang epidemic. Make no mistake about it: we can choose to short-circuit a brewing gang epidemic or we can be party to its fermenting. What is required now, and what this book is about, is a critical examination of the street-gang organism—what is it, how it works and what is it about gangs that attracts thousands of young Canadians. The tragic stories that I tell and the discussions that follow are here to cast a spotlight on the inner workings and grim realities of the modern Canadian street gang. It is a daunting exercise, but nonetheless a useful one, for it will show us much about the roots of brutality and the nature of the intoxicating pull of gangs. By exposing their fundamental DNA, we can implement prevention and suppression strategies that actually work, rather than simply mollify fearful residents with ill-conceived get-tough approaches that have failed time and time again.

We need look no further afield than the United States, which, I contend, is indeed gripped by a street-gang epidemic. According to the National Youth Gang Center, part of the U.S. Department of Justice, it is estimated that in 2004 youth gangs were active in more than 2,900 American cities with a population of 2,500 or more. It is also estimated that approximately 760,000 gang members and 24,000 gangs were active in the United States during that same year. In the past twenty-five years, the U.S. Department of Justice estimated, more than 70 percent of all murders in big American cities were gang related.

In 1980, though, the U.S. Department of Justice had reported only 2,000 gangs, comprising some 100,000 members. In twenty-four years Americans experienced a 660 percent increase in youth gang membership. As the American example illustrates, once gangs take root in a community, they can proliferate rapidly. But the interesting story-behind-the-story is what U.S. politicians and law enforcement officials did about it. They spent buckets of money in the fight against gangs, financing gang intelligence and geo-mapping information systems, supporting aggressive suppression programs such as street sweeps and zero-tolerance curfews, and increasing front-line police deployment by creating a whole new breed of law enforcement officer, the gang cop. Under programs such as Operation Safe Streets, Operation Hardcore and Community Resources Against Street Hoodlums, U.S. law enforcers threw a lot of money at the gang problem.

But the money has produced, at best, superficial results. The problem has grown so bad that the FBI has all but publicly announced that gang violence, not foreign terrorists, is now their number-one priority. America's annual $100 billion investment in their criminal justice system pleases law-and-order zealots, but increasing investments have not correlated with lower crime, especially gang-related crime, or decreased the community's fear of crime. While it would be convenient to blame America's fascination with guns—all 250-plus million of them—that would be a gross oversimplification of how gangs develop and transmute. Deeper societal problems such as poverty, which does correlate with increased crime, have been given short shrift. Today many agree that when it comes to U.S. gangs, get-tough approaches have failed.

What can we, as Canadians, learn from America's long-running battle with street gangs? Can we leverage ourselves by avoiding their many mistakes and expanding on their successes, and take a different path? Can we, Janus-like, employ well-conceived approaches that balance the need to suppress gang activity, seeded long ago, while preventing the formation of new street gangs tomorrow? Can the flurry of recent Canadian anti-gang proposals have a meaningful impact on our street-gang situation? Can we, as a populace, take responsibility for the creation of our own gang problem and work together to stem the rise of Canadian street gangs?

The short answer to these questions is yes, if we make intelligent choices. We don't have a problem with gangs or a problem with guns. What we have is a problem with people—and their lack of willingness to act. This book provides the longer answer needed to achieve success in what is one of our country's most challenging criminal justice issues ever.

PART I:
The Lure of the Street Gang

1: INNOCENCE LOST

How Street Gangs Have Taken Root in Canada

My desire to join a gang was kindled in Ottawa in the spring of 1977. Just shy of my twelfth birthday, I witnessed a fight in which a young man's jaw was broken by a stiff right cross in front of a slew of cheering bystanders. It was not the episode of violence per se that stoked my aspirations. For most people, witnessing an act of violence both attracts and repels, the latter because of the uniquely human trait of empathy. It was the environment in which the fight took place that spoke to me, and eventually that set me on a course of gang involvement that would consume two years of my life, from age seventeen until I finally smartened up, just after my nineteenth birthday.

The youthful combatants, intent on spilling each other's blood after several months of thrusting, parrying and escalating aggression, were surrounded by members of their gangs, who were goading them on to settle the score. The elemental "us versus them" nature of the confrontation appealed to my almost-adolescent self, as did the ready dispensation of street justice, devoid of the strictures of regular society. The two warriors, although engaged in a one-on-one battle with a sworn enemy, were fighting for a higher purpose: their own crew and its reputation, or "street cred." Most of the members of both gangs had left home long ago, some as young as fifteen or sixteen, to join their new "family" and adopt its colours, further its aims of power, learn its modes of communication, and make some money. Freed from neglectful fathers, doting mothers and the confines of the education system, they were able to pursue their individual dreams of money, power and status, all within the protective fold of the gang, where fellow members always watch your back.

Even at that young age I could see that gang members had an undeniable swagger, reinforced by the fear they instilled in some and the adoration they provoked in others, especially (as I was told) young women, who would freely share their bodies in the hope that they would be invited to join that unique subculture and all that it offered. The sense of camaraderie and common purpose; the private unity of the pack; the rebellious nature of their enterprise; the sanctioned, testosterone-stimulated aggression; the freedom from parental influence; the opportunity to make it big; the girls and the sex were an intoxicating mix. I knew that someday I wanted to join the gang.

Back then (and today as well), gaining entry into a gang was not automatic. You had to be deemed worthy and of value to the gang in order to justify their investment in you of trust and training. All gang members had to have a shared sense of teamwork, a desire to defer to the collective in pursuing group goals and achievements. Some were chosen for their propensity for violence; others for their ability to stir up the muck. Some were selected for their ability to defend the gang; others for their smarts and generalist skills. I fit into the last category, and five years later I was invited to join, in the summer of 1982, while I was toiling as a part-time gas jockey for the princely sum of $3.50 an hour.

I considered the invitation carefully over a few weeks. As it was for other young men my age, the restlessness of adolescence was palpable. I saw gang life as a heroic (and acceptable) rite of passage into manhood, a test of my ability to make it on my own, away from a caring but demanding father whom I referred to derisively as "the old man." Socially awkward, sometimes shy and rarely feeling understood, I was often teased by others for being the son of the "spic" mother with the thick accent. I thought that gang life would provide an opportunity to instantly remake my persona, to create a "new me" in order to escape the ordinary old one, which, from my restricted adolescent perch, seemed to lack a compelling purpose. Gang life was appealing also in that it offered immediate escape from a loveless, tension-filled and somewhat dysfunctional middle-class family life. My mother and father had an obvious and perpetual hatred for each other; it was clear they were sticking together only because of the kids. They spoke to each other only during fights over the finances, slept on different floors of the house and lobbied me and my older sister for support in their predicament. They were united only by surname and a shared responsibility for crushing 18.5 percent mortgage payments.

The gang would also provide me with the option of escaping high school. There I performed well when I felt engaged by the subject matter, but my boredom with the routine and an unquenched wanderlust earned me regular detentions and visits to the principal's office, especially from corpulent Mr. Gerow, whose chalkboard I often festooned with Bic pen–issued spitballs. Entrepreneurial by nature, I found the money possibilities of gang life compelling too, especially since I wanted to prove to myself and to the old man that I could do better—much better—than the income from what seemed to me an uninspired and soul-crushing existence as a federal civil servant. To me, life in the gang was an elite pursuit, one that would clearly distinguish me from most others my age. I saw a way out of the humdrum life I envisioned that would consist of finishing high school, going to college, getting a job, settling down, having kids and buying a station wagon. My emerging oppositional and deviant side was gaining control of me, and my disaffection was peaking for everyday life as a regular teenager in a regular community with regular opportunities. I relished the opportunity to join the gang and thus expedite my journey towards becoming a man of power and distinction.

The gang subculture, fundamentally meritorious in nature, represented to me an appealing game of high stakes. While the odds of success were slim and the risks of failure undeniably high, I knew that if I put in my time and did good work for the gang, I would someday distinguish myself and ascend to a position of leadership and eminence, where the rewards were quite possibly limitless.

An invitation to join the gang was one thing; to be accepted was entirely another. The few friends who had gone before me into the way of the gang prepared me for what was to happen next. I could expect to be challenged by established gang members and their leaders through physical intimidation and fights. I could expect to have my strength tested, along with my masculinity and my ability to protect both myself and the gang. If I passed those initial tests, then I would be subjected to a humiliating alcohol-fuelled initiation challenge, which I had to accept without protest, as all the others before me had done. Then, and only then, would I be formally accepted and entrusted with the task of strengthening the gang and forwarding its purpose. I was told that even after that initial acceptance, however, challenges to my worthiness and loyalty to the gang would never cease. Would I continue to fight? Would I continue to defend the honour of the gang and its standing relative to others? Would I continue to hone my own unique blend of skills that would benefit the gang? Would I continue to embrace the lifestyle, including consuming more booze than I wanted and chasing the gang "sluts," to prove I was a man through and through? Would I remain always a team player?

My resolve never wavered and my commitment to the gang remained steadfast. At seventeen, after running the gauntlet of fights, initiation rituals and endless tests of worthiness, I was accepted into a fellowship of kindred spirits, my fellow gang members, to play the game in our unique tournament of life.

WHAT IS A STREET GANG?

While their existence has gained broader public awareness only in the past half-decade in Canada, street gangs composed largely of young people have been a part of civilized society for hundreds of years. Gangs are clearly not a creation of twentieth-century American culture, however much some wish to believe they are.

The word *thug* derives from the Hindi *thag*—in the Indo-Aryan language Marathi, *thak* (a cheat, swindler)—and dates back to approximately 1200 CE. It referred to gangs of young murderers and robbers who strangled their victims. Descriptions of urban life in England in the fourteenth and fifteenth centuries note the mayhem that street gangs were responsible for, including theft, extortion and rape. Gangs that went by names such as the Mims, the Hectors, the Bugles and the Dead Boys "found amusement in breaking windows, demolishing taverns and assaulting the watch . . . and fought pitched battles among themselves dressed with coloured ribbons to distinguish the different factions."[1] France was also home to such gangs in the Middle Ages, as was Germany in the seventeenth and eighteenth centuries.

Street gangs, composed largely of new European immigrants struggling to find their way in early-nineteenth-century America, took root in the United States around 1820, with the Forty Thieves gang claiming turf in the Five Points district of lower Manhattan. This gang later spurred the creation of rivals such as the Plug-Uglies, the Dusters, the Bowery Boys and the Kerryonians, as portrayed in Martin Scorsese's 2002 film *Gangs of New York.* The Toronto Police Service Museum archives show that gangs were a significant city problem in the 1850s and 1860s, after a massive wave of Protestant and Roman Catholic Irish immigrants fled the great potato famine of 1845, bringing with them sectarian violence. The rapid growth of street gangs in Chicago in the late 1800s and early 1900s has also been well documented. Street gangs seem to be simply part of the human condition.

That street gangs have existed for hundreds of years, and will no doubt exist for hundreds more, troubles many people, especially those who have vowed to eradicate them. The spike in gang activity in Canada over the past five years has come with a set of fundamental questions: What defines a street gang and a street-gang member? Who are Canadian street-gang members? Where do street-gang members live? How did they become involved? And, perhaps most troubling, why did they get involved in the first place?

What defines *gang* generally, and *street gang* specifically, varies across Canada. Indeed, definitions vary throughout the world, since gangs, or "criminal organizations," come in many forms. Besides street gangs, there are youth gangs, organized-crime gangs, drug gangs, terrorist gangs and prison gangs, among others. Most gang experts would agree that the attributes of a gang, irrespective of its stripe, would include that it

- consists of a static or fluid organization, network or collective
- possesses identifiable leadership or a leadership structure
- associates on a continuous basis
- has as a main purpose or activity the facilitation or commission of a variety of offences planned or undertaken to generate material benefits or financial gain
- has the potential for violence or intimidation to facilitate its criminal activities
- consists of three or more members

According to these attributes, a street gang looks a lot like an organized-crime group such as an outlaw biker organization, but they are different animals. I would therefore distinguish street gangs from these more "traditional" groups by adding that they

- identify with a particular geographic area (territory, or turf)
- largely feature individuals under the age of twenty-eight

- have a fluid leadership structure and member participation
- may display common colours, insignia and communication patterns (for example, hand signs, codes, graffiti)
- are less sophisticated in terms of organizational structure, rules of conduct and nature of criminal activities

Several Canadian police agencies define a street gang simply as "a self-formed group of juveniles and/or young adults interacting with each other, who engage in a range of criminal behaviour . . . it may be loosely or well organized with established rules of conduct." I would further distinguish street gangs from "youth" street gangs by adding that the latter, generally speaking, consist of members under the age of twenty-one.

With these definitions, one might think it easy to define a street-gang member. However, there is no national consensus or government-mandated definition in this country. While it varies from one jurisdiction to another, police generally require that, before they "profile" individuals as street-gang members and enter them into a database, that the person must have been directly or indirectly involved in a gang-motivated crime and must meet at least two of the following additional criteria:

- reliable source information attesting to gang affiliation
- directly observed association with other gang members
- individual acknowledgement of gang association or involvement
- physical evidence proving gang affiliation
- previous court findings (including sworn testimony) that person is a gang member
- signs or symbols of gang identification or paraphernalia (name, turf, colours, signs, symbols and/or distinctive dress, tattoos, rituals or graffiti)

The more criteria a police agency chooses to satisfy, the fewer individuals they will define as gang members, and vice versa, which is why it is difficult to get an accurate accounting of how many street-gang members there actually are in Canada. This is not just an academic conundrum but also a practical one, as it complicates the process of allocating resources to a problem that is difficult to pin down. Just as important, the lack of consensus as to what defines a street-gang member masks the fact that not all street-gang members are the same; there can be no apples-to-apples comparisons. A fringe "wannabe" in one jurisdiction and a violent "shot caller" in another may both be considered street-gang members, but they are not the same breed of gangster. And the lack of a clear definition allows for some unfortunate politicking: some police agencies may purposely over- or underestimate the size of their street-gang problem—to get more resources or to satisfy citizens they are doing a good job—by manipulating the definition accordingly.

The questions of the who and the where are much less vexing. As I noted in the Introduction, findings from my 2002 national gang survey highlighted the cross-Canada and multi-ethnic composition of Canada's estimated 7,000-plus young (under eighteen) gangsters. Regional differences in gang composition are demonstrated in the data as well, with Asian gangs dominating on the West Coast, Aboriginals in the Prairie provinces, and African-Canadians in central Canada. Despite the widely held view that street-gang members align along ethnic lines (for example, all black or all Asian), data showed that gangs are increasingly hybrid in nature. This means that, more and more, they are multi-ethnic in composition; they are involved in every conceivable criminal activity that produces money; they do not display the typical characteristics of traditional street gangs (such as displaying colours, which today attracts unwanted attention); and their members display fluid affiliations, sometimes belonging to more than one gang.

Street-gang members exist in most provinces in Canada, with the highest per capita concentrations being in the western provinces, which speaks to the growing problem of young Aboriginal gang involvement. According to the 2002 youth gang survey, these are the top twenty Canadian cities by number of gang members:

City	**# of Gang Members**	**# of Gangs**	**Principal Racial/ Ethnic Composition**
Toronto	1,100	62	African-Canadian
Brampton	960	30	East Indian/Pakistani
Saskatoon	580	11	Aboriginal
Vancouver	550	35	Asian
Montreal	500	20	African-Canadian
Edmonton	300	20	Aboriginal

Regina	275	1	Aboriginal
Ottawa	250	15	African-Canadian
York Region	200	20	African-Canadian
Hamilton	200	3	African-Canadian
London	175	10	African-Canadian
Burnaby	150	28	Asian
Oshawa	125	11	African-Canadian
Winnipeg	100[2]	4	Aboriginal
Victoria	100	4	Caucasian/White
Surrey	75	15	Asian
Thunder Bay	50	3	Aboriginal
Brandon	40	2	Aboriginal
Windsor	40	2	Latino/Hispanic
New Westminster	40	7	Asian
TOTAL	**5,810**	**303**	

If these numbers are recast according to the per capita concentration of gang members in the cities where gang members are active, a different picture emerges, with Saskatoon having the highest concentration of young gangsters in the country. The top twenty cities by youth-gang member concentration are as follows:

City	**Per Capita**
Saskatoon	2.57
Regina	1.42
Brandon	0.98
Brampton	0.97
Burnaby	0.77
New Westminster	0.74
Toronto	0.44
Thunder Bay	0.41
London	0.40
Victoria	0.35
Edmonton	0.32
Ottawa	0.31
Hamilton	0.30

Vancouver	0.28
York Region	0.25
Oshawa	0.23
Surrey	0.22
Winnipeg	0.15
Montreal	0.15
Windsor	0.13

This snapshot of young street-gang members, taken in 2002, will soon be replaced by new data from a similar survey I will be conducting for the federal Department of Justice. I have no doubt that this picture will change—for the worse. Indeed, in the 2006 annual report of the Criminal Intelligence Service Canada (CISC), *Organized Crime in Canada,* the CISC estimated that there were 11,000 street-gang members and associates in Canada, located in every province except Prince Edward Island and Newfoundland and Labrador, as well as in the Northwest Territories. A map of the CISC's findings looks like this:

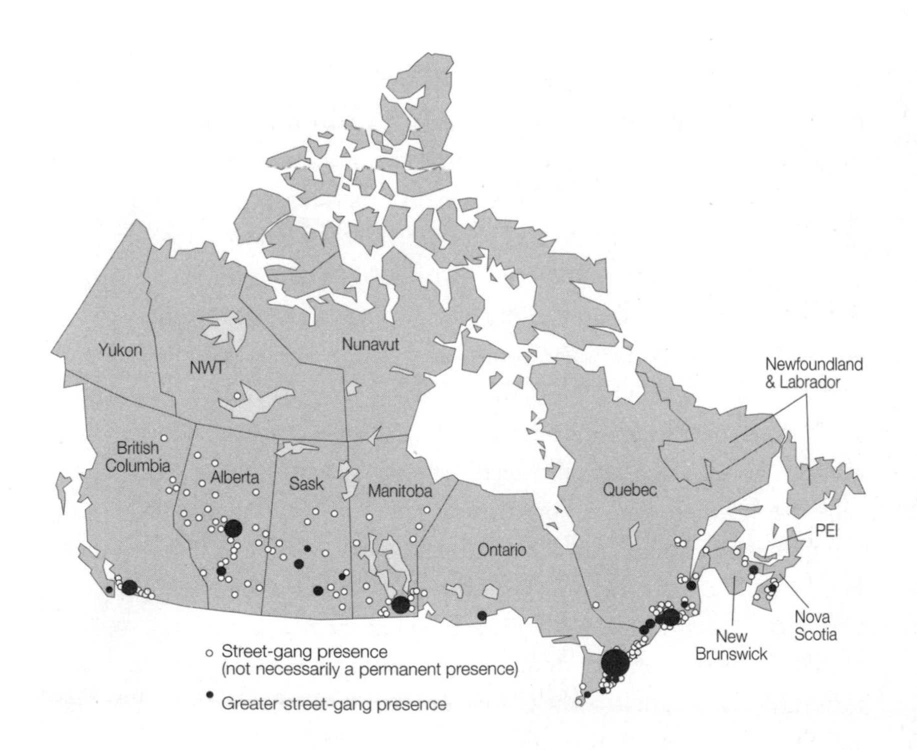

WHY YOUNG PEOPLE JOIN GANGS

We now know in which Canadian cities street gangs are active. The next, and perhaps most important, question is "Why do young people join gangs in the first place?" Since street gangs have existed for centuries, international social scientists, criminologists, pundits, concerned citizens and many others have posited a dozen or more fairly well-reasoned theories of gang formation and participation. The existence of so many theories, many at loggerheads with each other, underscores the reality that the street gang is a complicated social organism whose progenitors are, in most cases, many. However, before we can properly assess these theories and their ability to explain the growth of street gangs in Canada or elsewhere, we must first examine two issues: first, the universal desire of humans to coalesce into and participate in groups; and second, our core attitudes about the young gangster.

Since time immemorial, humans have come together to form groups. We are, fundamentally, creatures that like to live in packs, and we value our diverse social networks: the sum of the parts is greater than the whole. In these networks we can share ideas, protect and care for each other, provide for our economic security, deliver valuable goods and services to others, derive the intangible benefits of camaraderie, mentor each other's progression, enjoy recreation opportunities and collaborate in the achievement of a common purpose, among many other things. In these groups we often establish leadership hierarchies, define objectives, determine formal and informal mechanisms of social control, and create unique group names and other identifiers. Whether these self-formed social organisms are church groups, corporations, nuclear families, swingers' clubs, educational institutions, non-profit agencies, police departments, army regiments, sports teams, community service organizations, book clubs, bereavement groups, political parties, knitting bees or packs of street hoodlums, they all reflect humans' aspiration to surround themselves with others whose objectives or circumstances are aligned. These groups are all "gangs," and their participants therefore are all "gang members"—a phrase that now has a more sinister connotation.

I have mentioned my own aspiration at the ripe age of eleven to participate in a gang, which culminated at seventeen in actual participation. I must now confess that, while every bit of that narrative was true, my gang wasn't a street gang at all. Rather, it was a Major Junior A hockey club in the elite Ontario Hockey League, the now-defunct Brantford Alexanders. My fellow gangsters—teammates, that is—weren't nicknamed, as street gangsters often are, with provocative labels reflecting their propensities or personal attributes (such as "Killer," "Psycho" or "Shorty"), but with stylistically truncated surnames such as "Probie" (Bob Probert), "Gretz" (Keith Gretzky) and "Corse" (Shayne Corson).

Our reasons for membership encompassed many that also drive street gang members: the desire for money, power and respect; the need to escape humdrum or troubled lives back home; the wish to embark upon a special rite of passage into manhood. As well, our membership matched many of the characteristics of street gangs: mutual protection; camaraderie; violence; a code of conduct; colours; consumption of drugs and alcohol; degrading initiations; economic pursuits; and sexual adventures with young women who wanted to hitch along on our apparently exciting journey. With the exception of conduct that transgressed our country's criminal laws, we were little different from a street gang, and I was little different from a street-gang member. We were, for all intents and purposes, a societally sanctioned gang that happened to play out its purpose on the ice rather than on the street. If we are to understand the organism that is the street gang, we must first understand that the aspiration to form groups is universal, and that the outcome of that aspiration, for some youth with a certain range of circumstances, attributes and deficits, will unfortunately be a street gang. This is not meant to excuse their actions, but simply to highlight that the drive is real—the aspiration to form groups is hard-wired in all of us.

Now to the issue of our attitudes. If I randomly assembled a sample of a hundred individuals from across the country, I would be prepared to wager a small fortune that a word association game would most often produce the following responses to the phrase "street-gang member": black, dangerous, gun-toting, crack-dealing, predatory, violent, criminal, inner city, poor, menace. This composite image of gangsters is culled from the mass media, promulgated by tough-on-crime advocates and derived from our inherent stereotypes; it is not the product of informed examination and critical thought. Although the majority of Canadians have very little insight into our street-gang phenomenon—save for "if it bleeds, it leads" media accounts—we seem to have already calcified our view of the situation. Regardless of where that image comes from, however, it serves to demonize young gangsters and stigmatize them as a single, well-defined class of undesirables, deserving of aggressive pursuit and incarceration. In cities such as Toronto, Vancouver and Winnipeg, where crime is a top-of-mind civic issue, few members of society are as vilified as the urban gangster (except perhaps for the elusive al Qaeda sleeper-cell terrorist). While it is true that many young gangsters match the description suggested by the words above, many also do not. The popular image does little to differentiate between the gang wannabe, who deserves our attention, and the violent shot-caller, who deserves our scorn. These are, indeed, two different breeds of gangbangers.

A discussion of our society's attitudes to the young gang member is neither a pointless philosophical exercise nor a wasteful investment of time better spent cracking heads. Perception is our biggest obstacle to ending gang violence. Demonizing gang members as the evil other, the barbarians at the gate—and therefore requiring the stern hand of our government protectors—will most certainly cloud our understanding of why they become gang members in the first place and, most important, what to do about the gang problem. Don't get me wrong—I am not an apologist for gang members and, like most others, I am appalled by the devastation they can create. I just don't believe that the simplistic gang-member-as-predator view will serve us very well if our goal is to staunch the flow of youth into gangs.

With these two points in mind we can properly filter the possible reasons why young people join street gangs. Those who believe that a gang member is nothing more than a heartless predator could be deemed to subscribe to what is sometimes referred to as the "moral poverty" or "biological" school of delinquency. In this view, gang behaviour, and delinquency in general, is born of hedonism, rational choice, faulty thinking and sociopathic tendencies. This Jeremy Bentham–esque argument has roots more than two hundred years old and was popular from the 1960s to 1980s; it has been echoed vociferously by several influential gang experts from the United States, the country with the world's largest street-gang problem.

One of Ronald Reagan's favourite law-and-order advisors, Stanton E. Samenow, author of *Inside the Criminal Mind*, wrote, "From very early, the oxygen of the criminal's life is to seek excitement by doing the forbidden." Another American neo-con pundit, William Bennett, wrote in his book *Body Count: Moral Poverty . . . and How to Win America's War on Crime and Drugs*, "the twin character scars left by moral poverty—lack of impulse control and lack of empathy—reinforce each other and make it far more likely that the individual will succumb to either the temptations of crime, or the blandishments of drugs, or, as so often happens, both." American street-gang policy guru James Q. Wilson has questioned whether there are root causes at all, and has dismissed root-cause thinking as simply a way to avoid taking aggressive action against crime. Advocating severe punishment (since rehabilitation, in their view, is a waste of time), these individuals give short shrift to root causes beyond moral impoverishment. This is the politics of scapegoating writ large: blame genetic defects and permissive liberalism foisted on us by lefties, but give no credit to the decaying inner cities, institutionalized racism, poor police–community relations, extreme poverty or massive economic shifts that render the gang, in some youths' clouded view, a viable option. If we set aside this simplistic view, we can then open our minds to the many ways in which a young person, emerging from childhood into tumultuous adolescence, gets set on the path towards gangsterism.

There is no broadly accepted general theory on youth gangs. Rather, a well-considered approach suggests that, as with other large societal problems—global warming, for instance—a confluence of contributing factors, in different measures and combinations, gives rise to youth-gang formation and participation. Various sociological theories, some of which were articulated almost a century ago, have merit in explaining gang formation. This school of thought suggests that street gangs form because of environmental factors, specifically elements of "social disorganization" that characterize modern-day urban society. This perspective views street-gang formation from an ecological or natural sciences perspective, in that human beings and human behaviour are influenced by their physical environment. Low economic status, multi-ethnic communities, mobile populations, high-density housing, unemployment and disrupted families, among other environmental factors, stimulate the creation of a gang subculture in opposition to dominant cultural values and norms.

An early pioneer in gang-formation research, Frederic Thrasher, interviewed and studied more than 1,300 gang members in Chicago in the 1920s. In his landmark 1927 book *The Gang*, Thrasher suggested that gangs arose in the "interstices" of society, which included both the immigrant experience and the challenging period between childhood and adulthood. Reflecting his belief that street gangs held positive appeal to young men rather than being the product of immoral addictions and acute criminal pathologies, he wrote that "the gang is a spontaneous attempt on the part of boys to create a society of their own where none adequate to their needs exists."[3] Gangs offered young men the thrill of conflict and provided members a sense of self, an identity, a substitute family and an opportunity to acquire status: "the gang offers a substitute for what society fails to give . . . it fills a gap and affords an escape."[4] To Thrasher, gang involvement was part of the immigrant experience and transitory in nature, later to be supplanted by adulthood, family and career.

Another interesting perspective was offered in the 1940s by highly regarded U.S. social theorist Robert Merton, whose "strain" or "means–end" theory sought to explain how certain cultures (such as that of the United States) could create deviance and disunity in greater proportion than others. To Merton, strain referred to an apparent lack of fit, or articulation, between the culture's norms of what constitutes success in life (goals, or ends) and norms of the appropriate ways to achieve those goals (means). Merton cited his society's preoccupation with pursuit of the American dream, with its absolute core values of achievement, fame, individualism and money. However, Merton believed that his society was less absolute, if not ambivalent, about its values with respect to the means to achieve that success. So, while hard work, thrift and ambition were valued, U.S. society still tolerated those who engaged in deviant behaviour to achieve their success. Merton believed that success was valued more than virtue: that for some, the ends did justify the means.

But he carried his argument further by layering on class dynamics. While success is emphasized for all, the opportunities to achieve this success are not equally distributed because of class, ethnic and racial stratifications. Not everyone is created equal, nor is everyone accorded the same access to the raw materials of success: money, education, access, contacts and acceptance. According to Merton, the fact of differential opportunity led people to adapt in one of several ways. They could simply accept their lot in life and conform or retreat from pursuit of the American dream. However, others might rebel and, in the case of youth, join a gang as a (deviant) means of enabling their pursuit of what society so intensely values: success, fame, prestige, fortune.

Merton's focus on the United States in the 1940s and '50s does not diminish his theory's validity as it pertains to other countries, including Canada, or to the present time. While there is no proxy "Canadian dream" in our collective conscious, the pursuit of money, fame and success is not foreign to us. Like Americans, we place a high premium on economic affluence and social rank for all members of our society, and we cannot boast a perfectly egalitarian culture in which there is equal distribution of opportunity and the resources to achieve success. The existence of so many competing theories about street-gang formation—from bad genes and bad parents to bad economics and opportunities and all points in between—confirms the complexity of gangs. However, from a Canadian perspective, my decade-long work in this field leads me to believe that to understand the roots of street-gang formation one must first look at the complex array of socio-economic factors that have affected Canadian families, especially in the past three decades or so. This is not to suggest that parents, genes or other factors have no influence, because they certainly do in some cases, but it is my contention that socio-economic factors are the principal drivers of street-gang formation.

HOW WE HAVE FAILED NEW CANADIANS

The ethnocultural richness and diversity of our country is one of its key strengths, and we have much to be thankful for when it comes to immigration. However, an objective assessment of the Canadian street-gang situation requires us to look at immigration policy, which has in part contributed to urban street gangs. Since discussions around race can be contentious and emotional, let me preface the discussion by saying that I am decidedly pro-immigration, especially since I am foreign-born myself, the son of 1960s-era European immigrants. We are a country built on the significant contributions of immigrants, and most of us would surely agree that immigration has had a positive influence. The critique that follows has nothing to do with specific races or cultures, nor does it centre on what immigrants have or not have done for our country as a whole. Rather, it is a discussion of the consequences of major policy decisions made about twenty years ago and, perhaps most significant, what we as a country have not done for our new Canadian residents.

According to the 2002 Canadian Police Survey on Youth Gangs, a majority of gang members (some 82 percent) are from the so-called visible minorities—African-Canadian, Asian, Hispanic, East Indian and the like. We can assume that many of these youth are first- or second-generation Canadians, the offspring of parents who emigrated to Canada over the past couple of decades. Immigration to Canada was predominantly a white phenomenon in the twenty-five years from 1945 to 1970. In that period Canada admitted some 3.5 million immigrants, mostly from Europe, other Commonwealth countries and the United States. In 1966, for instance, the year my family emigrated from England, where I was born, 87 percent of Canada's 194,743 immigrants were of European origin. Buoyed by a post–Second World War expansionary economy and supported by solid white- and blue-collar skills, this cohort of immigrants did relatively well for themselves and were able to establish solid home, work and family foundations.

Things began to change markedly in the late 1960s and early '70s. In 1967 the federal government adopted a points-based immigration system that lifted many of the previous restrictions based on race, colour and national origin. The system gave pre-eminence to education, availability of employment in Canada, age, the individual's personal characteristics, and degree of fluency in English or French. Later, in 1969, Canada signed the 1951 Geneva Convention relating to the Status of Refugees and its 1967 protocol. This guaranteed protection for refugees in Canada, thus opening the doors for those facing civil war, drought and dictatorships—including Vietnamese, Cambodians, Sri Lankans, Somalis, Ethiopians, Haitians and Latin Americans, among others. Later still, in 1971, Prime Minister Pierre Elliott Trudeau announced the government's official policy of multiculturalism, further emphasizing the ethnocultural changes resulting from the immigration system.

The wellspring of many street gangs and street-gang problems lies in violent resistance, dispossession and migration. In the United States, for example, the colonization of Puerto Rico displaced thousands of immigrants, who settled in Chicago. There, one of North America's most feared gangs, the Latin Kings, formed because of the discrimination that Puerto Ricans faced in America. A civil war in El Salvador seeded what is North America's most violent and well-organized gang, Mara Salvatrucha, or MS13, which currently has members in Canada. British colonial rule in Ireland in the early 1800s, combined with a devastating famine, produced the early gangs of New York City.

The same dynamics hold true for Canada, facilitated in part by our immigration and refugee-processing systems. The war in Vietnam produced scores of "boat people" who would later give rise to secretive drug-dealing Vietnamese and Cambodian street gangs in Canada. Montreal's decades-long problem with Haitian gangs can be traced back to the migration of people from Haiti in the 1970s and '80s, escaping the brutal and oppressive political regime of dictator Jean-Claude "Baby Doc" Duvalier. Paid political gunmen in Jamaica, considered a liability after the 1980 election of Edward Seaga, relocated to North America and formed the violent drug-dealing Jamaican Posse street gangs that have troubled Canadian law enforcers ever since. Civil war, famine and natural disasters in the Horn of Africa, especially in Somalia and Ethiopia, produced a bumper crop of refugees—and the raw materials for new Canadian gangs that now troll our streets.

An offshore gangster apprenticeship or being brought up in a civil war does not necessarily make an immigrant or refugee into a domestic gangster. We must look to other contributing factors, of which there are many. In the ten-year period from 1971 to 1981, when Trudeau was mostly in power, approximately 1.43 million immigrants came to Canada—a manageable number. When Brian Mulroney assumed power in September 1984, he maintained low immigration levels for two years, with a total of 99,219 in 1986. However, Mulroney saw both a partisan advantage in increasing immigration and an economic advantage, because of a declining birth rate, and began a massive increase in immigration levels over the next five years, from 152,098 in 1987 to 230,781 in 1991. By the end of the Mulroney era in 1993, immigration levels were at 255,000, the single largest cohort (more than 20 percent) being children under the age of fourteen. These numbers were maintained by Jean Chrétien: about 200,000 to 250,000 per year. Canada's immigration figures for 2005—262,236 (23 percent of them under fourteen, and 81 percent from Africa, the Middle East, Asia and the Pacific, and Latin America)—gives this country one of the highest per capita immigration levels in the world. [5]

The economic ramifications of the immigration decisions made since 1987 have been felt most acutely in our major urban areas. Wanting to live close to people of the same background and where jobs seem to be most available, immigrants have flocked to our three biggest cities, with

Toronto, Vancouver and Montreal respectively receiving approximately 50 percent, 18 percent and 12 percent of all immigrants annually. In Toronto's case, 100,000-plus new Canadians flood into the city each year, making it one of the world's most multicultural cities: more than 44 percent of its citizens are foreign born. Under ideal socio-economic conditions, a large, wealthy and tolerant city such as Toronto would be capable of welcoming all these people and ensuring their personal path to success. The problem is, however, that for Toronto and the many other Canadian cites that receive tens of thousands of immigrants annually, conditions in the past couple of decades have been less than ideal.

It takes immigrants several years to acclimatize and establish themselves in their new country. Education and in-demand work experience certainly help; about two-thirds of immigrants today are considered "economic class": people with university degrees, skills and entrepreneurial experience. Compared to the rest of the Canadian population, immigrants are highly educated. However, while we have been acquiring people of immense education and skill, we have done an inadequate job of equating their foreign qualifications with equivalent Canadian credentials—as if a degree from the University of Punjab were third- or fourth-rate compared to one from Brock University. The lack of a consistent, intelligent prior learning assessment (PLA) system in Canada means that many foreign-born scientists, doctors and business professionals, lured by promises of a land of opportunity, are relegated to low-paying service jobs in the retail, food service, health and hospitality industries. Grab a taxi in Toronto or Vancouver and ask the cabbie—almost always an immigrant—about his education, and you'll likely discover that you are being chauffeured by a highly educated person.

In the early 1990s, when the economy was in recession, labour market conditions had deteriorated markedly for new immigrants. This was compounded by discrimination, language difficulties and poorly regarded degrees. As a result they lost considerable ground compared to workers born in Canada. In 1996, only 61 percent of recent immigrants aged twenty-five to forty-four held jobs, compared with 78.4 percent of the Canadian-born population in the same age group, a gap of 17.4 percentage points.[6] The gap persists today. Despite their better education, recent immigrants are less likely to be working in jobs that require a degree. For example, 10.4 percent, 12.0 percent and 9.7 percent of Canadian-born males in Toronto, Vancouver and Montreal respectively work in low- or moderate-skill jobs, compared to 24.8 percent, 25 percent and 21.2 percent respectively for male immigrants.[7] According to a Canadian Council of Social Development study, while a fifth of immigrants who came to Canada before 1986 live in poverty, half of the immigrants who came to Canada after 1991 live in a state of poverty.[8]

But immigrants' difficulties are more widespread than lack of PLA. They extend to our government's historical unwillingness to fund English as a second language (ESL) training to match the number of immigrants we accept. While the Canadian immigration system awards points based on language competency, young immigrants, and especially refugees (of any age), often lack the requisite language skills to succeed. It is ironic that the government has lavishly financed French instruction in support of official bilingualism while the ESL requirements of immigrants—our prime drivers of growth in an increasingly global economy—have been so inadequately addressed. This is especially true in the crowded elementary and secondary school systems, a no-man's-land as far as the federal government is concerned, since education is a provincial responsibility. This disconnect between rash federal government decisions (trebled immigration levels) and the provincial ramifications (inadequate ESL funding) is unfortunate, as it affects mostly the young new Canadians we ought to ensure are equipped with the English skills they need to succeed.

THE EFFECTS OF OUR CHANGING ECONOMY

The challenges posed by our country's inadequate transitioning of new immigrants have as their backdrop an economy that has changed over the past fifteen years. In the post-war economy many new immigrants entered the manufacturing sector, which was growing rapidly to keep pace with the emerging consumer age. More recently, however, the Canadian manufacturing sector has been in a decade-plus period of decline, shedding the jobs that many immigrants heretofore held.

Statistics Canada data show that manufacturing jobs declined from 2,229,000 in 2001 to 2,207,000 in 2006. During the same period, in the entire goods-producing sector (agriculture, resources, utilities, construction), employment rose from 3,779,000 to 4,002,000 jobs. Gains in the lower-paid service sector were even more marked, with employment numbers rising from 11,166,200 to 12,167,300, an increase of more than 8 percent. In fact, in every industry sub-sector that was tracked by Statistics Canada—trade, health care, public administration, finance and insurance, agriculture, transportation and more—employment levels rose, with the exception of manufacturing, which declined by 1 percent. In a phenomenon that began in the 1970s, employment has shifted from manufacturing towards the knowledge and service industries, and labour demand has shifted in favour of skilled workers (for example, engineers, tool-and-die makers, IT professionals, finance and legal experts), who typically enjoy higher employment rates and incomes. With immigrants struggling to establish themselves and to win the respect they deserve for their prior achievements, it is no wonder that many have a hard time adjusting to life in Canada.

These declines in manufacturing are due to several factors, including the appreciation of the Canadian dollar over the past few years, Canada–U.S. free trade, the early-1990s recession, and factor substitution, the process by which human labour is replaced by machinery and advanced automation processes. More important, however, is that the emergence of global supply chains, and the related offshoring of domestic jobs to low-cost/high-productivity regions, has major implications for all Canadians, especially new ones. In the 1960s and '70s, low-value domestic factory jobs, such as those in manufacturing clothing, toys, electronics, shoes and hard goods, began their flight to offshore jurisdictions where labour was cheap and plentiful. Through the 1980s and '90s, global outsourcing continued, with higher-value but routine tasks (such as call centres, computer programming and core banking processes) leaving as well. Since then, offshoring has continued with even more valuable jobs moving, such as those in advanced technology, research and development, engineering, medicine and even financial analysis.

These global economic changes have no doubt benefited Canadians. Consumers and businesses alike have enjoyed lower-priced and more available foreign products and services, and our economic performance over the past decade (one of the most dynamic in the G8 group of countries) attests to the continued prosperity of our country. The shedding of commodity-based production jobs to offshore in favour of high-value ingenuity-based production jobs means that our largest cities have grown to become significant command centres of capital, especially Toronto, whose stock exchange handles the third-largest stock market in North America, and the seventh-largest in the world by market capitalization. In Toronto's case, its role as a world financial power means that highly skilled, specialized, mobile and well-paid professionals from the service and knowledge sectors—lawyers, accountants, venture capitalists, management consultants, computing specialists, research engineers, investment bankers, risk specialists—must be hired. Well-paid people, of course, must be served and catered to. This recomposition of our job market has stimulated the creation of hundreds of thousands of relatively low-paying unskilled jobs in the retail, hospitality, construction, wholesale and distribution, administrative and general service industries, the ones where immigrants tend to find employment.

As much as some people wish to believe that "a rising tide raises all boats," this is not the case. There is a growing gap in this country between the rich and the poor. Income inequality is measured by the ratio between the income of a family in the ninetieth percentile (the family compared to which 90 percent of other families have lower incomes and only 10 percent have higher incomes) and a family at the tenth percentile (the family compared to which 90 percent of other families have higher incomes and only 10 percent lower). By 2000, families in the ninetieth percentile of income distribution in Canada had incomes about four times higher than those of their counterparts in the tenth percentile.[9] This was an increase from ten years earlier, because the gains associated with economic expansion in Canada went mainly to higher-income families. While incomes among the richest 20 percent of families were rising by about 10 percent, between 1990 and 2000 total family income stagnated among the poorest 20 percent of families.

Statistics Canada data also show that so-called "persistent low income" during this period was concentrated among five groups: single parents, recent immigrants, people with work disabilities, unattached people aged between forty-five and sixty-four, and Aboriginal people. In 1980, for example, 25 percent of recent immigrants were living on low incomes, but by 2000 this had increased to 36 percent. What is particularly telling, however, is that the low-income rate among Canadian-born people during that period fell, from 17 percent to 14 percent.

Even skilled immigrants are falling behind. According to 2001 census data, male immigrants with a university degree who came to Ontario in the late 1990s were earning, after six to ten years in Canada, only 54 percent of what similarly qualified native-born Canadians were making. Compared to the pre-Mulroney era, the most employable immigrants (men aged twenty-five to forty-four) did worse as well, with their employment levels falling from 75.7 percent in 1981 to only 65.8 percent in 2002. At the same time, employment of non-immigrants rose from 74.6 percent to 81.8 percent.

THE CRISIS IN MAJOR URBAN CENTRES

As noted earlier, the vast majority of immigrants (along with a majority of all Canadians) settle in big cities. In contrast to the American experience with "white flight" that emptied city cores of mostly white, middle- and upper-class citizens and the companies they worked for, we have not abandoned urban life. But all is not well in our major cities. The housing boom, fuelled by the low interest rates of the past decade or so, combined with the gentrification of downtown cores, has driven property values in urban centres through the roof, making the prospect of urban home ownership for many new Canadians a pipe dream. For the flood of new immigrants and rural Canadian migrants who settle in cities, finding an affordable and decent place to rent is a big challenge. This represents a huge impediment to successful integration and is yet another consequence of the sharp increase in immigration rates. According to statistics from the Canadian Mortgage and Housing Corporation (CMHC), from 1991 to 1996 the net increase in the number of rental units was 186,000. But from 1996 to 2001 that slowed to 2,000 net units. CMHC estimates that just to catch up with the demand from more and more low-income renters, about 45,000 new rental units per year must be developed in each of the next five years—inventory that will never materialize because of high urban property values and eroding urban tax bases.

Judged by their financial health, our biggest cities are sick and require emergency care. In her final book, *Dark Age Ahead,* acclaimed urban planner and critic Jane Jacobs discussed how successful medieval cities benefited from subsidiarity: the principle that government works best, most responsibly and responsively, when it is closest to the people it serves. Today over 80 percent of Canadians live in cities with more than 10,000 people (for example, in satellite communities, such as Kanata, Richmond Hill and Surrey, which are adjacent to Ottawa, Toronto and Vancouver). Over 50 percent of our population live in one of Canada's five largest cities. Because of anachronistic tax regimes that reflect the Canada of the nineteenth century, when people mostly lived in rural areas, cities still have only minor tax powers, and their sources of public revenue—mostly property taxes—are inadequate to meet their needs. So while the citizenry of major cities send billions to Ottawa every year in the form of GST, excise taxes and income taxes, they get a fraction back to help finance their increasingly burdened operations. With the federal government's belt tightening (a.k.a. downloading) of the past decade, cities have felt the brunt of the pain, compounded by a massive influx of people with real needs competing with each other for fewer and fewer places to live and work. The result: urban deterioration.

People have to live somewhere, so new city dwellers are being pushed farther and farther afield to find suitable accommodation. In many big cities the comfortable middle-class suburbs of the 1950s and '60s are becoming inner-city slums of rundown apartment buildings and social housing complexes. At the same time, while quality of life crumbles in urban areas (crowded public schools, closed community centres, deteriorating roads, increased crime and rising property taxes), the mobile middle class and their employers have begun a flight to the suburbs, where houses are cheap, rents affordable, big-box retail stores plentiful, community centres available and taxes more reasonable. Urban sprawl is upon us. We are producing, in a very real sense as far as our cities are concerned, an increasingly stratified society of very rich and very poor urban neighbourhoods with little in common, surrounded by the middle class in the suburban regions. This is a troubling dynamic that is undermining the social cohesion that has been the hallmark of Canadian cities—witness our emerging street-gang problem—because safe and harmonious cities tend to be those that are reasonably diverse and multi-layered. Of course, these structural economic changes have affected not only immigrants; all Canadians have felt them, but immigrants—and their children—have fared less well.

POOR ABORIGINAL CANADIANS IN THE CITIES

Also considered a visible minority, Aboriginal Canadians, faced with few economic and educational opportunities in remote and reserve communities, began coming to the cities in the 1950s, after the courts quashed a law that prevented them from leaving reserves without authorization. Approximately 1.3 million Canadians claim Aboriginal ancestry (North American Indians, Metis and Inuit), and about half of them live in cities of more than 100,000 people, up from about 7 percent in the early 1950s.[10] However, one of Canada's dirty little secrets is that in many cities across the country with large concentrations of Aboriginals—among them Winnipeg, Edmonton, Regina, Saskatoon and Vancouver—we have urban Aboriginal ghettos where the poverty and despair resemble that of black ghettos in the United States.

Even before their departure to the cities, many Aboriginals were burdened by memories of colonialism and the effects of physical, sexual and emotional abuse experienced in the government-funded residential schools that were, ironically, supposed to prepare them for life in white society. Lacking paid work experience, separated from traditional kinship networks and facing persistent racism, grim social housing and few decent economic opportunities, many Native people have had a difficult time adjusting to their new homes. This is reflected in part by Aboriginal income, which is 75 percent that of non-Aboriginals, despite equivalent labour participation rates.

The transition to city life should have been eased by the federal government's $9 billion annual budget for Aboriginal programming—equivalent to $6,900 per Aboriginal man, woman and child—which is constitutionally guaranteed under the Indian Act. However, the majority of these funds are sent to, and managed by, powerful rural band councils, who are under no obligation to assist those living off the reserve or those who have not maintained their status on the Indian Register. Consequently, while 70 percent of Aboriginals live off reserve, less than 5 percent of Aboriginal money makes its way to urban programs and assistance, underscoring the lack of portability of Aboriginal rights. Particularly troubling about this situation is that these disparities affect a population that, compared to the rest of Canada, is disproportionately young. The Aboriginal birth rate is about 50 percent higher than the non-Aboriginal rate. According to

2001 census figures, the median age for the Aboriginal population was 24.7 years, while that of the non-Aboriginal population was at an all time high of 37.7 years. Children aged fourteen and under represented a third of the Aboriginal population in 2001, far higher than the corresponding 19 percent in the non-Aboriginal population. So, although the Aboriginal population accounted for only 3.3 percent of Canada's total population, Aboriginal children represented 5.6 percent of all children in Canada. Many of these children will grow up poor in urban slums with high crime rates and rampant Aboriginal-on-Aboriginal violence, such as that seen in Winnipeg and Regina, which together boast several thousand young Aboriginal gang members.

Faced with these trying conditions, immigrant, refugee and Aboriginal migrant families produce a disproportionate share of Canadian street gangsters. Restricted opportunities, uncertain futures and economic desperation breed crime and manufacture an overarching sense of danger and despair among the people who experience these conditions. As can be expected, enduring economic stress produces family stress too. The Aboriginal community, for example, faces a pervasive problem of family breakdown: only half of Aboriginal children living in cities with more than 100,000 people live with both of their parents, compared to 83 percent overall in Canada. According to 2001 census data, of Canada's 1.3 million or so lone-parent families, more than 80 percent are headed by females who earned (in constant 2004 dollars) only $34,000 per year, just 40 percent of what two-parent families earned. It's no wonder that many young Aboriginal men, lacking an involved father to act as a positive role model, facing dire economic conditions and living in troubled communities, see the gang as a way out, offering them what Thrasher so cogently described eighty years ago: a substitute for what society fails to give.

All these things provide the fuel for street gangs, but there is more. An important added dimension to the street-gang situation—one that amplifies economic disadvantage in those who experience it—is the highly aspirational nature of Canadian society and the example set by our "culture of consumption." We are a country in which the majority of people are saddled by a high level of debt. We want it all, and we want it now. Low interest rates and financial institutions' desire to "increase shareholder value" have made it happen. Data from the Survey of Financial Security (SFS) reveals that, when 1984 is compared to 1999, the percentage of Canadian families with debt remained unchanged at 70 percent. [11] However, the aggregate amount of debt in real terms more than doubled over this time, increasing from $207 billion to $458 billion. Therefore the median debt of families increased from $12,567 to $29,000. From 1992 to 2002, average (real) outstanding consumer debt per adult Canadian grew at an average annual rate of 9.3 percent, but disposable income grew at an average annual rate of only 3.7 percent over this same period.

As debt has increased, savings have decreased. Canadians' personal savings rate—the difference between current personal income and expenditures measured as a share of disposable income—is now approximately zero, compared to the high-water mark of 19 percent set in 1982. Some economists argue that the personal savings rate does not take into account the net equity in homeowners' increasingly valuable properties, which could be considered a surrogate for sound but illiquid financial planning, so long as the housing market continues to perform well. However, home equity is of little consequence for poor folks whose dreams of home ownership may never materialize.

Popular culture also stimulates our collective desire to make it big quickly. It masks the reality that success is still, and will always be, largely the product of hard work and diligence. Self-help books on financial independence, favouring quick-fix remedies and strategies, many couched in quick consumption parables, are among our country's bestsellers. Professional sports creates the false notion that success is possible quickly and at a young age. And what explanation regarding the dot-com fiasco of the late 1990s can one offer other than investor greed run amok? Laypeople and educated financiers alike believed that their investment in a company with no intrinsic value, no products and no viable business model could somehow, post-IPO, earn them sufficient capital to make all of their dreams come true.

If we are honest, we'll admit to aspiring to a life of material riches. We want it today, not tomorrow. The irony is that we criticize the same aspiration if it is held by poor, uneducated, disenfranchised inner-city immigrant youths with few opportunities when they give it meaning through their apparently only viable option, a drug-dealing street gang. A September 2006 editorial in the *National Post*, commenting on the "rash" of youth stealing other youths' expensive athletic shoes, blamed wannabe gangsters and the "gaudy materialism" of ghetto life, as if inner-city youth were the only such Canadians guilty of the label. Somehow it is okay for brand-conscious, financially strapped, middle-class Canadians to buy more house than they can afford, fill it with "Don't Pay a Cent Event" furniture and lease two upscale SUVs while saving nothing for a rainy day, but it's not okay for a similarly financially strapped ghetto kid to wear Nike shoes, gold jewellery and FUBU clothing. A double standard indeed.

Perhaps now you can understand why some youth, set within these socio-economic conditions, decide to enter the gang life. To be sure, a confluence of factors may motivate a young person to join. But, far and away, the most contributive element today is socio-economics, not video games, rap culture, bad parents, U.S. influences or psychopathic genes (although these factors may influence some young people towards a street gang). We Canadians, by our actions and by our decisions, have produced street gangs. When he is faced with a future flipping burgers at McDonald's for minimum wage, a troubled home life, an absent dad, a crime-infested community and stifled dreams, the pull of a gang and all that it offers may be just too strong for a young man.

The actual manner in which a young person becomes involved in a street gang varies widely. Youths with gang-involved older siblings may simply grow into a gang from a young age—as young as eight in some places, such as in Winnipeg and Regina's large Aboriginal communites. If a street gang is established, has sufficient critical mass, enjoys steady proceeds from crime and is not involved in any heated rivalries, it may not need to recruit new members, preferring them to come through existing members. In contrast, an emerging gang wishing to earn its stripes in a market or displace existing gangs may actively seek out members whom they believe are amenable to joining and who can bring added capacity to the gang in the form of muscle or drug-dealing abilities. (The street gang's modus operandi for recruiting women is unique, as you will learn in the next chapter.)

RECRUITMENT AND HAZING

Active gang-recruitment techniques vary, from simple direct requests to join through to manipulative strategies, such as giving gang life an attractive veneer by offering at-risk youth a taste of free drugs and hookers at a wild party. For the vast majority of new gangsters, entrance to the gang rarely happens overnight. Young people, even if they are courted by a gang, usually carefully consider joining as they are increasingly exposed to the gang lifestyle and to active gangsters. They will weigh the benefits and risks, reconciling them with the gangster life that may soon follow. Thus a youth does not usually go from good kid one day to street gangster the next; the process is more often evolutionary rather than revolutionary.

Irrespective of the form of recruitment, most prospective gang members must proceed through some form of initiation. Essentially ritualized harassment, initiation, or "hazing," is used to determine suitability for membership in a defined group, promote group loyalty, and establish camaraderie through shared suffering. The fact that initiation is commonplace across many walks of life should come as no surprise: fraternities, service clubs (including the Freemasons), sports teams, military units and police forces, to name just a few, have used initiation as an accepted, if degrading, rite of passage. Like other social groups, street gangs use initiation to control, to subordinate and to test. Gangs don't want members who will run at the first sign of trouble or complain when issued instructions.

A youth may have been courted by a street gang, but the process of recruitment does not guarantee actual membership, at least until the youth has passed his or her test of initiation. The extent to which initiation is used by street gangs is generally in proportion to their power base and size. Small, relatively disorganized and emerging gangs, needing to build their power base, will often have a relaxed initiation protocol to ensure that the price of admission does not deter prospective members. Likewise, strong and well-organized gangs may often employ more rigorous initiations to separate the wheat from the chaff and to ensure that prospective members are highly motivated. This makes sense if you think of it in terms of the job market—young, upstart, undercapitalized companies, which do not have sufficient brand identity to attract the best and brightest in a competitive job market, tend to have a very relaxed screening process compared to the robust selection systems of industry heavyweights. Like young companies, young gangs often take what they can get.

As to be expected, gang initiation is firmly rooted in a culture of violence and criminality. Gang initiation rituals vary, but most often take the form of being "beat in" or "jumped in"—an act of love, according to some gangs. In a beat-in, the prospective recruit must withstand a beating by one or several members of the gang as a test of commitment and toughness. As well, new charges are sometimes asked to commit a crime to prove their commitment to the gang, such as transporting drugs, assaulting a rival gang member, writing gang graffiti on enemy turf or participating in a drive-by shooting, although the last example is rare. Some prospective members are forced to decorate their skin with gang tattoos, using either ink or a makeshift branding iron to burn the skin and create a permanent scar. For girls wishing to join a gang, initiation may also include beatings (from other female gang members), but given the male-dominated nature of gangs, it most often involves a sexual act, such as having to perform oral sex on some or all of the gang leaders.

As for exiting gangs, conventional wisdom suggests that once you are in a gang, you are a member for life, but this is not necessarily true. Unlike media portrayals of life membership, rank-and-file members of today's increasingly hybrid street gangs can move in and out of the gangs. For many street gangsters their final departure from the gang is often a result of their age—they simply "grow out of the gang" and decide that the gang lifestyle is no longer for them. Of course, for others, like gang leaders and those with significant criminal records, the street gang life may lead to a long-term criminal life in a more sophisticated organized-crime group.

LIFE AS A GANGSTER

Post-initiation, many active gang members (as opposed to wannabes or part-time gangsters) begin their tour of duty selling drugs such as marijuana, crack and methamphetamine or by participating in various frauds. These tasks are driven by the desire to maintain the gang's economic turf and, of course, to make some big bucks. As young gang members soon discover, however, the life of a drug-dealing gangster is a substandard one. There is a constant threat of violence from rivals wanting to take you out and organized-crime drug suppliers trying to hold you to your commitments. Bad weather compounds matters, as does the constant risk of arrest, because to make drug sales, you need to be visible. To distinguish yourself within a gang, you must demonstrate a violent and fearless streak, which magnifies the personal danger.

Despite the popularly held perception, the pay is poor. Drug dealers at the very bottom rung of the illicit drug market don't make that much money when drugs are plentiful and the competition is stiff (more on this in Chapter 5). And then there is the everyday boredom. The life of a street gangster, notwithstanding the real dangers, is typically not filled with daily threats, drama and intrigue. Gangsters go to school, live at home, have part-time jobs and just hang out like other young people, the difference being that they sometimes choose to bookend their otherwise lacklustre days with moments of sheer excitement and danger.

Often attracted to the street gang in the first place because of its apparent group camaraderie and unity, its members soon learn the disconnect between perception and reality. The typical street gang's members treat each other according to the "What's mine is mine; what's yours is yours" philosophy. Because most street gangs lack a well-defined hierarchy and control structure, this means that if a group of five gang members belonging to a gang of fifty went out and successfully robbed a bank, they would not necessarily share the spoils with the other members. With no central collection and redistribution of the proceeds of crime, as is typical with a traditional organized-crime group where members are expected to contribute to the communal wealth, street gangs represent *dis*organized crime, but a crime group nonetheless.

A DANGEROUS EXISTENCE

There is also, of course, the risk of death. In 2002, police agencies estimated approximately 7,000 gang members under the age of twenty-one in this country. Now, this definition excludes many more street gang members over twenty-one through to about twenty-eight, the upper age limit of most street gang members. My experience suggests that this group could conservatively represent another 6,000 members. Allowing for street-gang growth in Canada between 2002 and 2005 of, say, 1,000 members, in 2005 the street-gang universe likely comprised about 14,000 members. In 2005 Toronto was home to approximately fifty gang-related murders. Add other major Canadian cities with gang issues, and let's conservatively assume perhaps a total of a hundred gang-related deaths across the country (there were seventy-one gang-related murders in 2004, so the assumption of a hundred deaths in 2005 is realistic, especially since it was a violent year). Let's also assume that, of this total, a conservative 85 percent were murders of people with some sort of connection to the gang or the drug scene. These eighty-five homicide victims could have been gang members, drug dealers or gang wannabes. In other words, these were people unlike you and me, who of their own volition became involved in the subculture, and therefore accepted the risks of involvement.

Statistically then, expressing the eighty-five homicides as a ratio of the estimated street-gang population of 14,000, a gang member in Canada in 2005 stood a 1:164 chance of being killed. Expressed in terms of the incidence of death per 100,000 people—a common measure of occupational risk—street-gang membership is by far the most dangerous "job" in the country, at more than 607 deaths per 100,000 "workers." This is more than five times to as much as ten times more dangerous than the jobs held by loggers, commercial fishers, oil-rig workers, structural iron and steel workers, farmers and coal miners (across all occupations, the fatality rate is about three or four per 100,000). Interestingly, the chance of dying today for a Canadian street-gang member is more than *ten* times that of U.S. soldiers who served in Vietnam, who suffered a fatality rate of 58.9 per 100,000. And if you consider the dangers of gangsterism in Toronto, with an estimated 3,000 gang members and the fifty confirmed deaths in 2005, the city's aspiring young gangsters enter the fray with a prospect of death of 1,666 per 100,000, or a one-in-sixty chance of dying every year. Most active street gangsters intuitively understand and accept the dangers of their profession as "the cost of doing business." One can only wonder, however, that if this level of risk is part of the job of being a gangster, how can we possibly think that the threat of a long prison sentence will deter them from their gangster ways?

With its attendant risks and poor workplace conditions, why do so many young gangsters live the life and keep toiling at their jobs? They do it for the same reason that aspiring young hockey players leave home at seventeen (as I did) to play junior hockey, skating every day, lifting weights, travelling in crowded buses, fighting and plying their trade in cold small-city arenas. Gangsters—like Major Junior A hockey players, who are one step down from the National Hockey League—want to succeed in an extremely competitive field where, if they reach the top, they'll make a fortune and receive untold glory. For many youth growing up in inner-city communities, being a leader of or an important player in a gang that deals drugs is considered nothing short of a glamour job, especially so since the available options (a "McJob" or no job at all) are considered a route to nowhere. The job of gang boss or leader brings with it money, women, cars, power, respect and, most important, a possible ticket out of the ghetto and, someday, to a life that is "legit." Most aspirants to the job likely understand that the chances of getting to the top are slim and the rewards fleeting, even if they do make it. However, the size of the possible prize and the lack of better options mean there is no shortage of young people wanting to participate in what is, for all intents and purposes, a giant tournament being played out on the streets.

ARE GANGS ACTIVE IN YOUR COMMUNITY?

Earlier I highlighted the many cities in which police agencies said that street gangs were operational in 2006. But how do you know if street gangs are active in your community?

For many people, graffiti vandalism in their community signifies that gangs are active and that drugs, guns and violence must be close by. Visit any downtown or suburban area in Canada where people congregate today, and within seconds I'll bet you will spot the often unintelligible markings of some graffiti artist. In my discussions with people who are concerned about gangs or the health and safety of their community, many are surprised to learn that, when it comes to the graffiti–gang connection, we have very little to worry about. Of all the graffiti we see, approximately 2 or 3 percent, maybe upwards of 5 percent in the most troubled inner-city areas, is actually gang graffiti. The majority (80+ percent) is so-called hip hop graffiti, the balance being a combination of hate, folk, political activist, satanic cult, stencil and "latrinalia" (washroom) graffiti. Let me explain the differences between the hip hop and street-gang forms.

From its 1970s New York City birth, hip hop culture manifested itself in music, dance, dress and a non-verbal communication style:

graffiti writing in highly visible public places. Hip hop graffiti is designed to be cryptic and unintelligible to the casual observer. Three distinct styles have evolved, two of which you have no doubt encountered. The "tag" is a one-dimensional, one-colour marking, usually of a logo or the stylized initials, moniker or nickname of the writer, located on a visible surface such as a storefront, mailbox or hydro pole. Taking only a few seconds to spray-paint, the tag denotes the writer's "brand"; the payment sought is simply respect—for artistry and productivity—from others in the subculture (that's why you will often see the same tag plastered all over an area). Simple taggers, derisively called "toys" by more experienced graffiti artists, often move on to painting "throw-up" graffiti, the larger, two-dimensional, two-colour bubble-style markings that take more time and artistry to create and therefore expose the artists to greater danger of being caught. Part of the thrill for many throw-up artists comes in painting hard-to-reach surfaces such as highway overpasses, water towers or the tops of multi-storey buildings, or mobile surfaces such as railway cars and delivery trucks, especially when the chance of capture is high. The more difficult or mobile the placement, the more respect and recognition earned within the subculture. And finally, there is the hip hop graffiti artist of the "piece"—short for masterpiece—the multicoloured, very large, very expressive and complex urban mural.

The police will tell you that collateral crime is associated with hip hop graffiti. In Toronto, for instance, Inspector Heinz Kuck of the Toronto Police Service, the country's foremost graffiti expert, says that 80 percent of the graffiti vandals they arrest admit to stealing their supplies, something they call "racking" (taking paint cans from racks in the store). However, other than the theft of supplies, trespassing, vandalism and the consumption of illegal drugs, which is part of the lifestyle, the vast majority of hip hop graffiti artists do not involve themselves in serious crimes or in gang activity. Their crime is one of misplaced and illegal artistry, of treating public spaces as their canvas to decorate, and not that of gangsterism.

In contrast, whereas hip hop graffiti in all of its forms is designed to be read, understood and appreciated only by those within the subculture, gang graffiti is usually clear, one colour, crisp and legible to most people, including cops, citizens and other gang members. There are five unique forms of gang graffiti. The "hit-up" is a form of graffiti—usually a logo, the gang name or initials—used to demarcate boundaries or assist with recruitment. It says to rival gangs, "We own this turf, so stay out," and informs at-risk youth, who may be contemplating the gang life, from whom they must seek membership. The "cross-out" is a combative form of graffiti where a rival gang, as the name suggests, crosses out another gang's hit-up markings; it denotes lack of respect for that gang or a challenge to the turf they claim as their own. A "roll call" is designed to intimidate a community and rival gangs: the gang selects a large surface such as the side of a building and lists all the members of the gang, sometimes several dozens of them, including members who have been accused of serious crimes. An "RIP"—for "rest in peace"—is a graffiti memorial to fallen gang members that may include their name, portrait and accomplishments. And finally, "threat" gang graffiti is just that—the issuing of a death threat to a rival gang member.

Even when they see what may appear to be highly communicative, specific gang graffiti messages, people in a community should not jump to conclusions about their source, as oftentimes gang wannabes mimic gang artwork. Any graffiti assumed to be gang work must be validated by the police against empirical data, including Crime Stoppers reports, informant information, prisoner debriefings and actual calls for service. An emerging problem, as far as gang graffiti is concerned, is that the more aware and better-organized street gangs understand that police appreciate the communicative value of their markings, especially hit-ups and roll calls, and that helps cops understand their turf boundaries and gang membership. Since police pressure on gangs has steadily been on the rise, many gangs are "going underground," reducing their reliance on outward modes of communication, including graffiti, distinctive dress, hand signs and tattoos, among others—hence the evolution of the "hybrid" gang that I noted earlier. With regard to dress, the situation is complicated by the fact that the "gang chic" look has been adopted by the broader hip hop culture. A group of kids "saggin' and baggin'" and looking like gangsters might just be a group of kids acting the part, not playing it.

It may be hard to tell if gangs are active in your community unless gang crimes are reported in the media. On a day-to-day basis you may see no visible evidence, and what you might see may in fact be misleading.

In the final analysis, police data, along with first-hand reports from your children, who may be exposed to gangs in schools, malls and other public places, are probably the only reliable indicators of whether gangs are present in your community.

WHAT ARE THE CHANCES OF BEING KILLED BY A GANG?

In many respects, people fear the wrong things. Street gangs and their thousands of members are among us and live in dozens of towns and cities across this country. However, it is important to keep things in perspective as far as gang violence is concerned and its impact on the 99+ percent of Canadians who have no involvement, either directly or peripherally, with gang subculture. In my previous risk computation I estimated that eighty-five of the assumed hundred gang-related homicides in Canada in 2005 were of people with some connection to the business of street gangs. In effect, then, the so-called collateral damage associated with Canada's gang problem—such as Jane Creba and Philippe Haiart, who were truly innocent victims—constituted only fifteen people (a generous estimate).

I may be criticized for setting aside the eighty-five deaths of people somehow involved in gangs for the numerical argument that follows. It is not my intention to make a value judgment on the worth of those lives, but rather to demonstrate that the chance of being killed as a result of street-gang carnage is low for the bulk of the population who have no gang involvement whatsoever.

Expressed in terms of Canada's total population of some thirty-one million, you have a 1 in 2,111,266 chance of being an innocent victim of a gang-related murder this year. To put things in perspective, let's look at the odds of other accidental deaths. According to Statistics Canada's 2003 mortality rate data, approximately 2,850 people died in Canada as a result of traffic accidents, 1,600 from accidental falls and 855 from accidental poisoning and exposure to noxious substances. According to other sources, about 350 people die each year from fires, about 500 drown, about 83 die in plane crashes (commercial and private), and about 30 die from food poisoning. So let's express these accidents in terms of your chances of dying this year:

Accident	1 chance in
Street-gang related	2,111,266
Food poisoning	1,033,333
Plane crash	380,000
Fire	90,482
Drowning	63,338
Accidental poisoning	37,039
Fall	19,793
Traffic accident	11,100

These numbers tell an interesting story about humans and the psychology of fear. Many people harbour a fear of flying, but, despite the fact that one is thirty-five times more likely to die this year in a traffic accident than in an airplane accident, every day we get into our cars worrying not at all about the attendant risk and only about the commute time and what we'll be having for dinner. The same holds true for accidental street-gang–related deaths. Many people, especially in urban areas, are concerned about the potentially fatal spillover effects of a gang feud, yet on hot summer weekends across the country these same people gleefully frolic in pools, lakes and rivers, oblivious to the fact that they are far more likely to die from drowning.

We also have a distorted fear of other dangers, the likes of which most of us will never come face to face. How much media space in 2005 and 2006 was devoted to the impending avian flu, despite only a handful of cases worldwide? We are constantly reminded about the dangers of carjacking, home invasions, flesh-eating disease, antibiotic-resistant superbugs, mad cow disease and other lurking scourges. Yet we give short shrift to real dangers such as cancer, cardiovascular disease and diabetes, many of them brought on by deliberate lifestyle choices, which collectively kill well over 100,000 Canadians every year.

While many Canadians fear violent crime and believe that it is on the rise, the statistics tell a different story. Crimes of violence (murder, assault, rape) have fallen from 984 incidents per 100,000 people in 2001 to 946 incidents per 100,000 in 2004. We have been conditioned to believe that firearms murders are on the rise, but they have actually fallen from 184 murders in 2000 to 172 in 2004. The same holds true for youth crime, a phenomenon that many Canadians believe is spiralling out of control. In 1999 a total of 71,305 Criminal Code cases were tried in respect to youth, which dropped to 57,880 in 2004. Specifically, crimes against the person (rape, homicide, robbery) dropped 10 percent in that period, from 22,432 to 20,416 cases.

I am not trying to make the case that we shouldn't be concerned about crime generally, or street gangs specifically, in favour of ruminating exclusively about the many dangers that are more likely to affect us. Quite the contrary—street gangs are a serious and growing problem. They produce an insidious form of harm that is sometimes evident and sometimes ambiguous, but costly nonetheless. Street gangs put innocent people at risk, drive down property values and reduce our feeling of community safety. Street gangs create drug-trade–related violence that sometimes spills over into the general community and they defraud people and businesses of millions of dollars of hard-earned cash. Street gangs endanger our children, who may become entangled in their affairs, even in settings (such as schools) that we otherwise consider to be safe bastions for our young charges. Unintended deaths caused by street gangs are, after all, only one measure of the damage these groups can generate. Just because it is highly unlikely that any of us will die as a result of gang activity does not mean that they will never harm us or our families indirectly. We must remain vigilant about gangs.

Rather than fear the fate that befell young Jane Creba and Phillipe Haiart, we ought to be concerned about the causes of the dangers we most abhor, because this is a much more productive application of our anxiety. Take poverty, for instance. Countless studies by sociologists around the world show conclusively that poverty correlates strongly with crime, child abuse, drug use and the incidence of street gangs. So too does income disparity between rich and poor, which displays a strong correlation with both higher crime and negative health outcomes. By and large, in regard to street gangs, we fear the outcome but not the cause, an unfortunate case of inverted thinking that perpetuates our culture of fear, and our gang problem.

Nineteenth-century social reformer Jacob Riis elegantly wrote that "the gang is a distemper of the slums; a friend come to tell us something is amiss in our social life." It seems to me that an enlightened approach would be for Canadians to direct their anxiety against the ingredients of street gangs. So, rather than recoiling from gangs, let's recoil from poverty, social exclusion, discrimination, neglect of new immigrants, decaying cities, income disparity, "affluenza" and the other social afflictions that drive youth to gangs in the first place. Nothing short of a massive shift in perspective, and acceptance of responsibility for a problem largely of our own making, will enable us to quash the growth of street gangsterism in our country.

2: GANGSTA GIRLS

The Troubling Role of Females in Gangs

Through the decades, the city of Ottawa has been considered, by residents and visitors alike, a somewhat boring, safe, homogeneous, aesthetically pleasing government town, devoid of the excitement, diversity and raw energy that emanate most often from larger cities such as Toronto, Montreal and Vancouver. Few would ever have considered Ottawa a street-gang hotspot, but in the early hours of October 26, 1995, Ottawa's dominant (and well-earned) image was temporarily overshadowed by a heinous gang crime. The incident forever changed both the lives of two young women who lived to talk about it and the community in which they lived.

The story began at 12:30 a.m. on this fateful day, when a cousin of the young women, seventeen-year-old Ottawa resident Sylvain Leduc, picked up the receiver of his ringing home telephone. Thinking the caller was his half-brother Andre, Leduc jovially answered the phone in the brothers' customary way: "What's up, nigger?"

Sylvain Leduc was not black, nor was his half-brother. And Leduc had no idea that the caller was indeed black, and a member of the violent Ottawa street gang Ace Crew. That innocent, if offensive, greeting would result in his shocking death less than an hour later, in an almost deserted apartment in the suburb of Nepean.

Variously referred to as the Ace's Crew or Ace Crew, this street gang first became known to the Ottawa Police Service in July 1994, during the investigation of a shooting in the city's popular Vincent Massey Park. Composed largely of young black men ranging in age from eighteen to twenty-five, during the early 1990s the gang established its turf, created its own hand signs and graffiti, chose colours and went about the business of pushing drugs. It also stocked its numbers with a necessary gang accoutrement, young females. Barely into their teenage years, these girls acted as sex providers and dope sellers. To display their ownership of the gang, the leaders would brand them, like cattle, in a most ingenious way. An everyday Bic lighter would be purchased. A gang member would flick it on and then turn the lighter horizontally for a minute or so, to allow the flame to heat the steel hood on the top of the lighter. Then several gang members would forcefully hold down the left arm of the girl initiate and press the top of the lighter against the back of her hand until the skin was severely burned. The result was a distinctive rounded A, the sign of the Crew.

Sylvain Leduc knew the Ace Crew sign, despite having no personal involvement with the gang. His two cousins Marie and Chantal were branded with the A, and they sold drugs for the gang.[12] But the girls' commitment to the gang had wavered in the fall of 1995 as the Ace Crew's activities grew steadily more violent. They had also become disillusioned by the poor treatment they received from the gang, and they wanted out, but, as they would soon discover alongside Sylvain, it is not easy to leave a street gang that is rising in prominence and a sense of self-importance.

At approximately 11:15 p.m. on October 25, another young female member of the Ace Crew convinced Chantal to leave an Ottawa house she was visiting to discuss $400 the gang owed to Chantal's boyfriend, as well as her desire to leave the gang.[13] Driving a car supplied by a gang member, the young woman met Chantal outside the home. A male Ace Crew member was hiding in the backseat. As she settled into the car, Chantal was confronted by the end of his sawed-off shotgun. Under his direction, they proceeded to an apartment at 33 Banner Road in Nepean that was being leased by two other female members of the gang.

The building at 33 Banner Road is plain but purposeful, twelve storeys high and consisting of 220 units, not unlike any other middle-class apartment building in any other large Canadian city. Its portico displays the pleasant-sounding name "The Arlington"; its owner, Minto Corporation, glowingly describes the building as being "steps to everything, yet worlds away," an "immaculately maintained building . . . nestled in a tranquil neighbourhood." It's likely, however, that the residents of the building on that fateful night in 1995 would describe it as anything but immaculate or tranquil.

Escorted at gunpoint by the male gang member into the apartment, which contained several Ace Crew members, Chantal was led into a small, empty storage room. Bound hand and foot with stereo cables and with her eyes covered by a gang do-rag, Chantal heard the male gang member hiss, "This is where we're gonna blow your fuckin' brains out." He then ordered his compadres to cut up green garbage bags and tape them on the floor and halfway up the walls, to facilitate an easier clean-up.

Chantal was questioned for approximately half an hour about the money owed to her boyfriend and her wish to leave the gang. Three male Ace Crew members wanted to know the whereabouts of her cousin Marie. In fear for her life, Chantal gave the gangsters Marie's Ethel Street address in Vanier, a somewhat rundown low-income francophone district less than two kilometres from the prime minister's residence and tony Rockcliffe Park. The men, accompanied by the same young woman who had brought Chantal to Banner Road, left the apartment to collect Marie. In her later testimony while under a witness protection program, the young woman claimed that after they left Banner Road, a male Ace Crew member called the apartment on a cellphone to instruct someone to turn on the curling iron—a heavy-duty commercial-grade unit—and set it to high.

Twenty minutes later, at 12:30 a.m. on October 26, the entourage arrived outside the Ethel Street row house that was being rented by Sylvain Leduc's mother. Still in the car, a male Ace Crew member called the home to ask for Marie. But Sylvain answered the phone and, mistaking the caller for his half-brother, uttered the unfortunate "What's up, nigger?"

"Wha? Who you calling a nigger?" demanded the gangster.

"Oh, sorry, I thought it was someone else," responded Leduc, who then passed the phone to Marie.

Identifying himself, the gangster asked Marie, "Who else is in the house?"

"My cousin and his friend are watching TV and my other cousin is upstairs in bed."

The gangster and two other male companions left the car and entered the apartment. Armed with a gun, they confronted Marie, Leduc and his friend Dan Chartrand.

"Who's the fucking redneck?" the gangster asked aggressively.

"What do you mean 'the redneck'?" Leduc answered, confused by the question.

"Who's the redneck?" the gangster repeated with even greater insistence.

Again Leduc responded, "I don't know what you mean!"

Growing impatient with the answers, the gangster then asked Leduc, "Who's upstairs?"

"My little brother."

The gun-wielding gangster then sent a comrade upstairs to collect Leduc's brother, but was greeted halfway up by a large, growling German shepherd dog and beat a hasty retreat back to the others. The gangsters then ordered Leduc, Chartrand and Marie to put on their shoes and coats and get into the back of the car. As they departed Ethel Street, one of the gang members hit the two boys on the head several times with the butt of the gun. Marie later testified that Leduc, with tears welling in his eyes, said "I don't wanna die"—it was at that moment that she knew he thought he was going to be murdered that night.

Just after 1:00 a.m., the gangsters and their quarry arrived at the parking lot behind 33 Banner Road. In a second-floor apartment overlooking the lot, a male resident of the building was watching television with his balcony door slightly ajar to allow in the unseasonably warm fall air. The man was startled to hear a commotion outside and a voice commanding, "Just shut the fuck up and you won't get hurt!" Curious, the resident sneaked a peak over his balcony railing. He witnessed a group of people removing three others from the back of a car: Marie, Leduc and Chartrand. Heads covered by what he thought were hoods or coats, the three young people were roughly led through the rear entrance into the building.

Uncertain as to what to do, the resident paced his apartment for a few minutes, then decided to report the incident to 911. Several Ottawa police units were dispatched to the building. Arriving at the entrance, they saw eight young people—Ace Crew members both male and female—scurry into the lobby and out the front door. Four sprinted into the darkness and two cops gave chase while the other officers corralled the remaining four in the lobby. After one of the escapees was captured and taken into custody with the others in the lobby, the police officers began to ask questions. The detainees' stories ran from the ridiculous to the sublime: one youth, dressed only in a T-shirt and completely out of breath from running, said he was out for a walk. Another told the officers that he was only at the apartment to buy a puppy. Names were run, and CPIC data indicated that several were wanted for assault and breach of probation conditions.[14]

With the youths securely confined in the lobby, the police received another call, from a third floor resident who indicated that a woman was injured on that floor. An officer ran upstairs and found Marie in the hallway outside apartment 310, naked from the waist down, frantically screaming in pain, blood on her thighs. Entering the apartment, the officer yelled, "Police!" and heard another female's cries for help coming from a closed room—the garbage-bag–lined storage closet. After untying Chantal he was joined by other officers, who spread out through the small apartment. In an empty bedroom they found Sylvain Leduc lying prone on the floor, dead, with a stereo cable wrapped around his neck. His friend Chartrand was beside him, viciously beaten, unconscious, but still alive.

Securing the crime scene, the patrol officers called in to headquarters to report the crimes. Soon after, at 2:30 a.m., a seasoned major-crime investigator, Detective Sergeant Patrick Lowell, was called to report to the scene. Lowell arrived within an hour. With the victims already removed by paramedics, it wasn't much of a crime scene. It appeared that the occupants of the apartment were in the final stages of moving. Beds and a few moving boxes were pushed up against the walls, revealing large expanses of inexpensive parquet flooring. Moving about the small one-bedroom unit, Lowell saw gang do-rags, stereo cables and a pair of discarded police gloves on the floor. A sawed-off shotgun wrapped in a towel and an overcoat, the pocket containing several shotgun shells, was also discovered.

Investigators of crimes such as this liken the process of working the case to peeling back layers of an onion. To be sure, victim testimony renders valuable information, but often victims are not in possession of all the facts, circumstances and nuances that allow investigators to produce a reasonable account of what actually occurred. Unlike *CSI*'s portrayals of tidy, hours-long homicide investigations using incredible technologies to lift fingerprints or extract useable DNA from pocket lint and capture licence plate images from orbiting satellites, the Lowells of the world must still employ dogged legwork and sometimes use the testimony of suspects to make their cases.

The Ace Crew case was no different. The testimony of five young females, all under the age of eighteen (and later placed in a witness protection program), helped Lowell and his partner, John Maxwell, turn a nondescript crime scene and uncooperative suspects into an airtight case. In hours and hours of interviews, the young females—the victims Chantal and Marie, plus the driver of the kidnap car and the two girls who lived in apartment 310—detailed a harrowing tale of brutality that began roughly the same time the second-floor resident made the 911 call.

Pushed into the apartment by two male gang members, Marie, Leduc and Chartrand were immediately tied up and thrown on the bedroom floor. For his faux pas of answering the phone the way he did, within a matter of minutes Leduc was savagely beaten with foot and fist by several gang members. His beating so severe, the attending coroner later reported, that young Leduc would surely have died from his internal injuries alone if he had not been painfully asphyxiated with thick stereo cables.

Turning their attention to Marie, gang members held her down while they attempted to remove her blouse over her head. Discovering that it was pinned to an undergarment at the shoulders, they left the blouse over her head while another girl placed her in a headlock. Her pants and underwear were torn off and she was raped with the hot curling iron until she passed out from the unfathomable pain.

Two youngsters victimized, two more to go—Chantal was in the closet and Chartrand was lying in the bedroom next to his dead friend. Picking up where they had left off minutes earlier, the Ace Crew members began to beat the young man. Within minutes he too was unconscious. If it hadn't been for the sound of sirens, the approaching police cars and a gang member yelling "Five-O!"the young man would likely have been strangled as well. [15] Hastily departing the apartment just twenty-two minutes after they entered it, the gangsters flooded into the lobby just as the Ottawa police were arriving.

Over the next few months, Lowell and Maxwell, with help from the RCMP and the Winnipeg and Vancouver police, apprehended the three Ace Crew gangsters who had escaped into the night on October 26. Altogether, five young offenders and three adults were arrested and charged. The young offenders were charged with an assortment of offences including manslaughter, kidnapping and various assaults. Of the five charged, two were convicted of all the offences, including manslaughter, while the balance were variously convicted of kidnapping and assault charges. Under the provisions of the much-maligned Young Offenders Act, each received a sentence of five years, composed of closed custody, open custody and probation. Considering the seriousness and sheer brutality of the crimes with which they had been involved, the meagre sentences created an aftershock in the Leduc family and the community at large.

Since the city of Ottawa experienced a record twenty-three murders in 1995—Leduc's clearly the most horrific—Justice Douglas Rutherford did not begin to hear motions in the murder trial of the three adult Ace Crew gang members until more than two years later. Each was charged with thirteen offences, including first-degree murder, aggravated assault, aggravated sexual assault, kidnapping, forcible confinement and various weapons charges. After several weeks of testimony the jury began to deliberate the case over the 1998 Easter weekend. Eight days later the jury re-entered a packed courtroom to render their decisions. Of thirty-nine charges, the jury foreman stated "guilty as charged" thirty-nine times. In his concluding remarks Judge Rutherford thanked the police officers for "presenting a near perfect case." Later, one of the defendants would be ordered deported to his native country at the conclusion of his twenty-five-year prison sentence.

To this day, almost a dozen years after one of Canada's most brutal street-gang crimes and months from his well-deserved retirement, veteran police detective Patty Lowell describes Ace Crew as a "good case" and is justifiably proud of his contribution. He is also mindful of the ripples of good fortune in a sea of evil: a warm October evening, an open balcony door, the curiosity of the second-floor resident and his decision to call 911 when he did.

"There is no doubt in my mind, no doubt in my mind at all, that all four of those kids would have been killed," says Lowell. "You can't kill a boy in front of two other people and torture another with a curling iron and say, 'Okay, you go tell the cops now if you want.' If we didn't get that 911 call and come when we did, they would have been killed and we would not have found their bodies for days."

Perhaps remembering the shocking Leduc death, the smell of burned flesh at 33 Banner Road, or the physical and psychological terror wrought upon the three young victims, each of whom he came to know well during the investigation, Lowell reminds those who will listen that the Ace Crew case demonstrates the danger, the capacity for evil and the wanton disregard for the value of life that lurks in today's street gang. He muses rhetorically that if all this pain could arise from an unfortunate racial epithet, what horrors could be created by young gangsters when the stakes are higher—money, turf, survival on the street?

To Lowell and others familiar with the crimes, the Ace Crew case also demonstrates the precarious and subservient role that girls play in gangs, and the brutality that can be inflicted upon them. Two young women, recognizing their earlier poor decisions, had tried to put their checkered drug-dealing, gang-affiliated lives behind them, but were denied that chance by the men they had once served and perhaps even trusted. Dedicated police officers finally ended their tenure in the gang, of course, but the murder of their cousin and the indignities they suffered served only to usher them into another private hell, one from which they will never escape.

:::

The workings of the criminal mind fascinate us and have inspired countless brilliant but often obscure criminologists, sociologists and psychologists to pen weighty tomes describing the results of their research and their theories about what makes the criminal do what they do. One such "-ologist" was the late Dr. Robert M. Lindner. In the early 1940s Lindner recorded forty-six hour-long psychoanalysis sessions with an imprisoned teenage psychopath known only as Harold. Using hypnosis to plumb the depths of Harold's suppressed memories, he was able to uncover the many incidents in Harold's infancy and childhood that later steered him in the direction of rebellious criminal behaviour, including armed robberies and assaults and an overall detachment from society.

Based on his research with Harold, in 1944 Lindner published an acclaimed book that he felt exposed the hidden psychodynamics of "criminal psychopathology"; it was titled *Rebel Without a Cause: The Story of a Criminal Psychopath.* Lindner's academic work, now sixty-three years old, owes its enduring recognition not to the quality of his insights but to Hollywood's 1955 release of one of the world's most famous films—*Rebel Without a Cause,* starring James Dean and Natalie Wood—which the book in part inspired. The actors poignantly embodied youthful angst and malaise in the film's sympathetic portrayal of teenage delinquency, gangs, defiance and rebellion against parents and post-war middle-class society in the United States. Natalie Wood's role as Judy, a pretty girl experiencing emotional turmoil because of her stoic father's withdrawal of affection, has also become emblematic of the curious phenomenon of some women's attraction to so-called bad boys.

Both men and women wonder what some young women see in bad men, including gangsters and even prison inmates. This phenomenon is particularly important when considering the involvement of females—girls, young women and adults alike—in the world of street gangs. Why do some young urban women, who face a dizzying array of choices insofar as potential mates are concerned, choose to love or give themselves over to men from a small, dangerous and most often dead-end subset of society, the street gang? And, just as important, what drives women to the even greater commitment of actually joining a street gang as a full-fledged (but likely secondary) member?

Just as it would be impossible to quantify how many women are in relationships with "bad boys," it is likewise impossible to quantify how many are in relationships with gangsters, although we can safely assume that the number across North America is in the many thousands. But what of the number of actual female street-gang members? Despite suggestions that they exist, there is no evidence of all-female gangs in Canada. Street gangs are, and always will be, a predominantly male organism.

In the 2002 Canadian Police Survey on Youth Gangs, I asked police service respondents to estimate what percentage of gang members (under the age of twenty-one) in their respective jurisdictions were female. The data revealed that, across the country as a whole, 6 percent of gang members were female, ranging from a low of 3 percent in Ontario to a high of 12 percent in British Columbia. In the seven provinces that reported gang activity, a total of approximately 425 female gangsters were thought to exist, about equal to the female population of an average city high school. Despite suggestions that they exist, though there is no evidence whatsoever of all-female gangs in Canada, street gangs are, and always will be, a predominantly male organism. U.S. data show similar numbers, with female gang membership variously estimated at between 8 and 11 percent across America, indicating some 70,000-plus female gangsters. I contend that both the American and Canadian numbers are understated, since police agencies may be less likely to classify a female as a gang member because of both inherent stereotyping ("Women are not as bad as men") and their generally lower level of criminality relative to males.

Whatever their precise numbers, the fact is that hundreds of girls in Canada are befriending gangsters, if not joining their gangs, of their own volition. Many parents no doubt tell themselves, "This won't happen to our family. My girl is a good girl; we live in a good part of town. Those several hundred or so that joined are obviously just 'bad seeds.'" Unfortunately, that is flawed thinking. Every parent should be concerned about their daughter's potential to become mixed up in the lives of street thugs.

Male street gangsters are acutely aware of optics—of the need to establish and present a personal "brand identity" of ferocity and success, one that will earn respect from those around them. In the fiercely heterosexual, testosterone-fuelled and somewhat misogynistic subculture of street gangs, the subservient and loyal gangster girlfriend—a.k.a. "ho" or "bitch"—is as much a part of the gangster's sought-after branding package as are the handgun, the expensive SUV and the twenty-four-karat gold trinkets. Possession of a gangster girlfriend not only denotes sexual prowess and unadulterated machismo, it also tells your volatile brothers-in-arms that you have contributed valuable capacity to the gang. Females play an important supportive role in the commission of crimes and the generation of funds for gang members' enjoyment.

Lacking an inventory of ready and able gangster girls, where are these power-hungry, respect-craving, sexually charged gangsters going to get them? That's right, the community in and around which they operate. Don't let that number 425 lull you into a false sense of security. Just because police say there are only 425 female Canadian gangsters does not mean that many more are not involved in some way, either peripherally or standing on the precipice of full membership. My current estimate of 14,000 or so street-gang members in Canada suggests that, conservatively, some 8,000 to 10,000 girls and women are involved in gangs or associated with their members in some way. In this respect, street-gang culture is no different than Major Junior A hockey. In my time in the league, players who did not have a steady girlfriend, or who spurned the "puck bunnies" who made themselves available to us in small town after small town, were accused of being "queer"—perhaps the most incendiary name you can call a young player who is one step away from the National Hockey League. Your little girl may be a sweet and loving child who has toed the line all her life, but if she falls in love with a drug-pushing gangster with "fuck the police" tattooed on his forehead, you and your family will have a boatload of problems to contend with, and none that any amount of berating or pleading can solve.

WHY GIRLS JOIN GANGS

Historically, the question of why females join gangs or get involved with gangsters has received scant attention, since gangsterism is largely a male phenomenon. When we think about gangs—street, organized or otherwise—we conjure up images of aggressive alpha males committing extreme violence, dealing drugs and terrorizing the communities around them. These are generally viewed as masculine activities in which females generally do not participate.

Asking people why they chose their lovers is no simple matter. For each person with sufficient self-awareness to offer a cogent answer, perhaps two others will stare blankly and answer, "I don't know." Ask a group of girls or women what attracts them to gangsters and other bad men, and you'll get a wide array of answers interspersed with plenty of blank stares. While I do not profess to be an expert on the matter or have empirical data that can withstand the scrutiny of a social scientist, the answers to this unscientific question render informative insights.

Some gang-involved girls will say it is the element of danger, the thrill of being with someone who lives life at the margins of civil society. Some will say that good boys are boring, too predictable, insufficiently risky and lacking mystery. They think that bad boys are Type A guys who exert control and take care of business, traits that many women find irresistible. Some women believe they can change a bad man into a pussycat, a feeling rooted in the maternal desire to make him a better person. Others like the drama associated with a gangster, his unabashed can-do attitude and his ability to make them feel safe and protected. And some women, like the many others of both genders who partake in unsafe sex, consume street drugs of unknown quality and participate in other high-risk behaviour, simply enjoy the rush associated with breaking taboos.

The various anecdotal emotional reasons why women choose to be with bad men explains, in part, how they become exposed to street gangs and provides some perspective on the process by which they come to assume a more active stance and actually join the gang. Conventional wisdom suggests that women are being aggressively recruited or coerced into joining gangs, which presupposes a mandate on the part of a gang to expand. But this is not always the case in the world of highly fragmented and relatively disorganized Canadian street gangs. Many young men and women gradually "grow" into a gang rather than wake up one day and say to themselves, "Hey, I should join a gang today." This evolutionary, rather than revolutionary, process is especially typical for women who befriend and fall in love with male gangsters. A lover one day may become a female gangster the next, although many male gangsters would prefer their legitimate love interests to stay away from the gang for their personal security.

It would be misleading to suggest that falling in love with a gangster is the only explanation for why girls join or grow into gangs, especially when you consider that some girls join regardless of their love interests. Women, like men, are not ruled entirely by emotion, and many make a conscious choice to join a gang for reasons that can easily be articulated and understood. Young women join or accept their place within a gang for the same reasons that young men do: a sense of belonging and identity, power, protection, respect, fear, prestige, money and, for some, paranoia stemming from the "victimize or be a victim" ethos that exists on many mean streets. The problem is, because such limited attention has been paid to young women in gangs, we have traditionally only defined them with respect to their sexual relationship to young men in the gang—as coerced sex toys and property—rather than considering their actual criminal activity, and therefore have clouded the real reasons underlying their decision to join.

The need for protection should not be underestimated when trying to understand why young women join gangs. If you are a woman who has bought this book, you probably do not live in constant fear of violence. But if you do, it is more likely to stem from your spouse or significant other than from conditions in the community where you live. While there are no hard data for me to quote in the Canadian context, I believe strongly that many Canadian girls and young women who elect to join gangs do so in large part because the gang offers a perceived sense of security, if not family—a fundamental need of every human being.

Young women face a different, perhaps more persistent risk of victimization as compared to men, who generally experience crime in the form of robbery and violent physical assault. In Statistics Canada's 2004 General Social Survey (GSS), 28 percent of Canadians aged fifteen and older reported being victimized one or more times in the twelve months preceding the survey, with the highest proportion being among Canadians aged fifteen to twenty four. Status of Women Canada, the federal agency that promotes gender equality and full participation of women in the economic, social, cultural and political life of the country, reports that of all crimes against the person, women and girls make up the vast majority of victims of sexual assault (85 percent), criminal harassment (78 percent), other sexual offences (74 percent), kidnapping or abduction (62 percent) and common assault (52 percent).

Female victims are more likely to be subjected to severe forms of violence, such as being beaten, choked and sexually assaulted, than male victims. Women also tend to be more fearful than men about being victims of crime in specific situations. As well, almost seven out of ten women feel somewhat or very worried while waiting for or using public transportation alone after dark, more than double the proportion of 29 percent for men. The 2004 GSS also indicates that factors such as being single, living in an urban area and having a low household income (under $15,000) greatly increase the likelihood of violent victimization. So a woman living in a low-income, rundown inner-city area in Saskatoon, Regina, Winnipeg, Sudbury or Halifax (which have the highest rates of sexual offences in particular, some more than double those of large cities) will not necessarily feel a great sense of security about her surroundings.

Young women join gangs partly as a means of protecting themselves from violence in the community and partly because of mistreatment at the hands of other men in their lives, such as boyfriends, fathers and stepfathers. Estimates suggest that about half of sexual offenders are men who are known to their female victims. In 2003, girls were the victims in eight out of ten family-related sexual assaults committed against children and youth, assaults typically perpetrated by parents and caregivers. The rates of family-related sexual assault were highest for teenage girls, especially for young teenage girls, aged twelve to fourteen.[16] Within a gang, girls are protected from violent male family members and gain the friendship of other girls, which may provide an outlet to help cope with abuse and other problems. The gang then becomes a surrogate family and provides a sense of security, acceptance and belonging that otherwise may be missing in a young woman's life. Thus the gang offers the same sanctuary to girls and young women as it does to boys and young men.

HOW GIRLS BULLY GIRLS

It is not just predatory men that girls and young woman need to worry about; often it is other girls—female bullies, that is. Bullying is increasingly prevalent among girls, especially among ethnic minorities and other marginalized youth, and is in many respects blighting the future of a generation of young women. According to the LaMarsh Centre for Research on Violence and Conflict Resolution at York University, 8 percent of girls surveyed reported being a victim of bullying. Moreover, Toronto Board of Education research suggested that one in five children in Grade 4 through 8 was victimized periodically, and one in twelve was bullied daily or weekly. Recent research indicates that 9 percent of Canadian girls between the ages of four and eleven participate in bullying other children, and 7 percent are victimized by bullies; 68 percent of children have been observed in both roles, as bully and as victim.[17] We will likely never know the precise numbers, but experts agree that in the past two decades the incidence of female bullying has risen dramatically in Canada.

My police and school contacts concur that female-perpetrated violence is becoming more frequent. Whereas boy bullying tends to be more physical and manifests itself in fights, destruction of personal property and other violent encounters, girl bullying is usually less physical and more psychological in nature, but equally as damaging. Female bullying is more covert and indirect. Because females place greater value on social relationships than males do, female bullies target their victims where it hurts, by attempting to destroy friendships. Shunning their victims, taunting them about their personal appearance or spreading nasty rumours—so-called whisper campaigns that are often sexual in nature—are just some of the tools of the trade for female bullies, as well as physical threats and extortion.

For many girls the scars of social ostracism and diminished self-esteem are far more damaging than a physical attack. While boys are more likely to strike back on a physical level, girls often withdraw socially or drop out of school with few or no qualifications, then go on to lead disaffected lives, including becoming involved in gangs, criminality and drug and alcohol abuse. Of particular importance is an interesting characteristic of bullying: the majority of it takes place in the presence of others. Faced with the bullying itself and the quiet acquiescence of witnesses who are their peers, it is no wonder that some girls turn to a gang to acquire the protection they need.

Recent Canadian incidents have demonstrated the real threat posed by bullying girls. On November 10, 2000, fourteen-year-old Dawn-Marie Wesley of Mission, B.C., hanged herself in her bedroom with a dog leash, leaving a note for her family that read, "If I try to get help it will get worse. They [the bullies] are always looking for a new person to beat up and they are the toughest girls. If I ratted they would get suspended and there would be no stopping them. I love you all so much." And many Canadians remember the tragic November 1997 murder of fourteen-year-old Reena Virk, who was incessantly bullied because of her weight, ethnicity and social awkwardness, then beaten and drowned near Victoria by a group of six girls (and one boy), all of whom were found guilty of criminal offences including, for Kelly Ellard (fifteen at the time of the incident), second-degree murder.

The desire for security and protection is real and, I believe, a key driver in a girl's decision to join a gang. As with boys, however, I cannot help but conclude that it is socio-economic factors that play the largest role in motivating girls and young women to join a gang. While girls from good middle-class families certainly become mixed up in the street-gang subculture, the vast majority of female gang members come from lower-income racial or ethnic minority families, a large proportion of them either headed by a single parent or generally in some state of turmoil. The socio-economic factors that have given rise to our gang problem are many, and they do not require much in the way of further elaboration. As a country we have not done enough to help smooth immigrants' transition upon their arrival in Canada, either by way of supportive jobs or through language and education programs. Massive systemic changes have occurred in our economy over the past two decades: from resource-based to knowledge- and service-based, bringing massive job losses in employment categories traditionally filled disproportionately by immigrants, females and ethnic minorities. The prospects for some young women look bleak indeed.

Women aged fifteen to twenty-four make less than 85 percent of what men do for equivalent work—what Statistics Canada refers to as the "persistent gap" in wages.[18] While women's workforce participation rates have climbed since the mid-1970s, women's work has become increasingly part-time, thereby producing less in the way of earnings. Overall, women continue to be overrepresented among people living on low incomes: the

2004 numbers indicate that men still earn substantially more at $40,300 per year, compared to $25,600 for women. The deck is stacked against women as far as income potential and job access are concerned. The market offers thousands of poorly paying unskilled jobs in the service and hospitality sectors that provide little in the way of a compelling future. It is no wonder that some girls see gangs as offering income potential and prestige to which they would otherwise never have access. For many youth, including females, the underground economy—including the trade in illicit drugs and the sale of sex—is the only economy within which they believe they can readily compete, succeed, obtain standing and earn a living wage.

While it is true that many girls and young women gradually grow into gangs as a result of family and peer associations, there is no denying that active gang recruitment of females is rapidly on the rise in Canada. Especially because of the girls' income potential as sex workers, male street gang members are becoming more predatory in their recruitment, targeting females as young as ten, eleven and twelve in places such as malls, schools, all-night dance parties (a.k.a. raves), foster homes and even, in the case of runaway girls, homeless shelters and other supportive facilities for youth. Typically these men will identify their prospects and shower them with gifts and attention, which for many marginalized and at-risk girls provides the affirmation and sense of belonging they crave. Gangsters will also give girls a taste for drugs, helping to create a chemical dependency that can soon be translated into a bond of a different kind: membership in the gang. Once they are in the gang they can be coerced into the sex trade, with threats of severe beatings, even death, to keep them in check.

THE BRUTAL LIFE OF A FEMALE GANGSTER

If the life of a male gangster can be considered a dangerous and substandard one, then the life of a female gangster is much worse. The traditional view of gangster-girl life has been defined by their sexual relationship to males in the gang, sometimes best summed up as passivity, property and promiscuity. This view is by no means derived from the prejudices or stereotypes of a male-dominated police and gang-research community. To a great extent, especially in countries where street-gang activity is just beginning to emerge as it is here in Canada, girls and young women play a subservient role to the men. Sex—consensual, forced or otherwise—is an ever-present part of their reality.

The auxiliary or secondary role of females in street gangs can be illustrated in the lead-up to full gang membership: the process of gang initiation. Some females, especially those who are accepted into a gang because of family ties or a love interest, such as a brother or a boyfriend in the gang, often bypass the initiation process by being "born in" or "blessed in" to the gang; they must simply pledge allegiance to the gang or receive a gang tattoo or other marking. However, most females who have grown into gang membership through their peer group, or who have been actively recruited by male gang members to expand the size and strength of the gang, are bound to be subjected to a more abusive form of initiation, just like their male counterparts.

As I detailed earlier in this chapter, initiation of females into the Ace Crew gang included painful branding with a red-hot Bic lighter, signifying to others that the girl belonged to the gang. This somewhat rare form of initiation is supplanted much more often by what is known as a "jump-in," where the female is beaten by a group of gang members (usually other females, as many as three to eight at a time) to determine her toughness, commitment to the gang and ability to both receive and administer a beating. Some gangs force females, as part of their initiation process, to commit either one or a series of crimes such as robbery, assault or auto theft. This is sometimes called "doing strikes" or "strykes"; hence some recruits are called "strykers."

Far more frequently, in male-dominated gangs, females are subjected to the degrading "sex-in" or "train-in," an initiation process that clearly demonstrates the deferential nature of girls in gangs. While there are many variations on the theme, the sex-in or train-in generally consists of forcing the aspiring female gang member to perform oral sex or have intercourse with multiple members, if not the entire membership, of a gang; the rank or seniority of the male gang member determines whether he gets to go first, last or somewhere in between. Gang researchers also know of "roll-in" initiations, in which the number of men the female aspirant must have sex with depends on the roll of a pair of dice. Aside from the physical and emotional trauma from the initiation process itself, females who are sexed-in to a gang have the difficult, if not impossible, task of shedding the negative stigma attached to the initiation. Perceived from the outset as promiscuous and submissive, females who enter a gang through this process may forever be relegated to the role of sex toy for their male counterparts.

Membership thus gained, street gangs led and managed by men then set about deploying their new female charges. As noted earlier, for some women (as many as 25 percent of female gang members, in my estimation) life in the street gang will largely be about providing sex to various male gangsters and helping to situate the gang's brand as viable, dynamic and legit. Recently I learned of street gang "spliff for brains" parties, where female gang members seeking marijuana or other illicit drugs must first perform oral sex on a male gangster in public. A variation on this theme is so-called chicken parties, where male gang members force female members to perform oral sex in public on a group of prospective gangsters being groomed for membership; picture chickens' heads bobbing up and down as they walk and you'll get the idea. Just as in the media, sex truly does sell, and a prospective young male gangster must find the thought of ample free sex within the gang to be virtually irresistible.

THE GROWTH OF TEENAGE PROSTITUTION

Gang members, constantly compelled to generate revenue, are not content to let "productive" sex-providing young women do so just for internal consumption. In Canada we have known for years that traditional organized crime syndicates have tight control over several criminal enterprises, including drug trafficking, auto theft and prostitution. What is good for the goose is certainly good for the gander, and street gangs have taken a page from the organized-crime book and have entered the fray of prostitution—more specifically, juvenile prostitution, forcing their female members to contribute to the gang's finances through paid sex.

Some startling facts should motivate Canadian parents to pay attention to the safety of their daughters. If you were to poll several large Canadian police agencies, you would learn that in this country the average age of entry into prostitution is considered to be thirteen or fourteen—sometimes younger—and many of these girls come from abusive backgrounds or are runaways. Today many girls targeted for prostitution are lured in by street-gang members trolling schools and malls, where young women are plentiful, as well as group homes and foster homes where girls may be living. Technology has facilitated this predation; my police sources suggest that gangs identify possible victims and initiate contact through MySpace listings and YouTube–posted videos. This should serve as a caution to parents about the need to keep your young daughters safe. The next time your twelve-year-old asks to be dropped off at the mall or left alone at the family computer for a couple hours of unsupervised browsing with a friend, I urge you to please think twice.

The demand for paid sex with pretty women has always been strong, but if the growth of teenage prostitution is a reliable indicator, Canadian men seem to be demanding a less common—indeed, illicit—experience that can be provided only by "fresher" teenage prostitutes. For men seeking such girls the options are limited. They can travel to exotic locations such as Thailand, Cambodia, Indonesia or the Dominican Republic, countries that are notorious for a tourist sex trade involving both young girls and boys. Of course, if international travel is too costly or inconvenient, these men will have to find teenage prostitutes locally. Entrepreneurial street gangs can always produce supply to meet the demand. They have filled the void because they—more so than their organized-crime counterparts—have access to young girls whom they can coerce into prostitution as part of their gang membership.

There have been a few high-profile examples of street-gang involvement in teenage prostitution rings. In 2002 a large-scale teenage prostitution network was disrupted by Quebec law enforcers as part of Project Scorpion. The ring, led by forty-four members of Quebec City street and biker gangs, included girls as young as fourteen. They were pimped out at up to $500 per hour to prominent Quebec City businessmen, including a popular radio host and an aide to a former premier. In 2004 six people linked to street gangs were arrested as part of a one-year investigation called Project Orion, which focused on a teenage prostitution ring of more than thirty females aged fifteen through nineteen. The investigation discovered that the girls were either runaways or foster children, and were often moved around to other cities by their gang pimps to avoid being traced by police. Later, in early 2006, the Montreal Police Service publicly acknowledged that twenty "major" street gangs, mostly split into Bloods and Crips factions and consisting of approximately 400 to 500 members, were involved in crimes such as drug trafficking and teenage prostitution.

The consumers of these teenage prostitution services, either wittingly or unwittingly, contribute to the growth of gangs. All Canadians, therefore, through either ethical behaviour or choices made on the periphery of accepted societal practice (such as buying street drugs or paying for a fifteen-year-old hooker), can play a role in either stopping or fermenting the growth of street gangs.

According to RCMP officials in British Columbia, more and more girls are joining the South Asian gangs in that province. Rosie Thakar, diversity coordinator for the Surrey (B.C.) RCMP, says that many Indo-Canadian girls join gangs, start off as prostitutes and end up as drug runners for male-dominated street gangs who see girls simply as cash. However, it must be said that not all girls are coerced victims forced to keep turning tricks at the end of a gun. Most gang pimps know that they've got to keep their girls reasonably happy or they'll bolt. For some girls and young women the income potential of turning tricks and the lifestyle it offers—compared to that provided by burger flipping or hotel room cleaning—keep them involved in their substandard profession. For these girls it can be a relatively circumspect choice: "My body is mine and it can earn me money—lots of it—so why not do it for a while?" This is perhaps the same line of reasoning that keeps strippers stripping and lap dancers dancing and adult escorts entertaining, all of their own volition, despite the availability of broader, though less well-paid, career options.

HOW GANGS REDUCE THE RISKS OF INVOLVING GIRLS

There is a certain risk in allowing any person—male or female—into the fold of the gang. Will they stand up for the gang? Will they remain loyal? Will they, if picked up by a cop, spill their guts about the activities, structure and membership of the gang? The risk associated with accepting a female into a street gang is greatly enhanced if she only provides sex to members or their customers. After all, there is nothing illegal in being a gang whore. However, entrepreneurial and street savvy as they are, male gang members know that their risk profile can be greatly mitigated (and their income potential enhanced) if they ensure that the female gangster participates in some way in criminal activity. Someone who is herself guilty of criminal activities within a group is less likely to rat them out than someone who is not.

The drug trade being so central to the street gang, females can play an important role in its operations. Because of the risks of theft and violence from rival gangsters, females are not deployed in street-level sales of illicit drugs to the same extent as males. This is and will likely always be a principally male task. However, females make good drug dealers in more controlled settings such as schools and dance parties, where the chances of violence are lower. Because of their overall lower level of criminality and reduced propensity for violence, law enforcers do not view females as suspiciously as they would males, especially, for example, black males who appear to be gang-involved. In 2005, of the 250,492 Canadians admitted to custody (prison or remand), only 10 percent were women. Among youth, boys are three to four times more likely to be charged with a criminal offence than girls. As a result, females play an important supporting role in hiding, holding and transporting drugs from one place to the next. A woman acting as a drug mule, the contraband safely stowed inside her vagina, is a favoured vehicle for transporting drugs into prison. A female gang member with an incarcerated boyfriend is likely to increase her drug dealing to help finance her life and her lover's requirements while he's in the prison system.

Females can also be deployed in street-level crimes such as robbery, shoplifting and extortion, helping street gangs to collect valuable merchandise that can later be turned into cash. Recently I heard of an operation in Ottawa that featured the combined crimes of shoplifting, drug distribution and money laundering all in one. A street gang that purportedly included female members was discovered stealing—are you ready for this?—mozzarella cheese and meats such as steak, ground beef, pepperoni and other deli products from local grocery stores. The gang would collect the food over two or three weeks and store them, unrefrigerated, at the home of one of the gang members. Periodically they would deliver the meats and cheese to a local pizza shop affiliated with the gang. The owners of the pizza joint would pay the thieves in crack cocaine, which they were importing but did not want to push at the street level. The gang would then sell the crack, using the proceeds as compensation for their meat-stealing activities, and the pizza place would make a large profit on their takeout dishes because the cost of their ingredients was so low. This seems a rather circuitous route to making money, but it has a certain elegance, especially for the pizza shop, which could operate as an ostensibly legitimate business.

In criminal enterprises, just as in legal businesses, information is power, and females can play an important role in brokering it for the benefit of a gang. American research shows ample evidence that females are often deployed by gangs to seduce rival gang members, either to obtain information about the gang's activities or to set them up by getting the rival to a secluded area so he can be beaten or murdered. Because the numbers of female gang members in Canada are presently relatively small, the extent of this infiltration activity is limited, but it is occurring with greater frequency as gang rivalries escalate. Infiltration is also an issue in witness intimidation. If gangs are aware of possible witnesses to a serious crime such as a shooting, they have been known to deploy females to determine who knows what and their likelihood of co-operating with the authorities. "Corrective" intimidation (such as threatening death) can then be implemented. Indeed, witness intimidation may be one of the biggest challenges law enforcement officials face when prosecuting gangs.

WHY GIRLS STAY IN GANGS

Earlier I suggested that life as a female gangster can be a brutal one. However, female gangsters do not spend all their time involved in prostitution, drug dealing or other criminal offences. A typical day in the life of a street-gang member, especially for young females, is not jam-packed with drama, constant danger and a variety of adrenalin-inducing excitement. In fact, it can be a pretty humdrum existence: going to school, working at a dead-end job, participating in family activities, maintaining relationships and just being a young person struggling to find a way in the world. The Pareto principle applies here also: 20 percent of gangsters (mostly men) produce 80 percent of gang-activity excitement, danger and violence, meaning that the vast majority of gangsters live fairly ordinary lives most of the time, punctured by brief periods of excitement induced by criminal activity.[19]

Within this context we can understand why some young women, especially marginalized ones for whom school, family, job or other institutions simply do not work, stay in gangs. Danger is a real, though intermittent, possibility, as is a subservient, oftentimes sexual-plaything role. Time has shown that some girls and young women, however, derive sufficient compensation from the gang. Camaraderie, companionship, excitement, acceptance, protection, respect, status and income derived from drugs and prostitution—all reasons that perhaps drove them to the gang in the first place—are often perceived as adequate compensation for the perils. For a while at least: like the two young female victims in the Ace Crew case, many girls eventually figure out that gang life is a ticket to nowhere.

The same cannot be said of many young women who have fallen victim to the manipulative advances and criminal artifices of predatory male gangsters who crave female companionship and the income stream they can produce—essentially as indentured sex slaves or drug mules. The choices available to these girls are few, and I consider them to be among the ranks of the true victims of street gangs. It is because these ranks are, regrettably, growing that we must pay special attention to street gangs and do everything possible to curtail their growth. All Canadians, especially men, must do everything possible to protect our country's girls and young women from the ravages of gangs and the clutches of male gangsters.

3: UNCLE SAM

Playing the Guns and Gangs Blame Game

The United States casts a long and influential shadow on Canada's economic, cultural and geopolitical affairs, a shadow we sometimes regret and have limited power to influence. Uncle Sam's sway in Canada is especially compelling from an economic perspective. While both countries are esteemed members of the Group of Eight (G8), the United States is first among equals: it boasts the world's biggest economy, some 10.5 times larger than ours. Roughly three-quarters of our trade is with the United States, as is most of the movement of capital in and out of this country. When the U.S. Federal Reserve chairman expresses fiscal concern and the Dow sneezes, the Toronto Stock Exchange immediately catches a cold. Our shared border's porosity in terms of military defence is matched by its openness to other influences, including America's ubiquitous popular culture. But what can be said about the social ills of U.S. gang culture and violence?

In late 2005 our political leaders began making "poor us" statements that led to a belief that Canada's gang problem is due in part to our American cousins. In the run-up to the January 2006 federal election, when the blood that flowed from Toronto's year of the gun was still fresh, former prime minister Paul Martin and Toronto's mayor, David Miller, allocated some of the blame for the city's gang problem on Americans and the "export of their gun violence." The typical citizen took that to mean the export of their culture of gang violence, of dangerous American-made firearms and, in some cases, of the gangs themselves. Searching for convenient sound bites to explain the mounting death toll, our politicians took the easy route, allocating at least some causality to outside our borders—to our favourite gang-culture whipping boy, the United States—rather than to Canadian causes of the violence.

As easy as it is to play the blame game and assign responsibility to the United States without offering proof, let alone reasoned argument, it would be just as easy to dismiss the politicos' assertions as nonsense, the stuff of electioneering and rampant scapegoating. After all, U.S. influence on our everyday lives is real. Setting side for a moment the possible impact of imported American culture and mass media, the core question is what influence the United States has on our emerging street-gang problem. More specifically, has the United States exported gangsters to Canada, along with the gun violence often associated with American street gangs?

THE MYTH OF GANG MIGRATION

No discussion of the possible effects of the United States on our gang situation is complete without exploring the idea that large, well-established, organized U.S. street gangs are exporting their gang "franchise" to new and less established gang locations, including Canada. The myth of migration is best illustrated in the context of one of the world's most storied and feared street gangs, the Crips. In 1969 a fifteen-year-old East Los Angeles youth, Raymond Washington, organized a group of neighbourhood youths into a gang, in part to protect themselves from other small but violent gangs that were roaming through South Central Los Angeles. Launched as the Baby Avenues, the gang emulated a larger group called the Avenue Boys, which had been carrying out minor crimes on behalf of the Black Panthers since about 1964.

Washington, along with Stanley "Tookie" Williams (who was executed in 2005 for the 1979 robbery deaths of four people) and several other members of the Baby Avenues, was increasingly fascinated by the hype surrounding the Black Panthers, and they sought to develop their nascent gang into a more violent and dominant force. A name change seemed necessary, so the gang began calling themselves the Avenue Cribs, since its members lived in and around Central Avenue ("crib" being a slang term for home). By 1971, for reasons that are still debated, the use of the word "crip" had become so common among the Avenue Cribs that it became their accepted name. By then known simply as the Crips, the gang was also identifiable by their trademark colour, blue, and their C hand sign.

Through the 1970s and early 1980s, as violence and crack cocaine swept through southern California, the Crips grew steadily, through aggressive recruitment, successful drug-market expansion and amalgamation with smaller gangs, to become the largest and most dangerous street gang in southern California. At one point its membership outnumbered that of rival street gangs by about three to one. The rapid ascent of the Crips forced other, smaller gangs to coalesce, most notably into the Crips' biggest rival, the Bloods, and the violence continued to escalate. Their notoriety in Los Angeles was firmly established and their profile outside of L.A. was thrust into the public consciousness by movies whose narratives centred around street gangs and gang life. The acclaimed film *Colors* portrayed a rivalry between the Crips and a fictional Hispanic gang, the White Fences; it begat other gang-themed movies such as *Boyz n the Hood, Menace II Society, New Jack City* and *American Me.*

While the meteoric growth in the sheer number of Crip foot soldiers in L.A. was remarkable, no similar growth occurred in their organizational capabilities. The gang—if it could still be termed properly in the singular—grew to become a disorganized, diverse, fractious and insular street entity without the formal structure and well-defined conventions of, say, a Mafia crime syndicate. Throughout southern California, dozens of independent Crip gang "sets" could be found that had no association with one another, their monikers highlighting their geographic origins, as in the Avalon Garden Crips, the Eastside Crips, the Inglewood Crips, the Westside Crips. While Crip sets would collaborate from time to time in major drug deals, often they fought brutally with one another. Law enforcement officials estimated that, in the peak years of Los Angeles gang violence, Crips killed each other at a rate of three Crips to every one of their sworn enemies, the Bloods, an indication of how ubiquitous—and violent—the gangsters had become.

Since the mid-eighties, Crip gang sets have been established all over the United States and in Canada, Europe, Central America and even Africa, although Los Angeles remains their stronghold. One set, the Rollin' 60 Neighborhood Crips, claims to be the largest black criminal street gang in the city of Los Angeles, with more than 1,600 active members—about the size of an army brigade, or three-quarters of the estimated street-gang population of Toronto in 2006. Today the Crips remain a force to be reckoned with throughout North America. But the Crips' bark may be worse than their bite, not because they are not dangerous and powerful (they certainly are, on a set-by-set basis), but because of people's mistaken belief that they are a "supergang" with many branches and strong centralized control, that the gang is migrating and that it has "franchised" its operation throughout the world.

According to this migration theory, powerful gangs located in major American metropolitan areas, such as the Crips and the Bloods, are desirous of new drug markets and less strident competition from rival gangs. Wishing to escape police pressure, they seek to expand their presence elsewhere, into smaller cities that have a less acute gang problem. Just as a franchise-based corporation such as Tim Hortons expands into underserved communities to increase market share and generate new sales, according to the gang migration theory, street gangs similarly seek to expand into emerging markets. This phenomenon is consistent with the expansion of organized-crime syndicates (the Hell's Angels is a good example), wherein a history of good service to the group earns a long-standing member or associate an opportunity to establish a new "chapter," and hence a new sphere of influence and economic potential for the organization.

Far be it from me to let a good story stand in the way of the facts. Evidence for this street-gang franchising or "colonization" theory is limited, yet it continues to help people explain how new gangs have taken root in their cities. According to the U.S. National Young Gang Center, a body funded by the Department of Justice that has studied this issue extensively, a majority (more than 70 percent) of U.S. police jurisdictions surveyed claim that they have experienced gang migration; that is, gang members from other areas have relocated in their cities. Similarly, in my 2002 Canadian Police Survey on Youth Gangs, more than 85 percent of police agencies surveyed reported that they had experienced gang-member relocation and migration. Neither body of research, however, sought to quantify the actual number of migrating gangsters, and my survey in particular did not ask respondents to indicate the source of the migration (from Canada, the United States or otherwise). Most police agencies will admit that the numbers relocating to a city in any given year are insignificant relative to the population of local gang members.

That gang members relocate to new cities should come as no surprise. They relocate for many reasons, some seeking to escape escalating gang violence, others to minimize the negative ramifications of their leaving a gang. Many young gang members still live with their families, so when the family moves, they move. When gang-affiliated inmates leave federal penitentiaries, they may have spent years getting to know gangsters from other parts of the country and developing new social and economic networks, so they may move to a new city to stake their claim. Others may move simply to isolate themselves from the negative peer associations that got them into trouble in the first place. Many gang members move because they are, like the estimated 20 percent of Canadians who change their addresses annually, looking for a fresh start in a city where they perceive a better future. From time to time Canadian law enforcement officials do encounter and arrest former members of American street gangs, including such large gangs as the Mexican Mafia, 18th Street, Mara Salvatrucha and the Latin Kings. However, these occasional arrests and incursions have not (at least, not yet) presaged the arrival of expansionary U.S. gangs.[20]

Whatever the reasons, the available evidence suggests that most moves are socially motivated rather than economically driven. Once they arrive in their new city, gang members are more likely to join an existing gang than to challenge the way things are and start a new gang, which can entail much more risk and violence. Again using my Tim Hortons analogy, rarely does a gang select a "franchisee," choose a location, build or import the required infrastructure and supply the product (drugs) for the new franchisee to turn into money. Yes, gang members sometimes move, but rarely do so-called supergangs relocate an operation elsewhere, especially in Canada. Gang-member relocation, from the United States or from other parts of Canada, ought not to be considered a leading culprit insofar as the Canadian street-gang situation is concerned.

So what then explains the existence of Crips in Canada? The reason comes down to one of simple branding. If you belong to a group of young people wishing to start a gang, for whatever reason, what name would you think best to choose? You would, of course, do what new professional sports teams do: pick a big, bad-ass, intimidating name. The rather benign names of the original six National Hockey League teams—Canadiens, Maple Leafs, Red Wings, Rangers, Bruins, Blackhawks—have given way to a much more menacing breed—Predators, Hurricanes, Panthers, Coyotes, Lightning, Sharks. Since your name is part of your gang's fundamental brand identity—your message to those with whom you come in contact—you need to pick a name with a certain *gravitas,* a name that inspires fear and makes rivals think twice. An Ottawa gang that named itself the Churchill Street Chuckleheads wouldn't stand a chance in the fear or recruitment department if it had to contend with a gang with a much more menacing name, like the Carlingwood Crips. So emerging gangs everywhere choose the Crip brand or, better yet, combination names that doubly reinforce their bad-ass gangster personas. Why stop at the Carlingwood Crips when you can be the Carlingwood Mafia Crips, or the Carlingwood Mafia Crip Posse, or the Carlingwood Mafia Crip Posse Low Riders? The bigger and badder your brand, so the reasoning goes, the wider the berth others will give you.

Crips (and Bloods) include gangs of every shape, size and description. Racially speaking, they have historically been black, but Canadian Crips (and emerging Crips in other countries) can be just about anything, including white, Asian, Aboriginal and combinations thereof, creating the modern-day hybrid, or mixed-race, gang. Whatever their description, the Crips' enduring power to instil fear rests with their powerful brand, built over years of bloodshed and with a healthy dose of ever-expanding folklore. To be a Crip means something to the uninformed: you are dangerous, you are street savvy, you are to be feared, you have a history and roots stretching back to Los Angeles, gang capital of the world. But the Crips are not a supergang—never have been, never will be. A young Crip in Ottawa, Halifax, Montreal or Edmonton has about as much in common with a Crip in Los Angeles as I had in common, when I was eighteen and playing defence for the Kingston Canadians of the Ontario Hockey League, with a pro playing in Montreal for the Canadiens. This is not to say that they are not a threat—a Crip gangster in Montreal or Vancouver can be every bit as dangerous as a Crip gangster in Los Angeles. Or he could simply be a punk wannabe trading on the name recognition of one of the world's most famous street-gang brands. So, while Crip gangsters in Canada share a name in common with their U.S. cousins, they do not share a common ancestral lineage that reaches back to the days of now-deceased Crip founders Tookie Williams and Raymond Washington.

As we struggle to come to grips with street gangs in Canada, perhaps it is just human nature for us to fear the evil outsider or the "outside agitator," the marauding interloper from afar who has come to despoil our environment despite our best defensive efforts. The notion of a storied American inner-city gang like the Crips spreading their tentacles further and further into Canada makes for good coffee-shop conversation and could, if it were true, readily explain our growing gang problem. But the notion is as misleading as it is intellectually dishonest. Fear of a colonizing supergang is also remarkably convenient, as it serves to cast the colonized (the community with the emerging gang problem) as the victim, powerless to tear the enemy asunder. Moreover, the colonizing supergang theory forestalls the acceptance of personal responsibility—"We didn't create this problem; it found us"—and excuses some from the tough job of looking within for the causes, causes that exist irrespective of any outside influence.

ARE AMERICAN GUNS FLOODING OVER THE BORDER?

If gangs do not migrate in large measure, what can be said of American guns, the most necessary of gang accoutrements? It is difficult for many Canadians to comprehend the sheer scope of American gun culture, especially since the focus over the past couple of years has been on our own billion-dollar arms registry boondoggle. The right of an American to carry arms, enshrined more than two hundred years ago in the Second Amendment to the U.S. Constitution, has resulted in an estimated quarter of a billion firearms (tripled from 1960) in circulation in the United States—a third of them handguns. It's one of the most armed countries in the world, with homicide rates two to ten times higher than in other developed nations. Approximately 40 to 45 percent of U.S. households contain at least one firearm. According to the FBI's *Uniform Crime Reports* for 2004, 66 percent of the 16,137 murders in America were committed with firearms, the majority being handguns rather than rifles. Startling numbers indeed, but it should be noted that the non-fatal firearm crime rate dropped dramatically from 1993 to 2004, from 5.9 to 1.4 victims per 1,000 people, leading some people (including U.S. economist John R. Lott, Jr.) to conclude that more private ownership of guns results in less crime.

If all these guns were in the hands of law-abiding, non-violent Americans and used only for sport and self-defence, that would be fine as far as most of us are concerned. But, regrettably, guns readily find their way into the hands of violent criminals in the United States. Many are stolen from cars and homes, especially in states that lack laws requiring safe storage of firearms, and where there are large numbers of gun owners and relatively high crime rates. Based on FBI data, nearly 1.7 million guns have been reported stolen in the past decade, of which only 40 percent were ever recovered. That's more than a million unrecovered guns on the streets of America and elsewhere.

But these numbers do not tell the whole story. Popular wisdom suggests that the source of gun violence is a shadowy black market somehow completely divorced from the legitimate firearms industry. The truth is, the illegal market in guns is just downstream from the legal market, since virtually every illegal gun in the United States began its life as a legal product, manufactured or imported by a company licensed by the federal government and sold by a licensed dealer. According to the Bureau of Alcohol, Tobacco and Firearms (ATF), 30 to 40 percent of all handguns used in crimes that were traced by the U.S. government were sold brand-new by a licensed dealer less than three years earlier. Beyond simple theft, these guns often enter the illegal market through so-called "straw purchasers"—otherwise law-abiding citizens who are permitted to purchase guns. They acquire a firearm from a licensed dealer and then resell it to a prohibited person with a markup. American gun traffickers abound, in part because U.S. federal laws do not limit the number of firearms a person can purchase in a single transaction, allowing traffickers to buy dozens of guns at a time. Because of poor regulatory oversight and lack of enforcement of criminal-check provisions, there have been many cases of licensed dealers selling firearms to both organized criminal rings and prohibited persons.

Gun shows also play a part in the illegal gun market. While licensed dealers must perform a criminal check on a gun purchaser, prohibited purchasers can easily gain access to handguns from unlicensed sellers, who are not required to conform to the background-check requirement. What with the sea of stolen guns and otherwise legally acquired guns now in the wrong hands, there is a glut of firearms in the illegal U.S. gun market. Disturbingly, according to an American Medical Association study, upwards of half of male eleventh-graders in the United States believe that they could easily get a handgun if they wanted one.

The unfortunate fact is that Canada sits just north of the United States—and, therefore, the world's largest cache of illegal guns—separated only by the world's longest undefended border. Since guns are so plentiful, their cost in the United States (even in the illegal black market) is insignificant, with some going for as little as $30 or $40. But in Canada, which has some of the most stringent gun licensing, storage and registration laws in the world, the supply of the illegal handguns that criminals want is anything but plentiful. As Economics 101 suggests, when the supply of a desired product or service is restricted, prices will be high. And when prices rise, new suppliers of the desired product will step into the breach to satisfy demand and capture some of those demand-induced profits. Insofar as the illegal Canada–U.S. gun situation is concerned, we have a compelling arbitrage opportunity in which major price discrepancies for similar products produce a dynamic black market.

With the growth of gang rivalries in major Canadian centres and the consequent increased demand for guns, U.S.-based black-market traffickers, as well as profit-hungry Canadian importers (often street gangs themselves), have enjoyed a steady trade. According to Canadian police sources, smuggled U.S. guns account for about half of the handguns recovered in crimes in large cities, with the balance largely from Canada. Guns are compact, profitable and easily shipped. Those who ship contraband guns via normal channels (such as cartage and courier companies) stand a good chance that their customers will receive their shipments. Canada Customs checks only 2 to 3 percent of all incoming trans-border shipments. In 2004, for example, only 1,099 gun seizures were made—a veritable drop in the bucket, given the sheer volume of trans-border traffic.[21] Guns are also readily shipped across unmanned border crossings. Problems arise in places such as the Mohawk Akwesasne Reserve, a twenty-hectare maze of islands and hidden inlets in eastern Ontario that is notoriously difficult to patrol. It is considered by some a smuggler's paradise for guns, drugs, cigarettes and even humans, since it straddles the borders of Ontario, Quebec and New York State.

Demand is particularly high for gun models that are not readily available in Canada. Gangster culture is very much about optics—style versus substance—and this carries over to the types of handguns most coveted through black-market channels. As you can imagine, it is difficult to create the necessary gangster swagger when you are packing a "Saturday night special" (a.k.a. junk gun, pocket pistol or mousegun), a pejorative term for a class of cheap ($50 to $60), small-calibre (under .25) and highly available handguns made by American companies such as Raven Arms and Jimenez Arms. If you are a Canadian gang member who wishes to intimidate others, in part through the type of gun you carry, you'll opt for one of the highly desirable models, the ones that command the greatest street price—like the venerable 9mm Glock 17 and the Glock 22, a gun favoured by law enforcers and civilians alike; the Lornic .380, now the ATF's most frequently traced firearm, and the infamous TEC-9.

The TEC-9 assault pistol enjoys the dubious distinction of being one of the most widely used "criminal" guns in North America. It has been used in several mass murders and was the weapon of choice for the shooters in the 1999 Columbine High School massacre. Known for its menacing appearance, fingerprint-proof finish, threaded barrel (to accept a silencer), fifty-round magazine and forward pistol grip, the TEC-9 is essentially a semi-automatic version of a Swedish machine gun. Production of the pistol was banned in 1994 under the U.S. Brady Bill, but not before its Miami-based maker, Intratec Firearms Inc., tripled production (producing 102,682 TEC-9s that year) as the bill gained momentum in Congress.[22] Since all existing guns were grandfathered under the legislation and since legitimate gun owners consider it to have no sporting value (because of its heavy weight, dismal accuracy and general unreliability), thousands of TEC-9s have found their way onto the street and into the hands of gang members throughout North America who seek to intimidate—and kill—others.

TEC-9s, Glocks and Lornics, sourced mostly through U.S. black-market channels, are among the most desirable on Canadian streets, and the prices have risen accordingly—so much that guns are now beyond the financial reach of many poor gangsters. This has given rise to an interesting entrepreneurial phenomenon that perhaps explains why some guns turn out to have been involved in multiple shootings: gun rental. Just as you can visit Home Depot to rent a posthole digger or carpet steamer for your weekend project, you can, if you're in the know, rent a handgun for a week or a weekend. Young, aspiring, short-on-cash gangsters no longer need to buy a gun—an expensive and risky proposition, especially when Criminal Code sentencing provisions enforce a minimum three-year prison sentence for unauthorized possession of a restricted or prohibited firearm with ammunition. Instead, they simply rent the gun, flash it to intimidate others or, worse, commit a crime, and later return it to the black-market dealer, thus perpetuating the cycle and the useful life of the gun.

In spite of the new sentencing provisions, gangsters will continue to seek out handguns, simply because the growing violence on the street demands that you be equipped, that you never show up to a gunfight carrying only a knife, a metal pipe, a baseball bat or some other less lethal weapon. Indeed, a case can be made that the proposed new sentencing legislation will actually stimulate the demand for even more handguns, as is often the case with any measure that seeks to prohibit consumption. The new provisions offer severe penalties for the carrying of guns, but guns are required to maintain fear on the streets. Rather than buy, use and store guns for future use, gangsters can buy, use and dispose of guns after committing a crime. Guns are therefore becoming a disposable item in the business of being a gangster, and demand for their replacements will likely increase accordingly.

As noted earlier, guns smuggled from the U.S. account for only half of those recovered from crimes, the balance originating from Canadian gun owners. It is a mistake to peg Americans as the sole source of gun violence. One cannot assume that they will provide the majority of the supply needed to satisfy what I believe will be an increased demand for illegal arms. We should remember that the gun used in the 2005 Boxing Day shooting of Jane Creba was stolen from a legitimate Canadian gun owner. Moreover, every year an estimated five thousand guns are stolen in Canada—about 1 percent of the half-a-million legally owned handguns in the country—and no doubt some of those guns are in the hands of Canadian gangsters.

While we can rightfully complain that the supply of illegal American guns is virtually limitless and importation opportunities are readily available, can we therefore conclude that the U.S. is indeed exporting its culture of gun violence, as our politicians are wont to say? In other words, does the propensity for gun violence somehow get shipped, as a companion accessory, along with the gun itself, to be consumed by Canadian gangsters?

If it were as simple as saying that the U.S. is exporting its gun violence, then we ought to compare Canadian gun violence statistics with U.S. figures. Statistics Canada last studied firearms-related injuries in Canada in 2002, which included homicides, accidental deaths and suicides. That year, 816 people, 94 percent of whom were men, died of firearms-related injuries in Canada. This represented a rate of 2.6 deaths per 100,000 people, down from 5.9 per 100,000 in 1979. In a cross-border comparison for the year 2000, Statistics Canada data show that the risk of firearms death was more than three times greater for American males than for Canadian males, and seven times greater for American females than for Canadian females.

Because more of the U.S. deaths were homicides (as opposed to suicides or accidental deaths), the American rate of gun homicide was nearly eight times Canada's, where homicides account for only 18 percent of deaths involving guns (although figures for 2005 show that gun murders spiked considerably, by as much as 12 percent, because of rising gang tensions). The fact is, Canada's rate of gun homicide shrank (to 0.4 per 100,000 people in 2002 from 0.8 in 1979). The difference is, however, that handguns moved into a dominant role, accounting for two-thirds of gun homicides in 2002, up from about half in the 1990s, says Statistics Canada. It is only in this respect that Canada mimics the United States, as it does in the overall decline of gun deaths over the past dozen or so years.

America has no monopoly on gun violence, or any other violence for that matter. The United Nations estimates that 600 million small arms are currently in circulation worldwide, in both open and black markets (small arms are assault rifles, grenade launchers, submachine guns and pistols). Small arms are responsible for much of the death and destruction in conflicts throughout the world, and are therefore the real weapons of mass destruction, rather than nuclear, biological and chemical weapons. In 2005, small arms alone were responsible for the deaths of more than half a million people—10,000 per week—of which the United States was responsible for just 3 percent, despite having approximately 40 percent of the world's stock of small arms. The extent of worldwide small-arms violence is further demonstrated by the fact that more than 14 billion bullets are manufactured globally each year, enough to put at least two bullets into every living human on Earth—way more bullets than even those "gun-crazed" Americans could possibly consume.

LET'S END THE BLAME GAME

I cannot help but think the idea that the United States is exporting its gun violence to Canada is another example of "poor us" thinking and part of the contagion that makes people blame others for problems they themselves have been instrumental in creating. Violence is a core part of the gang lifestyle, whether guns are plentiful or not and regardless of whether the guns are sourced from Canada, the United States or elsewhere. Illegal American guns, like large American gangs, are not the wellspring of Canadian gang violence nor are they the accelerant behind the growth of our street-gang problem. Rather, deteriorating economic conditions for marginalized people, combined with the brutal competition that results when people sell illicit drugs for huge profits (among other key factors), have much more to do with gang violence and gang expansion in Canada than guns ever have, and ever will.

Of course, if a gang is known to be well stocked with weapons and if tensions are running high, rival gangs will seek out guns, playing out a Cold War–inspired arms race that supposedly will deter others' aggressive actions against them. And, of course, the more guns there are, the more that gangsters become desensitized to them, and therefore the greater their indiscriminate use, simply because they are so effective at intimidating and killing compared to other weapons. But if we are to truly get a handle on the street-gang problem and protect future generations of children from the harm they cause, then we must understand that the source of most gang aggression and violence lies elsewhere. It does not somehow spring forth from the hunk of metal that is the American handgun.

So let's stop the blame game insofar as the influence of the U.S. is concerned; it's not their guns, it's not their gangs and, as you'll see in the next chapter, it's not their popular culture. We have largely created our own street-gang problem. But the good news is that we have the power to solve it.

4: GANG CHIC

Popular Culture and the Glamorization of Gangs

At 10:20 p.m. on January 24, 2006, forty-six-year-old Tahir Khan, a Pakistani man who had lived in Canada for six years and was set to receive his Canadian citizenship in just three days, was driving his taxicab south on Mount Pleasant Road in Toronto when he began to make a left turn onto St. Clair Avenue. At that precise moment, two cars travelling north on Mount Pleasant at an estimated 140 kilometres per hour (in a 50-kilometre-per-hour zone) passed through the same intersection. One car slammed into Khan's cab, killing him instantly.

The incident appeared to be the outcome of a teenage street race gone terribly wrong. Toronto Police alleged that eighteen-year-old schoolmates Alexander Ryazanov and Wang-Piao Dumani Ross—both graduates of Aurora's prestigious St. Andrew's College boys' school—were racing their parents' Mercedes-Benz sedans when one of them struck Khan's cab. Both youths were charged with criminal negligence causing death, and Ross received an additional charge of failing to stop after an accident causing death.

This tragic death received widespread media attention in Canada and also, surprisingly, throughout North America and beyond. Other people who died at the hands of reckless street racers have received far less media attention (such as Rob and Lisa Manchester, who in May 2006 were celebrating their seventeenth wedding anniversary when they were killed by street racers in Richmond Hill, Ontario). What made the Khan case different was what police found on the passenger seat of the car that struck Khan: a copy of the popular street-racing game *Need for Speed.* One of the most popular titles from gaming giant Electronic Arts, the game allows players to race high-octane luxury cars through busy urban areas while attempting to evade police. The discovery of the game in the car stimulated yet again discussion of the possible impact of video games on the behaviour of young people.

The comments of two Toronto police officers were notable. Detective Paul Lobsinger, who was assigned to the case, refused to point his finger at the video game, telling Global News, "There are a small percentage who have difficulty separating reality and simulation, fantasy. It's a very, very small percentage. This was not the game's fault. There are millions who play this game and don't go out and do this." In contrast, veteran York Regional Police Sergeant David Mitchell, one of the founders of Project ERASE (Eliminate Racing Activity on Streets Everywhere), stated publicly that the tragedy was a case of "life imitating art." In an interview with the *Toronto Sun,* Mitchell said, "Video games and everything our younger generation is exposed to definitely has something to do with [street racing]. Some kids raised on high-octane race games may blur the line between fantasy and reality."

Whether the game really had the power to influence the alleged reckless behaviour of Ryazanov and Ross we may never know, but what is certain is that the discovery of the game in the mangled Mercedes had the power to restart a debate that will likely never be resolved.

HOW MUCH DOES THE MEDIA AFFECT US?

We live in a world saturated with mass-produced media. Television, film, radio, music, websites, blogs, books, billboards, video games, newspapers and magazines all vie for our attention. The breathtaking prevalence and scope of the mass media in our lives has been stimulating healthy debate on its overall effects for almost ninety years, polarizing people into "powerful effects" and "limited effects" camps. Each camp views human nature in different ways, thus coming to different conclusions about the impact of mass media on all of us, but especially young people.

The powerful-effects model holds that the effects of mass media are immediate, significant and sometimes harmful. According to this view, the media project false or contrived images of reality into consumers' minds and can lead to copycat behaviour, where people thoughtlessly mimic what they see and hear. This model says that a media stimulus invariably provokes a response, and that humans are malleable creatures prone to the "hypodermic" effect of powerful and ubiquitous media messages. This power to influence human behaviour means for some that the media must be controlled and subject to constant censorship.

In contrast, the limited-effects model acknowledges that the media can and do influence people but that the influence is not a primary basis for a person's actions or beliefs. This theory suggests that other factors in a person's life will determine how a media message is interpreted and acted upon, including personal and societal values, socio-economic status, age, gender, religious beliefs and ethnicity, to name just a few. This perspective holds that the media stimulus does not create a response in isolation, but is filtered by a person's unique life circumstances, ensuring that any given message will have only limited effects on the overall public.

The effect of the media on people has been one of the most enduring and politically charged issues of the past hundred years. Researchers, think-tanks, advocacy organizations, political groups, industry associations and lobbyists have sponsored and conducted thousands of studies over the years to prove their own theories or disprove competing ones. The impact of the mass media has always been hotly contested as far as youth crime is concerned. Now, with an increasingly visible and menacing street-gang problem on the rise, the debate about the impact on youth of films, the gaming industry and music is being revitalized like never before. Wherever people congregate to discuss the reasons for the vexing existence and growth of gangs, the media are almost always mentioned as a responsible agent alongside other factors such as poverty, psychopathy and the breakdown of the traditional family. The general belief is that the media, especially violent video games and "gangsta rap" music, glorify gangsterism and thus stimulate impressionable young people to adopt the lifestyle and its violence. As we struggle to meet the challenges posed by street gangs, we ought to assess this theory critically. Should the media shoulder the blame for the growth in gangs, or are the media an easily attacked scapegoat, chosen to mask the real causes of our problems?

SHOULD WE BAN VIOLENT VIDEO GAMES?

Much has changed in the world of video gaming since Atari's *Pong* made its first appearance in 1975. Massive technological advancements have allowed video-game console and personal computer manufacturers to pack incredible computing power into small, affordable packages. Video game software programmers have taken full advantage of this power, scaling dizzying heights of digital graphics and special effects. Not to be outdone by the techies, video game creative directors have been responsible for incredible progress in the complexity and richness of narrative treatment and subject matter, spawning twenty or more different game genres, such as first-person shooters, sims and multiplayer fantasies, facilitated by the Web and the availability of high-speed Internet connections.

What hasn't changed much about video games are the protests of critics. The internationally revered (and sometimes reviled) American paediatrician Dr. Benjamin Spock wrote about video games: "The best that can be said of them is that they may help promote eye–hand coordination in children. The worst that can be said is that they sanction, and even promote, aggression and violent responses to conflict. But what can be said with much greater certainty is this: most computer games are a colossal waste of time." On the other hand, American writer Steven Johnson, in his book *Everything Bad Is Good for You,* claims that they encourage what he calls "collateral learning," forcing players to probe, learn, project, strive, deal with setbacks and make reasoned decisions in an environment of uncertain information.

The massive advances in narrative complexity, creativity and engagement of today's most popular games have been overshadowed recently by their blatant violence, their portrayals of illegal activity, their moral vacuum and glorification of the gangster lifestyle. Consider one of the most popular game series of the past few years, one that is approaching a staggering fifty million copies sold. Early editions of *Grand Theft Auto* had players assume the role of a small-time criminal who could rise through the ranks of an organized crime syndicate by completing missions, such as bank robberies and assassinations, assigned by underworld figureheads. The game also allowed players to have sex with a prostitute, then beat her to death with a baseball bat and take back their money. If confronted by police, players could decapitate them, kill them with a sniper rifle or massacre them with a chainsaw, and then, as a final indignity, set them on fire. The recent *Grand Theft Auto: San Andreas* focuses on urban street gangs and a bloody rivalry between the Grove Street Families and the Ballas, reflecting the real Crips-versus-Bloods rivalry currently disrupting many American cities. Featuring more than 150 hours of play and celebrity voices (Samuel L. Jackson voices the corrupt Officer Tenpenny), the game includes levels that require players to murder police characters before the game will advance. Reviewers consistently rate it as action packed, highly engaging and fun.

Other games have raised the ire of politicians, police agencies and media critics. The release of *25 to Life,* a third-person-shooter game that pits street gangsters against police, prompted the National Law Enforcement Officers Memorial Fund to petition for a ban of the game. Another panned game is *50 Cent: Bulletproof,* where the game's protagonist, hip hop superstar 50 Cent, hunts down the street-gang hit men who attempted to murder him. *Crime Life: Gang Wars* is set in the fictional Grand Central City, which is infested with gang wars, where the Outlawz fight with their rivals, the Headhunterz, to restore their former glory as the city's most powerful gang. None of these street-gang–themed games have sold well, however, not because of their content, but because of their poor gaming quality and production values. Yet this has not slowed down criticism one bit.

Today, whenever citizens gather to discuss what to do about street gangs in Canada, there is a good chance that the video-games-produce-gangsters argument will surface. Last spring I attended a community briefing organized by the York regional police on their still-in-development street-gang strategy. Gang-unit leaders spoke to the audience about the troubling connection between violent video games and emerging gangsterism, without putting forth a shred of evidence in support of their assertions. During an open question period I voiced my objection to this claim and to other aspects of their presentation, such as showing a video of a young boy, perhaps four years old, flashing gang hand signs while holding a 9mm handgun—purporting to demonstrate intergenerational gang membership, an immaterial phenomenon in Canada. I spoke of the difficulty of proving the video game critique, pointing out that the research did not clearly support the hypothesis and that, if we are to understand gang formation, we ought to look beyond simplistic notions to manifest socio-economic causes.

Little did I know that voicing a moderate, fact-based opinion would cause me to be scorned by community leaders. One council member, ironically a defence lawyer, stood up and said, "I don't care what that gentleman said about video games. I don't need proof that a connection exists and I think we should ban them outright!" I later suggested to this person that if violent video games were to be added to the prohibition list despite lack of proof, then we ought also to ban things with a proven correlation to gang behaviour, such as unemployment, inner-city social housing projects and families headed by poor, single females. As I have stated before, it is easy to blame outside agitators—in this case, violent American-made video games featuring gangster themes—for our street-gang problems, but doing so will only mask what really needs to be done to short-circuit the growth of gangs.

We are all entitled to our opinions on these games. Personally, I can appreciate the games' incredible technical mastery, their creative genius and the sheer volume of human capital invested, since some of them take more than four years to develop. I can also appreciate the complex and emotionally charged narratives of some of the games, however violent they may be, since good stories often begin at the outer reaches of a society's accepted beliefs and conventions. At the same time, I object to their disturbing content and declining moral and behavioural standards, which add little value to society and do not improve the human condition. But I recognize them for what they are—games, not a call to action for our youth to shoot cops. To each his own, I say. If you want to play these games or allow your child to do so, that is your decision to make in a largely free society. However, if you want to criticize them, petition to ban them, boycott the stores that sell them, punish your children for playing them or just ignore them altogether, as we do with many things in life we find disturbing, that too is your right.

Perhaps the most disturbing element of these games is not their violence but the associated discourse that links—using scant and oftentimes methodologically poor scientific evidence—the fictional violence in these games to actual violence on the streets, in what is becoming an all-too-frequent and, I believe, ill-informed belief that life is imitating art. Perhaps this stems from the powerful-effects model's (unspoken) dim view of the capabilities and intellectual capacity of adolescents. Traditional developmental psychology promotes the idea of a universal individual who must develop through various stages from incompetent childhood to rational, logical adulthood. Children are defined not so much by what they can do as by what they cannot do. With respect to social problems, therefore, children are cast as the innocent victim because of their inherent inadequacies and incomplete social progression. Many studies show that people as young as ten or twelve are in fact media literate and thus able to critically assess and converse intelligently about the media. However, the powerful-effects theory portrays young people as highly impressionable and thus incapable of distinguishing fact from fiction or resisting the highly suggestive allure of the media they consume.

Examples of these "proven" links abound. Lieutenant Colonel David Grossman, a former West Point psychology professor and author of *On Killing* and *Stop Teaching Our Kids to Kill,* has argued that unethical video game publishers train children in the use of weapons and harden them emotionally to the act of murder. The past president of Canada's Media Watch, René Caron, has stated that "violence has been used by the [media] industry to capture the attention of boys, to captivate them and manipulate them," an approach that has had "abominable repercussions." Craig Anderson and Brad Bushman of Iowa State University, after reviewing dozens of studies of video gamers, reported in 2001 that children and young people who play violent video games, even for short periods, are more likely to behave aggressively in the real world, and that both aggressive and non-aggressive children are negatively affected by playing. Prominent media critic L. Rowell Huesmann of the University of Michigan has argued that fifty years of evidence show "that exposure to media violence causes children to behave more aggressively and affects them as adults years later."

Despite what many believe is a weak (at best), correlation between media violence and real-life aggression, the Canadian Paediatric Society has declared media violence a public health issue, a move that Canada's Media Awareness Network seems to cautiously endorse: "After all, governments don't wait for scientific certainty before they act to protect the public from smoking or drinking; all that's required is proof of a risk. If there is evidence that an activity or substance will increase the probability of negative effects, then the state is justified in intervening." All the way back in 1977 and the days of *Pong,* the Ontario Royal Commission on Violence in the Communications Industry connected violence in the media and incidence of violent crimes in society, as did the House of Commons Standing Committee on Communications and Culture in 1993, with its report, *Television Violence: Fraying Our Social Fabric.*

If I had the space and you the interest, I could quote hundreds of studies purporting a link between media violence, including that found in video games, and actual aggressive behaviour. I could also quote you another several hundred refuting that link (more on this later). Media critics know this, but they have real-life examples to draw upon to make their case. These include the tragic death of Tahir Khan and the Columbine High School massacre, when two Colorado teenagers, Eric Harris and Dylan Klebold, killed twelve fellow students and a teacher and wounded twenty-four others before committing suicide. The young men were heavy players of violent first-person-shooter games such as *Doom, Duke Nukem, Redneck Rampage* and *Wolfenstein 3D*, as well as fans of the Leonardo DiCaprio movie *The Basketball Diaries*, in which a student kills his classmates. Critics claimed that the games had a causative role in the massacre. The family of the murdered teacher, Dave Sanders, filed suit against Time Warner Inc., Palm Pictures and eleven video game makers, including Sony Computer Entertainment America, Activision and id Software, the maker of *Doom*. The suit claimed that they should have known their products might have led Harris and Klebold to carry out the massacre, and that the products should not be protected by the U.S. Constitution's First Amendment, which guarantees free speech. The complainants alleged that "absent the combination of extremely violent video games and these boys' incredibly deep involvement . . . these murders and this massacre would not have occurred."

In his judgment, U.S. district judge Lewis Babcock wrote that the makers of the games and movies could in no way have reasonably foreseen that their products would cause the Columbine shooting or any other violent acts. Babcock rejected the plaintiffs' claim that video games should not be protected by the First Amendment, ruling that a decision against the game makers would have a chilling effect on free speech. He also wrote: "Setting aside any personal distaste, as I must, it is manifest that there is social utility in expressive and imaginative forms of entertainment, even if they contain violence." I believe that these cases do not demonstrate convincing proof of a connection. Rather, they are good examples of mistaken causality, or what could be called post-hoc fallacy: the belief that, because event X occurred before event Y, X caused Y. Leaping to a causal conclusion is always easier and faster than actually investigating the phenomenon, and while it is true that causes do precede effects, it is not true that precedence makes anything a cause of something else.

Of course, one couldn't have such a contentious cultural debate without powerful special interest associations weighing in on the matter.

According to the Entertainment Software Association (ESA), a U.S. group of video and computer game publishers, the average video game player is thirty-three years old and the average buyer is thirty-seven, dispelling the notion that it is largely youngsters under eighteen who are playing and buying the games. As well, the ESA makes the point that if violent crime were preceded by violent video game playing, then one would expect to see a rise in youth crime. But while computer and video game sales have doubled since 1996, from $3.2 billion to more than $7 billion, total violent crime offences, particularly among young people, have steadily declined in the United States. And finally, the ESA points out that violent video games are also sold in foreign markets, in many countries where rates of violent crime are considerably lower than in America. For the ESA, "this suggests that the cause of violent crime lies elsewhere."

Independent researchers (not on the payroll of the ESA or other, similar bodies) have much to say as well. In her 2004 article "Does Viewing Violent Media Really Cause Criminal Violence?" in the scholarly journal *Aggression and Violent Behavior,* Dr. Joanne Savage reviewed the research purporting to show negative effects of media violence on youth. She concluded that there is no causal link between media violence and violent crime. "The question addressed here is not whether or not the effect is plausible, but whether the effect has been demonstrated convincingly in the scientific literature—and the answer is 'not so far.'"

In a 2004 article in *American Psychiatry,* Cheryl K. Olson, a professor of psychiatry at the Harvard Medical School's Center for Mental Health and Media, concurred with Savage's view that no demonstrable evidence supports the games-make-youth-violent hypothesis. She suggests, "It's time to move beyond the blanket condemnations and frightening anecdotes and focus on developing targeted educational and policy interventions based on solid data. As with the entertainment of earlier generations, we may look back on some of today's games with nostalgia, but our grandchildren may wonder what the fuss was about." Dr. Karen Sternheimer, in her book *It's Not the Media: The Truth About Pop Culture's Influence on Children,* looks deeper into societal dilemmas to see what other common factors could be affecting children:

> Blaming media for changes in childhood and societal problems has shifted our public conversation away from addressing the real

> problems that impact children's lives. The most pressing crisis facing American children is not media culture but poverty . . . we want research to support our fear so badly that even a minor study filled with flaws will be published and circulated throughout the news media.

I could go on and on listing positions contrary to the powerful-effects theory. And for every citation I provide from esteemed, Ph.D.-laden researchers who deny the connection between video games and violence, I could cite another that argues the contrary. That's the problem when debating a contentious social issue where there is, at best, only an emerging body of research findings. The "he said/she said" path generally leads to entrenched positions rather than true enlightenment. If you set aside the content of the polarized debate for a moment and look at the science underlying these studies, you will find some glaring problems that render most of the arguments void and lead me to believe that we really have little to worry about, that violent video games are not producing gangsters.

First, a good study on this issue ought to employ empirically validated, normative, proven reliable, standardized measures of aggression and exposure to media violence, yet few of them do. Then there is the notoriously difficult task of defining and measuring media violence—is it the *threat* of violence or aggression or an actual act of violence? Do you include violence in cartoons and games, despite their often comical, unrealistic presentation, or fictitious acts captured on film? Most of these studies fail to account for so-called third variables, which could include personality, socio-economic status, exposure to actual family violence and the like, all of which could explain why someone acts violently independent of media influence. As well, many studies produce data that show a "statistical significance," which critics grab for to make their case. However, because two variables show a statistically significant relationship does not necessarily mean they produce a meaningful effect size, that is, how large the relationship is between the two variables.

Setting aside arcane discussions of scientific methodology, I urge you to consider some common-sense numbers before you conclude that violent video games and other media are responsible for our street-gang problem. In the past two decades we have experienced an explosion in media violence. Laval University professors Guy Paquette and Jacques de

Guise studied six major Canadian television networks over a seven-year period, examining films, situation comedies, dramatic series and children's programming. Their study showed that, between 1993 and 2001, incidents of physical violence increased by 378 percent. If media or video game violence truly had an effect on the mind and behaviour of the person viewing it, especially a young person, we would logically expect to see supporting crime data in the real-world experiment called life. In other words, for the powerful-effects theory to hold true, media violence should correlate with actual crime statistics. However, in this period of unprecedented media violence, including increasingly violent video games, violent crime statistics in Canada over the past decade actually *declined* by about 10 percent, including crimes associated with youth. Moreover, powerful-effects theorists cannot explain why countries such as Japan and Canada, which have media violence rates equivalent to the United States, have materially lower crime rates. Nor can they reconcile the fact that, while video games have been around for only about thirty years, street gangs have been around for centuries.

Conventional wisdom suggests that violent video games, set within a culture of gangsterism, help create gangsters, which in turn leads to violent behaviour. But consider these facts. The vast majority of new gangsters in Canada are poor, marginalized, inner-city youth, mostly Aboriginal or from racial minorities. If we are to believe that *25 to Life*, *The Warrior* and *Grand Theft Auto* create gangsters, then we must believe that these emerging gangsters—whose precarious families frequent food banks, live in squalid conditions and are chronically underemployed in menial jobs—somehow found the resources to purchase an expensive game console and a few $50-plus games. Carrying this line of reasoning further, are we also to believe that the socio-economic conditions in which these at-risk youth live are merely secondary influences? Viewed from this perspective, the gaming-leads-to-violence argument seems tenuous at best.

I believe that media-effects research has most often started in the wrong place, in that violent media are shown to young people and the possible effects are measured. What if we collected, say, two hundred gangsters who have been convicted of violent offences and attempted to trace their behaviour back to media usage, contrasting this sample to a control group of two hundred youth with no gang affiliation? I would venture a guess that the impact of violent media would be minuscule at best. A 1994 British study of young offenders by Ann Hagell and Tim Newburn used this model, and they found that young offenders watched less television and video than their counterparts, had less access to the technology in the first place and had no particular interest in specifically violent media. If you want to believe that at-risk youth are motivated to join the violent, substandard world of street gangs because of games or Hollywood movies, so be it, but no data exists to prove that this contention is true.

We may never know if there is a positive correlation between exposure to fictional media violence and actual violent behaviour such as gang crimes, but even if there were some correlation (I believe, by the way, that there is, but to a very limited degree), the effects are much weaker than the other social trends that contribute to and shape gang behaviour in our society. The media-violence debate is nothing more than a political red herring, especially as it pertains to the growth of gangs. Rather than addressing the significant root causes that lead youth to join gangs, we are offered the fight against video games, which in effect substitutes practicality with yet another unsubstantiated moral panic. It's time to get serious, folks—forget about video games, and focus on the real issues that are giving rise to street gangsterism.

RAP'S BAD RAP

Our perception of socially accepted art forms of the past tends to colour, if not cloud, our judgment of emerging ones. This point may have particular meaning for many middle-aged Canadians who grew up listening to the Beatles or Queen, especially when we consider the sometimes incendiary and purposely shocking art form known as gangsta rap. Gangsta rap has emerged as the powerful-effects lobby's new whipping boy, widely criticized for its lyrics, which often espouse violence, materialism, misogyny, drug use, promiscuity, hatred of authority and—of special significance to this book—the gangster lifestyle. Like *Grand Theft Auto* and *25 to Life*, gangsta rap must now, according to some, be held accountable for the street carnage it somehow helped create.

Rap music grew out of the experiences of marginalized, inner-city, mostly African-American youth in the 1970s in New York City. Characterized by rappers, known as MCs, chanting lyrical semi-autobiographical stories or improvised street poetry set to a music track or beat, rap has been criticized by the white majority for years as the obscene, anti-white, anti-establishment rantings of discontented black youth. Rap music's supporters, however, have long contended that rap and its underlying poetry are social commentary writ large. Its themes, protesting isolation, oppression and racism and calling for autonomy, justice and survival, featured prominently in the works of early rap stars such as DJ Kool Hertz, Afrika Bambaataa and Grandmaster Flash. From this perspective, early rap—and even the rap of today—is not so different from rock 'n' roll, with its long-standing pedigree of social activism established in the 1960s by artists such as Bob Dylan, and continuing to this day with U2, Green Day and Bruce Springsteen.

By the mid-1980s, around the time of Run DMC's smash hit "Walk This Way" and the breakthrough of rap and hip hop into the mainstream music scene, what would become its most controversial sub-genre, gangsta rap, appeared, its lyrical focus the trials and tribulations of violent street gangsters. Philadelphia rapper MC Schooly D is credited with originating the form in 1986, with his release of the single "P.S.K." (purportedly referring to the Park Side Killers gang). In 1987 Tracy Morrow, better known as Ice-T (and now a television actor), released what is considered to be the first gangsta rap album, *Rhyme Pays,* which features songs such as "6'n the Mornin," whose engaging narrative describes a police bust of a gangster. Ice-T initiated the West Coast gangsta rap scene, with Dr. Dre and Niggaz With Attitude (NWA) soon joining the fray. NWA later released the groundbreaking 1988 album *Straight Outta Compton,* which describes the growing unrest and despair of black ghetto life in South Central Los Angeles.

One cannot possibly understand the roots of gangsta rap or its violent and aggressive narratives—as well as why it struck a chord among the marginalized inner-city youth who first embraced it—without understanding the social context of the time, especially in Los Angeles and New York City, where gangsta rap first took hold. The 1980s were the Ronald Reagan years, in which his administration made significant cutbacks in social funding to urban areas, affecting schools, community centres, housing projects and playgrounds, while at the same time increasing investments in the criminal justice system. Meanwhile, the American "rust belt" phenomenon that had begun in the late 1970s continued to erode manufacturing employment in urban centres in favour of increasingly automated plants in suburban areas, exacerbating "white flight." By the early 1980s intolerable poverty, unemployment, crumbling schools and housing projects, and racism were an oppressive reality for inner-city youth in Los Angeles and other big cities. With few viable paths to success, many turned to the underground economy to survive; for some, it represented a better, although more violent, career path than preparing fast food. This in turn accelerated the growth of street gangs, aligned primarily along ethnic lines, that claimed—and fought for—specific geographical turf.

An already tenuous situation spiralled out of control with the sudden appearance of cheap and highly addictive crack cocaine. Through crack sales, young people suddenly had money to buy guns, and an urban arms race ensued. Crack made people more violent; rather than fighting for turf only, gangsters fought for lucrative drug markets. The crack epidemic intensified gang conflicts and led to thousands of deaths of young men over the next fifteen years as they jockeyed for control of drug sales markets. Over seven thousand gang-related homicides occurred in Los Angeles between 1979 and 1994, 93 percent of which were of black or Hispanic individuals. The corresponding intensification of the government's "war on drugs" led to mass incarceration of black and Hispanic youths and charges of rampant police corruption and brutality (accusations that have plagued the LAPD for decades now)—the Rodney King beating of 1991 represented a poignant exclamation point.

Ice-T was once a member of a Hoover Crip gang set and was well-known even then as an intelligent artist who used his music to comment on racism, police brutality, drug abuse and prison conditions. He released his 1992 song "Cop Killer," performed with his heavy-metal band Body Count, just weeks before the Rodney King riots. The song, vilified as obscene by U.S. politicians, attacked LAPD policing with its incendiary lyrics and reinvigorated the debate about gangsta rap. Was it simple hate-mongering or a legitimate form of social commentary—ghetto reportage designed to cast light on crime, violence, the drug trade and police brutality?

As gangsta rap grew in popularity in the early 1990s, the big record companies sensed that they could exploit this genre to make money, and lots of it. In 1991 *Billboard* magazine, through its Soundscan service, reported that over 60 percent of rap music was being sold in suburban malls and music stores, largely to white, middle-class audiences, and the demand seemed insatiable. To satisfy the masses, the music industry fast-tracked many artists who were not as capable of ghetto reportage and social commentary as gangsta rap's pioneers. The music in many respects began to devolve into a misleading caricature, a cartoon, as it were, of the world it claimed as inspiration: the inner-city ghetto. Marshall McLuhan wrote, "Violence, whether spiritual or physical, is a quest for identity and the meaningful. The less identity, the more violence." This was perhaps the underlying driving force of gangsta rap from the early 1990s to the present day: select artists of sometimes questionable quality, often with a contrived and mythologized pedigree as hardened street gangsters; package them and their lyrics with a sensational wrapping of violence to situate their identity and titillate the masses; and amp up the public relations machine to lay down the artist's street cred (think Curtis "50 Cent" Jackson, whose branding as a bullet-riddled crack-dealer-turned-rap-star is a stroke of genius)—sales will follow.

David Samuels, in an article in the *New Republic*, wrote that the more rappers were packaged as violent, menacing black criminals, the bigger the white audience for rap became. By 2000, according to a *Newsweek* poll, 75 percent of people between eighteen and thirty listened to rap music. This approach seemed to tap into the white community's fascination with the enduring myth that black men are dangerous, anti-social and sexually insatiable, and therefore must be studied so that we can properly stand guard against them. It was a successful strategy. Today hip hop music, judged by sales, is the largest music genre in North America. And most of it is bought not by poor, inner-city minority youth, but by middle-class youth everywhere who have grown up listening to (and fabulously enriching) the likes of Snoop Dogg, 50 Cent, Kanye West and many others.

Let's return to the question that has plagued this genre of music and that is the focus of this chapter: what role, if any, has gangsta rap played in the growth of street gangs specifically, and the whole "gangster chic" ethos generally? The critics—and there are many of them—have long contended that gangsta rap's lyrics encourage violent, materialistic and misogynistic behaviour. Some have tried to causally link the growth of gangsta rap since the mid-1980s to the growth of U.S. gangs, according the music equal responsibility to issues such as poverty, the crack epidemic, racism and massive economic shifts.

Some have even tried to link rap with specific crimes (without concrete proof). Three cases in gangsta rap's birthplace, New York City, come to mind. An African-American community group, the New York Leadership Alliance, blamed gangsta rap for the disgusting 2000 Puerto Rican Day sexual assaults in Central Park and launched a Save Our Sons (SOS) campaign against record labels. In 1993 the city's public pools experienced a spate of "whirlpooling" crimes committed by young men who stripped and sexually assaulted girls in public pools, in some cases while singing rap group Tag Team's song "Whoomp! There It Is." And in the famous Central Park "wilding" incident of 1989, twenty-nine-year-old Trisha Meili was beaten, raped and left for dead by several men; some commentators attempted to link rap to the act of rape, specifically Tone-Loc's song "Wild Thing."

Criticism of gangsta rap has been particularly acute lately in the black community, whose leaders object to its caricatured, exaggerated, corporate-promoted portrayal of black life. Edmund Gordon, a professor emeritus at Yale and chair of the National Task Force on Minority High Achievement, has criticized gangsta rap by suggesting that black males have neglected their education in order to perform rap and hip hop. Al Sharpton, a black Pentecostal minister and political activist (and 2004 presidential hopeful), said that rap's vulgarity was "desecrating our culture—it is desecrating our race." The brilliant comedian Chris Rock, in his 2004 HBO special *Never Scared,* says that he loves rap music but is tired of defending it, because of its vulgar lyrics and rhymes. In a March 2005 speech at Toronto's Ryerson University, acclaimed African-American filmmaker Spike Lee opined that many black students are neglecting school because gangsta rap and its promotion of violence and materialism have convinced them that it's cool to become pimps or "video hos." Lee has also said that many of hip hop's heroes are minstrel performers; while they're not the whites in blackface of the late nineteenth and early twentieth centuries, they are nonetheless presenting a falsified and damaging image of what it means to be black.

Rap's critics can sometimes be one-dimensional in their critique of what is a complex and diverse musical style. It is indeed difficult to find much value in the brutish and gratuitously violent lyrics of some gangsta rap, but one ought to look more closely at what can be compelling art. We tend to fixate on the nasty gangsta rap and pay little attention to the songs with valuable messages. Gangsta rap can vividly portray the brutality of street life, and some artists have used their songs as cautionary tales about the risks associated with the gangster lifestyle, for instance, Notorious B.I.G.'s "Niggas Bleed," BDP's "9mm Goes Bang," and Ice-T's "High Rollers." Rap artists have also used their music to preach anti-drug messages; Melle Mel's song "White Lines," which rails against cocaine use, is an example. More recently, Grammy-winning rapper Kanye West spoke out on MTV (in words, not song) against hip hop's homophobia, drawing comparisons between African Americans' long struggle for civil rights and the present-day gay rights movement.

If rap has the power to hurt, so too does it have the power to heal, especially for youth who embrace the sound and poetry of the hip hop scene. Toronto rapper Tristan Graham, who goes by the name Collizhun, partnered with the non-profit agency 411 Initiative for Change to offer Grade 4 to 6 classroom workshops to teach youth how to write and record their songs, with the proviso that lyrical content must focus on positive messages about diversity and ending violence. In Edmonton's tough Boyle-McCauley area, the inner-city Beat of Boyle Street program helps at-risk youth express themselves through song and dance. Led by Jeremy Cooper, the full-to-capacity Beat program lets its participants sing, dance, rap and beat-box (a form of hip hop) about their personal experiences. It has been credited with helping turn around the lives of several young people.

I think that we sometimes put too much emphasis on the lyrics of music. To be sure, music has the power to move, motivate and stimulate debate, but most people respect and enjoy the total music offering—the instruments, the voices, the beat, the emotions evoked, the words used and even the volume—rather than getting fixated on disentangling and interpreting the intended meaning. Who among us understands the narrative intent of every song we enjoy listening to? I love U2 and respect Bono's decision to use music as a form of political activism. I can probably name and hum most of the tracks on the band's finest album, *The Joshua Tree*, but I can't say I understand the meaning of all the songs or the deeper theme of the entire album, except that it is probably about the complexity of relationships. The album is to me simply a compilation of great songs sung by one of rock's most talented performers, and it's enough for me to simply sit back and let the music wash over me without thinking too hard about every word and its socio-political ramifications. And if we really paid as much attention to lyrics as the critics suggest, there would certainly be fewer of us mangling the lyrics to Manfred Mann's smash hit "Blinded by the Light."

Many of the arguments I make in the discussion of violent video games can be offered here as well. Those who promote a causal link between gangsta rap and actual violence, especially in Canada, seldom offer a scrap of proof of this troubling connection, preferring to rely on innuendo, superstition, anecdotes and, quite frankly, prejudice to make the case. If gangsta rap truly had such a violent effect, we would expect to see a corresponding rise in gangster behaviour among those who consume the most music: young, middle-class, suburban kids, particularly white kids who really seem to enjoy stories of ghetto gangsterism as told by their young black counterparts. Rap music, including gangsta rap, is incredibly popular these days, and notwithstanding the violent gang clashes that occur from time to time on Canadian streets, youth crime specifically—and violent crime generally—is on the decline. Gangsta rap began in New York in 1986, but the "gangs of New York" made famous by Martin Scorsese's 2002 movie surfaced there around 1825—160 years earlier—so something other than questionable music lyrics must be at play in producing gangs. No such definitive correlation exists, so rap critics ought to look elsewhere for the significant causes of gang violence.

Rap's critics contend that gangsta rap MCs are terrible role models. But what do the youth who enjoy gangsta rap aspire to? Becoming a gangster, or becoming a rich, popular, famous rapper surrounded by beautiful young women? As a young man I aspired to make it to the National Hockey League. When some of my Major Junior A teammates were drafted by the NHL, I got a first-hand view of the lifestyle a pro hockey career could offer, and my aspiration shifted. I became more interested in the rewards (money, fame, women, achievement, nice cars, travel) than in the opportunity to grind it out nightly in the world's top hockey league. In other words, the perceived spoils superseded the role I wanted to play. I believe that the same holds true for young people who enjoy gangsta rap. The aspiration is to become an MC, not a gangster, and such an opportunity, however fleeting it may be, may provide a sense of hope, especially for inner-city youth whose other career choices may be less desirable.

The "stupid, impressionable youth" argument is wearing thin. The principal consumers of rap have brains, and many readily understand that gangsta rap can represent a contrived, fictionalized, hyperbolized and caricaturized portrait of real ghetto life. I believe that young people can also appreciate the strong social messages of disaffection contained in the better rap music, as well as take heed of the cautionary tales of gangster life that it offers. Although some gangsta rap portrays life in a gang and all that purportedly goes with it, that does not necessarily mean that youth will be motivated to join. Let's give our young people more credit than that—they can readily appreciate that gang life is a violent, substandard existence that will likely lead nowhere except to jail or an early death. Young people, whether exposed to fictitious gang members on television or real ones in their schools and communities, don't simply decide that it is "cool" to join a gang the way they may think it's cool to smoke cigarettes or try pot. They join for a host of more substantive reasons—for money, for protection, for camaraderie that they don't get elsewhere.

It's a chicken-and-egg case: rappers may describe violent realities and buff the rough edges off the image of street gangs, but I don't believe that their street talk is a prime stimulus of violence or gang membership. For those who believe there is a connection between gangsta rap and gang violence, I offer this recommendation. Go to a troubled inner-city community in your city and see for yourself. Go there with an open mind and ask the question "Does rap motivate gangster behaviour?" Ask the people who actually live there.

I did this a few years back when I was directing the evaluation of a $900,000 crime-prevention program, Project Early Intervention, in Ottawa's Banff–Ledbury community, home to the aggressive Ledbury Banff Crips. The area, which is composed almost entirely of run-down rent-geared-to-income townhouse blocks owned by the Ottawa Community Housing Corporation, suffers from geographical isolation from the broader community around it. Bordered by railway tracks, an elevated major roadway, a hydro field and vacant land, Banff–Ledbury carries the same social stigma as other poor Ottawa neighbourhoods such as Caldwell Avenue and Bayshore.

The evaluation protocol required my team to interview parents of participating children so that we could complete standardized surveys that measured the improvement in social functioning brought about by the program. I vividly recall meeting with a mother of six children under the age of ten, recent refugees from war-torn Somalia, whose educated husband toiled eighteen hours a day driving a cab and delivering food for Pizza Pizza. I sat with her in a sparse two-storey, two-bedroom townhouse unit, perhaps all of six hundred square feet, that was also home to hundreds of cockroaches (including inside the refrigerator). Utterly poor, but blessed with a dignified and stoic spirit, she quietly lamented the presence of drug dealers and gangsters in the neighbourhood and wondered how their community (owned by the city but patrolled infrequently by uniformed police) had gotten so bad and dangerous for her children. Naive as I was at the time, I asked her what impact, if any, gangsta rap had on the lives of youth in her long-suffering neighbourhood. Moments after I asked the question and saw her blank stare, it struck me how incongruous, how utterly uninformed and unaware the question really was. Her simple and restrained answer was telling: "Music did not create this."

I would ask this question again and again, to virtually the same response, because the critics' brilliantly compact gangsta-rap-produces-gangsters hypothesis needed, in my curious mind, to be thoroughly tested while I had the chance. And it was only when I saw people struggling in these communities of neglect, violence and sheer poverty—set within one of Canada's most prosperous and influential cities—that I began to appreciate that this single music form, however violent its lyrics were, played virtually no role either in breeding gang behaviour or in stimulating it to expand to capture other impressionable youth.

I do not support the hypothesis that gangsta rap produces gangsters, that it somehow legitimizes the gangster life as a viable option in the minds of youth, or that it trumps other causes of street gangs such as socio-economics. However, I do support the proposition that gangsta rap specifically, and the massive hip hop culture generally, has had a broad influence in our society that is reflected especially in dress and in the urban patois. This "gangsta chic" ethos, however, has been propagated as much by multinational brand giants that have glommed onto the culture—Nike, Reebok, Tommy Hilfiger, Pepsi—as the hip hop culture itself. Visit an urban shopping mall on a Saturday afternoon and you'll discover a sea of young people dressed and speaking in hip hop style, and sometimes in the stereotypical gangster mode (bandana, low-rider jeans, rope jewellery, ball cap turned sideways, tattoos, "Whassup, dawg?"), the latter in most cases poseurs rather than the real gangster McCoys. The fact that many people consider it cool to look or speak like a gangster does not mean that they are real or wannabe gangsters, or that they consider it a desirable lifestyle in which to actually participate. In the early 1980s the urban cowboy look was hot, in large part because of the John Travolta film of the same name. I admit that I sometimes wore cowboy boots, a Stetson and a sheepskin jacket, but I had no desire to rope steers or ride a bull—I was acting a part. For better or for worse, this is what happens when an art form catches the attention of youth and the popular media; some people will adopt its outward elements until the next big thing comes along.

As to whether gangsta rap has helped desensitize us to violent words and imagery, I would generally agree. These are no longer the days of imagined small-town innocence, when life seemed to exist on a different plane of grace, decorum and empathy. As a society we have allowed our world to become full of violent imagery and have become more used to aggression, so it is unfair to shoot the rapping MC messenger. We watch and enjoy violent movies such as *Goodfellas, Scarface* and *The Godfather,* and television shows such as *The Sopranos*, which also happen to portray the gangster life. We tune in nightly to "breaking news" that profiles war and civil strife around the world. And, judging by the pay-per-view receipts, mixed martial arts, brilliantly marketed by the Ultimate Fighting Championship (UFC), is one of the world's fastest-growing spectator sports.

This apparent heightening of aggression in society does not mean that the popular media are stimulating or perpetuating violent behaviour. As long as people have lived together with competing aims and differing circumstances, we have had periods of unfathomable violence. Was not the Second World War, with its Holocaust and the bombing of Hiroshima, violent? What about our present-day "war on terror" and the associated loss of life of tens of thousands of people? The vagaries of the human condition have produced violence since time immemorial. The key difference between then and now is that today we have instantaneous communication. The Internet, the multi-channel universe and the massive media apparatus are chock full of probing, talented storytellers—including rappers—who give scope and dimension to the pain we inflict upon each other. Violence is not more ubiquitous, only those who tell the stories of violence, and we have become desensitized as a result.

The jury will be out on gangsta rap for a long while, as the music still has legs some twenty years after its debut. Some rap—pardon the pun—deserves its bad rap. But if your position is that it is dangerous to youth, what would you propose society do about it? Ban it outright or control its transmission into Canada? Government censorship is a slippery slope, so be careful. Rather than pull your hair out wondering how we can stop the scourge of gangsta rap, try exposing your children to lots of different kinds of music. Speak to them about why and how artists use music to express their ideas and perspectives. Engage them in a frank and informed discussion of rap's positive and negative influences. Teach them when they are young how to distinguish between good and bad, and trust that, when faced with decisions in their lives—such as what music to embrace—they'll take the right path. I say let youth enjoy their rap and hip hop culture, with the informed guidance and supervision of committed and aware parents.

The genie is out of the bottle. Rap, in most of its forms, is mainstream now and here to stay. It is a powerful voice of resistance and expression, bringing to light many of the problems that affect our society. Rather than just accuse it of promoting gangsterism, we ought to investigate the clues inherent in its expression, and do something about the true causes of gang behaviour.

5: SHOW ME THE MONEY

Street-Gang Economics 101

The job is considered a pretty good one by those who hold it. Unlike most other jobs, it requires no formal experience or education, but simply demands that you be prompt and loyal to your employer and enjoy driving around the city. You are required to work eight-hour shifts in teams of two, one driver and one "runner." You are each paid $100 per shift for five shifts a week, sometimes more, because demand for your product seems never to abate. As well, it is understood among those who hold this job that you can skim a little of the product off the top to resell later on your own account. By doing so you can increase your weekly net earnings to maybe $1,000, almost double the gross pay of an unattached Canadian male worker.

Your employer, because he wants both of you to succeed, happily supplies you with all the tools you need to do your job well. On-the-job training, ongoing mentoring, an ample supply of product, security and collection services if you need them, a comfortable prepaid rental car, as well as one or several cellphones or Blackberry devices—all provided for free. Operating on call during your shift, you simply respond to phone or Blackberry PIN messages, take the order, deliver the product and collect and submit the payment to your employer at the end of your shift, in return for which your daily earnings will be paid in cash. You can get a job like this when you are as young as thirteen or fourteen. And on top of the financial incentives, it provides a crash-course street-based MBA that teaches you important disciplines of business management, including procurement, inventory control, distribution, marketing, financial control and customer relationship management.

The only downside of the position, of course, is that it is illegal. It makes you part of a street-gang "dial-a-dope" operation. Taking a page from the fast-food industry's book, street gangs now offer the ultimate convenience of delivering drugs right to the customer's door, rather than forcing them to hunt down a dealer on a street corner in a dangerous part of town. Whatever a customer's heart desires—cocaine, crack, marijuana, hash or chemical drugs such as ecstasy, Rohypnol, GHB, ketamine and methamphetamine, qualified or repeat customers just need to call a number, get their cash together and await delivery from a street-gang runner.

THE BIG BUSINESS OF DRUGS

Of the many attractions of the street gang—camaraderie, protection, a sense of shared identity, power—the opportunity to make lots of money is undeniably part of its allure. That the pursuit of the almighty dollar is a street gang's leading preoccupation should come as no surprise, since the pursuit of money drives most of the rest of us as well.

Money itself has no intrinsic value. It is not money per se that gang members or anyone else wants, it's what money represents: purchasing power and its ability to finance the lifestyle we wish to live. The street gang's love of money and what it offers was summarized by one of film's most famous fictional gangsters, Tony Montana, played by Al Pacino in *Scarface.* His rags-to-riches ascent demonstrated what is possible when you live life on the margins: "When you get the money, you get the power . . . when you get the power, then you get the women."

However, if making money were truly the primary motivation for street-gang members, most of them would join high-paid professions in Canada's financial districts, high-tech parks and oil-patch facilities. The desire for money and the desire to make money quickly, by whatever means possible, are the combined drivers of street-gang activities. They serve to differentiate gang members from the rest of us who earn money the traditional way, through hard work and commitment to our vocation.

From the 2002 youth-gang survey, along with police data, we have a good idea which drugs street gangs sell. Marijuana leads the way, but gangs will sell pretty much anything they can get their hands on and make a profit from. We also have a good idea where they sell their drugs. If you are in the know, you can score drugs on inner-city street corners, in retail malls, on public transit, from cars and bikes, in organized crime–controlled strip joints, through dial-a-dope operations, from crack houses and at house parties. For a fashionable mind-expanding hallucinogenic such as ecstasy (a.k.a. Adam, XTC, X, Versace, hug, beans or the love drug), the "all ages" dance parties (formerly known as raves) that teenagers like to attend are often crawling with well-stocked street-gang dealers. In collaboration with the party promoters, street-gang members will dispense colourful, candy-like pills of varying composition for $20 a pop, alongside others offering water to avoid dehydration, baby pacifiers or sports mouthguards to avoid teeth-grinding and massages to reduce muscle rigidity—all side effects of ecstasy.[23] Once the dance is over, they'll also be there to sell marijuana to bring the patrons down from their hallucinogenic high. According to Louise Logue, a youth intervention coordinator with the Ottawa Police Service, registered nurse and internationally recognized expert on chemical drugs and the dance scene, so ubiquitous are recreational drugs today that most young students known how to score, even at school. She says that if you poll an average Grade 6 or 7 class in an average school in an average Canadian city (something she does frequently as part of her job), about half will admit to having tried drugs and a majority will know where to buy some within minutes—hard or soft. Equally troubling for parents, according to Stu Auty, president of the Canadian Safe Schools Network, a favoured drug retail location for gangs is the school parking lot (high school or elementary), which hundreds of young people traverse every day.

CANADIAN DRUG CONSUMERS BREATHE LIFE INTO GANGS

Lest you think that marauding gangsters are "pushing" dope on impressionable young people or drug-addicted Canadians on the margins of society, know this: millions of Canadians consume illicit drugs every year. This consumption is supporting the underground trade in drugs and, of course, helping street gangs and other criminal enterprises earn the money they need to maintain their operations.

Much is known about the drug habits of Canadians. Every year millions of Canadians consume cannabis (mostly marijuana, but also hash and hash oil) and many hundreds of thousands consume harder drugs such as methamphetamine, cocaine and ecstasy. Canada's national addictions agency, the Canadian Centre on Substance Abuse (CCSA), conducted the Canadian Addictions Survey in 2004 by polling a random sample of more than 13,000 Canadians over the age of fifteen. According to the survey,

44.5 percent of Canadians had used cannabis at least once in their lifetime, and 14.1 percent reported using it during the twelve months prior to the survey. Using 2006 population projections for people over fifteen and assuming that the 2005 consumption statistic holds true today, this means that almost 3.8 million Canadians will consume cannabis this year. Younger people are more likely to have used cannabis in their lifetime; almost 70 percent of those between eighteen and twenty-four have used it at least once. Younger people are also more likely to be past-year users of cannabis: almost 30 percent of fifteen- to seventeen-year-olds and just over 47 percent of eighteen- and nineteen-year-olds.

Excluding cannabis, the most common illicit drug type used during one's lifetime was reported to be hallucinogens (for example, PCP or LSD), used by 11.4 percent of respondents, followed closely by cocaine (10.6 percent), speed or amphetamines (6.4 percent) and ecstasy (4.1 percent). The portion of respondents who reported use of any of the five drugs other than cannabis (cocaine or crack, hallucinogens, speed or amphetamines, heroin and ecstasy) was 16.5 percent. In other words, 4.4 million Canadians have at some time in their lives consumed hard drugs.

By comparing numbers from their survey to the 1994 Canada Alcohol and Other Drugs Survey conducted by Health Canada, the CCSA was able to determine that self-reported rates of illicit drug use are increasing in Canada. The proportion of Canadians reporting any illicit drug use in their lifetime rose from 28.5 percent in 1994 to 45 percent in 2004, and usage in the past twelve months increased from 7.6 percent to 14.4 percent over the same period. The lifetime use of cannabis increased from 28.2 percent in 1994 to 44.5 percent in 2004. For cocaine, use rose from 3.8 percent in 1994 to 10.6 percent in 2004. For LSD, speed and heroin, the rate rose from 5.9 percent in 1994 to 13.2 percent in 2004. The collected data also allowed the CCSA to extrapolate that the number of Canadians who have used an injectable drug at some point in their life increased from 1.7 million in 1994 to a little more than 4.1 million in 2004. Specifically, 269,000 Canadians were estimated to have used a drug by injection in 2004, compared with 132,000 in 1994. Public surveys have their inherent limitations and are never a hundred percent accurate, but the sound methodology of the CCSA research supports the proposition that Canadians demonstrate a robust interest in and consumption of illicit drugs. It is no wonder that street gangs are striving to perfect their craft as drug dealers.

The global retail market for illicit drugs is estimated to be worth from $250 billion to as high as $400 billion.[24] Unfortunately no reliable estimate of the size of Canada's illicit drug market is available, but the usage numbers outlined above tell us it is substantial—well into several billion dollars at retail prices. Whatever the number, the illicit drug market is one of the world's largest industries, and one of its most profitable. Despite the fact that modern nations have hundreds of laws prohibiting importing, manufacturing, growing, distributing, selling and using these drugs, supported by punitive penalties for transgressing them, illicit drug use is common in most countries and demand remains high and stable. Because of the large and growing demand for drugs, their illegality and associated criminal sanctions, those willing to trade in them—drug cartels, organized crime syndicates, so-called narcoterrorist groups and street gangs—can demand high prices and derive great profits.

THE HIERARCHY OF THE DRUG TRADE

Understanding the role of street gangs within the drug trade hierarchy is essential to understanding the changes afoot that support the growth of gangs—and what to do to stunt this continued growth. Since street gangs across the country are actively engaged in street-level sales of crack and powdered cocaine—nervous-system stimulants in strong demand in Canada—it is convenient to begin our analysis here.

Colombia is far and away the single largest manufacturer and exporter of cocaine, supplying an estimated three-quarters of the world's market. Farthest from the end consumer are the growers, farmers of coca leaves located mostly in Peru, Bolivia and Colombia itself. Farmers sell their raw, unprocessed leaves to large drug cartels in these countries, who pay poor local workers to first convert the leaves into cocaine sulphate, or "paste," by placing them in a plastic pit with water and dilute sulphuric acid. The resulting paste is then processed in a stew of kerosene, methyl alcohol, more sulphuric acid, potassium permanganate, benzole and sodium carbonate to render cocaine hydrochloride, the fine, pure white crystalline powder most commonly seen.

The cartels are the best-paid players in the cocaine trade. They contract with Colombian brokers to export the product as pure, or almost pure, bricks of cocaine hydrochloride. Paid drug smugglers transport it (for a healthy fee) by air, sea or land through Mexico, then the brokers deliver in bulk—sometimes hundreds of pounds at a time—to the first post-production purchaser. The next stop is either a U.S. or Canadian crime syndicate that deals largely, if not exclusively, in the drug trade. Once the powder is received, to increase its volume and thus their financial proceeds, the pure cocaine hydrochloride is mixed, or "cut," with inert white substances such as powdered sugar, lidocaine, talcum powder or corn starch, or with other drugs such as procaine, benzocaine or amphetamines. This reduces the purity of the cocaine to perhaps 80 percent. Acting essentially as a wholesaler, the syndicate then sells the reduced-purity cocaine—with a markup, of course—in smaller quantities to a regional organized crime or drug gang somewhere in Canada, transporting again by land, water or air. The process is then repeated: the cocaine received is further cut, or "stepped on," to render more volume at less purity, reducing it to perhaps 50 to 60 percent of its original potency. At this point some of the cocaine may be processed into crack cocaine, cocaine hydrochloride that has been treated with ammonia or baking soda to free its potent base material.

Canadian organized crime syndicates act as drug distributors rather than retailers, preferring to leave the risky retail street-level sales to others, such as smaller drug gangs and individual dealers. In street gangs, however, traditional organized crime syndicates have a wide array of money-hungry retailers at their disposal to do their dirty work, making the nook-and-cranny, community-by-community street sales that they are unwilling to undertake. Once the two groups find each other, to get the relationship started the organized crime group will provide the gang with cocaine on consignment (at about 30 to 40 percent purity) for about $1,500 an ounce, or about $26,000 to $33,000 per kilogram—which, of course, the street gang will cut again to about 20 to 30 percent purity. Then the leaders of the street gang will pass on their new inventory to their members to sell, on commission, to what is usually the end consumer, at a price of about $100 a gram or $280 for a 3.5 gram (an eighth of an ounce) "eight ball." To complete the cycle, the street gang pays the larger gang for its coke and is paid a commission either in cash or in drugs, which they can sell in turn for their sole financial benefit.

The traditional cocaine business model or supply chain in Canada is a multi-layered one, with cocaine passing through many hands. It looks something like this:

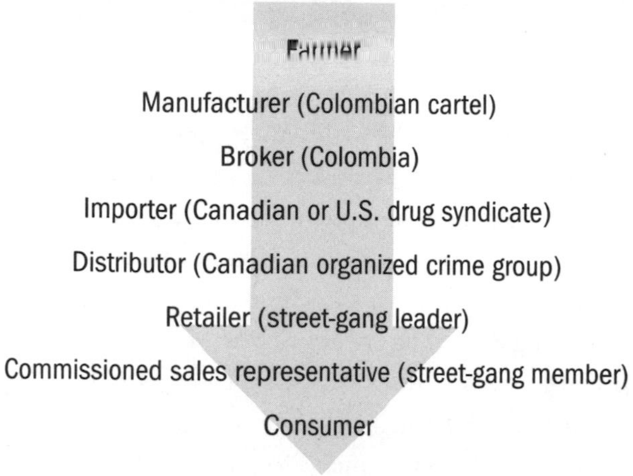

Farmer

Manufacturer (Colombian cartel)

Broker (Colombia)

Importer (Canadian or U.S. drug syndicate)

Distributor (Canadian organized crime group)

Retailer (street-gang leader)

Commissioned sales representative (street-gang member)

Consumer

Each player makes money, but those at the top of the drug chain—the manufacturers, brokers, importers and distributors—make much more than those at the bottom—the street-gang sales reps—despite the fact that the per unit value of the increasingly impure product keeps going up as it proceeds down the line. This is due in large part to the fragmented, competitive and fluid nature of the retail drug market, which is dominated by relatively disorganized street-gang members and other independent entrepreneurs who rely on word of mouth and social networks for their sales, which are often used to offset their own consumption. These dealers sell their product for the street price (constantly changing) that prevails at the time and sometimes compete for sales with other members of their own gang, because the gangs generally lack a central system for collecting and redistributing the proceeds of their crimes. In spite of some lucrative dial-a-dope opportunities, most small-time street-gang dealers enjoy relatively modest, even insignificant, incomes. Their leaders, who handle the relationship with the organized crime group and derive income from the dealer-members they supply, may do very well for themselves. However, the average rank-and-file, low-level dealing gangster, despite popular perceptions of wealth, often just scrapes by financially.

A by-product of the competitive and fragmented nature of the retail illicit drug market is the danger and the violence we have come to expect and increasingly read about. The majority of street-gang violence is directed at other gangs, and stems mostly from drug deals gone bad, money owed and the desire to protect trade within a given territory. Low-level dealers and their street-gang leaders do not consider themselves to be pushing their drugs aggressively, as is the popular image. They feel they are selling to willing consumers, of whom there are many, including respectable people who enjoy recreational drugs and the high they produce. From this perspective, street-gang dealers consider themselves to be businessmen and have no trouble justifying their behaviour, which includes aggressively defending their valuable customer base from rival street dealers by whatever means necessary. If a gang discovers that a rival gang has encroached on their sales territory by offering drugs at a lower price or of a better quality, they may resort to physical violence, threats or the stereotypical drive-by shooting, or they may simply adjust their prices or improve their product quality accordingly to win back lost business. To street gangs and their members, protecting their markets through violence is just part of the business of being a gangster, surviving in a dog-eat-dog world where the risks are high and the rewards often meagre.

HOW CHEMICAL DRUGS ARE CHANGING THE BALANCE OF POWER

Violence also stems from the changing market dynamics of the drug trade and from consumers' broadening tastes. The traditional cocaine-trade business model has as its basis dependent relationships. Each player requires other selfish criminals to do their job in order to get the product to the consumer. These disparate and tenuous dependencies and the need for every intermediary to take a financial cut along the way make it difficult for street gangs to control the price and quality of the product in their hands, and its availability. Their self-identification as "businessmen," especially among the leaders of larger and more established street gangs, means that more and more of these gangs are trying to go it alone, to obtain more favourable terms for their drugs with respect to price, quantity and purity. Sometimes they attempt to cut out their Canadian organized-crime suppliers by dealing directly with U.S. importers, which has been known to cause violence between the street gang and the (likely more powerful) organized crime group. Going it alone means that, in the case of some drugs such as marijuana and so-called club or designer drugs, a street gang tries to make their own product, introducing a new source of supply to a market. Whenever a new supply of an illicit drug enters an established market, however, the existing order is destabilized and violence often follows.

Consider the growth in recent years of club drugs such as ecstasy, GHB and especially methamphetamine, which is gaining in popularity throughout North America. Methamphetamine was originally synthesized in Japan in 1893 from ephedrine (an organic compound found in the ephedra plant). It was distributed to Japanese and German troops during the Second World War to stimulate their stamina, energy, wakefulness and fighting spirit. The drug, which can be snorted, smoked, injected or ingested, is a powerful psychostimulant that acts on the brain's reward pathways by releasing norepinephrine, dopamine and serotonin. Inexpensive and highly addictive, methamphetamine delivers a long high since it metabolizes slowly in the body. Also known as meth, speed, chalk or jib, it produces acute feelings of euphoria and restlessness and increases sexual energy, metabolism and tolerance to pain, among other possible effects. In Canada it is popular among young people aged fourteen to twenty-nine, club/rave partygoers, sex trade workers, the gay community, at-risk youth, rural youth and even in the mainstream, including athletes, long-distance truck drivers and men and women who want to lose weight.[25] At about $10 a hit for upwards of a twelve-hour high, it is no wonder that meth is often called "poor man's cocaine."

In North America the drug was manufactured and used legally in the 1950s to treat a number of conditions including narcolepsy, obesity, Parkinson's disease and depression, and it is still used today under the trade name Desoxyn to treat narcolepsy and attention deficit hyperactivity disorder (ADHD). However, in the 1960s clandestine labs began sprouting up in California to manufacture methamphetamine for a much broader market of recreational drug users. Unlike cocaine, which is derived from coca leaves that grow only in tropical regions and require sophisticated production facilities, methamphetamine is most often produced in the country of consumption, thereby eliminating the need for elaborate and cumbersome trafficking networks and expensive intermediaries. For domestic criminal organizations, the advantage of methamphetamine is that, while it can be hazardous to make because of the volatile chemicals involved, it requires little investment in the way of skill, human resources or capital. A meth "cook" needs only some simple chemistry equipment and a recipe that can be downloaded from the Internet. He also needs one of two precursor substances, ephedrine and pseudoephedrine, which are found in cold medicines and weight-loss supplements. Then just a few easily obtainable (but sometimes hazardous) chemicals are required to synthesize the conversion process; the long list of candidates includes acetone, drain cleaner, iodine, lye, red phosphorous, hydrochloric acid, Freon, chloroform, hexane, ammonia and hydrogen peroxide. With steady nerves, some experimentation and a little luck he can produce hundreds of thousands of dollars worth of methamphetamine in a tiny, hastily assembled clandestine lab located virtually anywhere—house, apartment or even trailer—and can do so in a short period of time.

In Canada, according to the RCMP, outlaw biker groups and Asian crime syndicates have led the way in the production of meth, especially in the western provinces. They continue to control the trade in stolen or fraudulently imported precursors, which are now considered controlled substances (under the Precursor Control Regulations) because of their essential role in meth production. But, as the drug's popularity has spread eastward, more and more independent producers are getting in on the act, including street gangs. It's not hard to see why, since meth production is enormously profitable. Whereas a gram of coke costs a street gang roughly $1,500 and sells, a gram at a time, for about $2,800—an 87 percent markup—the profits associated with meth can be almost 500 percent. So profitable is meth that street sales of only one or two pounds can pay for the entire cost of a small clandestine lab and suitably remunerate someone for the dangers involved in its production, including toxic fumes, explosions and arrest. So a lab can be quickly assembled and put into production, and its rapid payback ensures that it can readily be abandoned if the gang fears the police are nearby.

Organizationally speaking, the flatter and less cumbersome supply chain for methamphetamine, ecstasy and even hydroponically grown marijuana can be likened to the "disintermediation" brought to the market by Dell Corporation, which revolutionized the personal computer market in 1984 by eliminating the middleman and going direct to the consumer. It can be represented as follows:

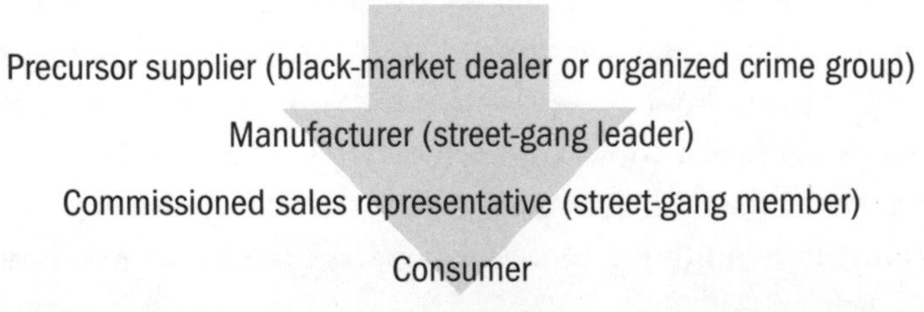

Precursor supplier (black-market dealer or organized crime group)

Manufacturer (street-gang leader)

Commissioned sales representative (street-gang member)

Consumer

New business models are, by their very nature, disruptive. The expansion of street gangs into new drug markets is destabilizing the current order and producing more fractious violence as money-hungry street gangs compete for business against other street gangs, organized crime groups and single-purpose independent manufacturers. Street gangs are still beholden to larger, more powerful and better-organized gangs for plant-based drugs such as cocaine and heroin, as well as to Canadian and foreign marijuana growers, notwithstanding the availability and ease of hydroponic grow-your-own technologies. But the chemical drug market can provide a vehicle for gangs to establish even more profitable ventures, at least in the short term, because drugs that can be manufactured by street gangs can be produced better, faster and cheaper by larger syndicates, even from afar. Indeed, in the United States, proficient, connected and well-capitalized Mexican drug cartels have essentially appropriated control of the methamphetamine market by establishing "super-labs" and flooding U.S. markets with inexpensive, high-quality product. In the process they have diverted customers from smaller producers such as street gangs. Whether this will happen in Canada—perhaps led by a traditional organized crime group, tired of street-gang incursion into its profit stream and therefore seeking to re-establish drug trafficking dominance—remains to be seen, but it does perhaps portend growing destabilization of the Canadian drug market in years to come.

With all this drug moving, drug dealing, drug making and drug consuming going on—all prohibited substances—it is no wonder that drug enforcement is a primary preoccupation of police, the courts and the government. Every year police invest hundreds of millions of dollars in drug enforcement to keep criminals away from money and Canadians away from the drugs they seem to desire so much. According to the most recent version of the RCMP report *Drug Situation in Canada*, in 2004 Canadian police and their government counterparts seized—in Canada and en route to Canada—more than 3,300 kilograms of cocaine, 88 kilos of heroin, 97 kilos of opium, 34,000 kilos of marijuana, 3,700 kilos of hashish, 496 kilos of liquid cannabis resin, 15,000,000 doses of ecstasy and 13,500 kilos of khat (a natural stimulant popular in Africa), and shut down forty clandestine methamphetamine laboratories. In 2005 police reported more than 92,000 drug-related "criminal incidents" (one incident can include multiple charges), down 6 percent from the previous year. Statistics Canada data from 2003 show almost 4,000 drug possession or trafficking cases against youth and, for adults, approximately 3,000 drug possession cases (dealt with by either prison sentence or probation) and 4,800 drug trafficking cases. Canada's National Drug Strategy, established in 1987 and designed to reduce the supply of and demand for drugs, has sucked well over a half a billion dollars to date from the federal government treasury. But in spite of all this activity and investment, drug use among Canadians continues to rise, lining the pockets of criminals everywhere.

STREET GANGS CASH IN ON THE BUSINESS OF FRAUD

With police pressure on the rise against gangs' primary revenue-generating activity, drug distribution, combined with the inherent risk and competitiveness of street-level drug sales, gangs are naturally turning to other ventures to feather their nests. One such emerging avenue of street-gang commerce is fraud. This "business" is already so big that if one were to aggregate the estimated Canadian losses associated with fraud and then treat this number as the annual revenue of a publicly traded corporation, "Fraud Canada, Inc." would be among this country's largest fifty companies. Its sales would be well into several billion dollars, and it would likely be our country's most profitable enterprise, since its cost of goods sold would be negligible.

Let's look at one sector with which, for better or worse, we are all familiar. Canada's property and casualty (P&C) insurance industry provides insurance protection for most homes, motor vehicles and commercial enterprises across the country. Not including government-owned auto insurers in Manitoba, Saskatchewan and British Columbia, more than 213 private insurance companies in this country directly and indirectly employ more than 100,000 Canadians and control over $100 billion in assets. By any measure, insurance is big business. In 2005, $33.3 billion in premiums were collected, while Canadian insurance companies paid out just over $20 billion in claims. Most, if not all, of us are accustomed to the periodic pain of paying insurance premiums. In doing so we take comfort in knowing that if we experience a loss, whether in the form of a house fire, a car crash or a business break-in, the insurance company will likely be there (after we have jumped through the necessary hoops, of course), chequebook in hand, to make us whole and ameliorate our inconvenience.

While most of us lament the ever-rising cost of insurance, we seldom hold the insurers themselves to account. Many people would be shocked to learn that an estimated 15 to 25 percent of all claims paid by P&C insurance companies in Canada contain some element of fraud. Fraud, like the people who use insurance products, comes in all shapes and sizes and includes so-called "opportunistic" and "premeditated" modalities. Opportunistic frauds are commonplace. Typically they are conducted by regular policyholders who, fed up with the high cost of insurance and years of premium payments for which they never made a claim, feel they are somehow entitled to claw back some of their hard-earned cash through an otherwise legitimate claim. So an automobile broken into with little corresponding damage or theft somehow morphs into a claim for an expensive laptop, a set of top-of-the-line golf clubs or an exclusive handbag for which receipts cannot be produced. Opportunistic claims are troubling to insurers, as they are hard to investigate and prove false without alienating what might be a legitimate (and profitable) claimant. However, they are generally considered a cost of doing business, much as a retailer would deal with "shrinkage"—the loss of saleable products caused by damage, employee theft, inventory errors and customer pilfering—for which a defensible accounting entry can be made.

The premeditated fraud modes, however, are the most problematic to insurers, and they represent an emerging new source of quick cash for gangs across the country. One is known as the "swoop and squat" scam, and it may unwittingly involve you, an otherwise legitimate insurance customer. Here is how it works. Five people from a gang or a criminal syndicate go to a car rental agency and rent a large sedan, ensuring that they pay the extra amount for the complete auto insurance package, which is always offered by the rental clerk. Insurance policy and car in hand, the five perpetrators will drive to where another car, driven by a collaborator, is waiting, and together they will set out on a busy highway.

This is where you, the legitimate car driver, may come in. The car with the five occupants will begin driving in front of you. Then the single co-conspirator will cut off the driver in front of you, forcing him to stop abruptly; if all continues according to plan, you accidentally drive into the back of the sedan. The five occupants feign expensive (and hard-to-prove) soft-tissue injuries such as whiplash, which are falsely diagnosed by medical providers—chiropractors, physiotherapists, massage therapists—who are also part of the scam. No treatment services are rendered, as no real injuries were sustained, and the insurance company experiences a claim loss of $100,000 plus, money that is shared by the medical providers and the perpetrators of the scam. Worse yet, you have been victimized. You will experience actual loss in the form of damage to your car (and, possibly, a real injury) and your premiums will likely be increased as a result of being charged for an "at-fault" accident—it was you who rear-ended the scammers' car.

It would be misleading to suggest that street gangs are perpetrating these insurance scams on their own. Criminal rings of all descriptions have been carrying them out for years. But street gangs are increasingly getting involved in these schemes to some degree, largely because of the easy money to be made, the limited chance of capture and the relatively light criminal sanctions associated with commercial crimes. Look at it this way. Assume you are a gang member looking to make some cash for you and a few of your homies. Faced with acquiring drugs on consignment from a more powerful organized ring (very risky, especially if you don't sell the drugs and return a profit in the allotted time) and then having to dodge the police and rival gang members during the sales process (also very risky), why would you not consider the relatively simple staged accident scam, which requires only a little organizational sophistication and the participation of like-minded individuals in the health-care delivery system?

Three things are driving the growth of insurance fraud. The limited chance of capture is a big factor, as police agencies naturally focus their investigative bandwidth on crimes against the person; allaying public anxiety about crime, after all, is good for business. Commercial crime units are notoriously understaffed and underfinanced relative to "hot" units such as Major Crimes, Gangs and Drugs, and there is still a sense today that commercial crime is victimless. As well, with courts full of more brutal cases such as rape, murder and domestic assaults, the few insurance frauds that do see their day in court usually earn a slap-on-the-wrist sentence, further disinclining our over-tasked police agencies to work fraud cases. Relative to capital offences, the penalties are light, and I have heard of cases where commercial crime perpetrators served as little as one-eighth of their sentence.

The growth in insurance fraud is due to more than these three factors. The money is good and the attraction is compelling, because insurance companies are, and will continue to be for the foreseeable future, extremely easy marks. Despite proclamations that they are committed to fighting fraud, the vast majority of Canadian insurance companies are essentially complicit in its growth. Ergo, they are financing Canadian gangs, including the street, the organized and perhaps even the terrorist varieties. I know I will be criticized by the Insurance Bureau of Canada and the insurance companies for saying this, but no insurance company CEO in Canada can truthfully claim to have ordered all possible actions to staunch the flow of funds to insurance fraudsters. Content to pass along the cost of fraud—in the form of higher premiums—to customers who, in the case of automobile drivers, are required by law to be insured, insurance companies are protecting their massive financial assets with, essentially, cap-guns. Curiously, this complicity exists despite the fact that preventive technologies are readily at their disposal. The banking sector has used them effectively over the past twenty years to detect and prevent fraud before transactions are even processed.

I know this issue first hand. In 2003, I co-founded a technology company to help insurance companies address this growing problem by offering them an outsourced fraud-detection service. In the course of sixteen months or so I met with dozens of insurance company executives and representatives (including several CEOs) to discuss their fraud problem and detection apparatus. For most of these companies their fraud detection apparatus, if it could be called that, consisted of a simple rules-based claims processing system (easy to defraud) and a small corps of people who manually reviewed a few of the many thousands of claims their companies processed each year. For example, an insurance company headquartered in Toronto that processed $600 million in auto claims yearly estimated that their fraud problem was costing $60 million to $100 million per year, yet they deployed only a single staff member to review anomalous claims. Claims executives were simply unable to obtain CEO approval to invest more against the fraud that was stripping their company of tens of millions of dollars annually. When the insurance companies' laissez-faire attitude coalesces with the criminal entrepreneurship of gangs, it's no wonder that insurance fraud is on the rise.

GRAND THEFT AUTO

In addition to incurring the cost of fraud schemes, Canada's property and casualty insurers also experience huge losses every year from auto theft. According to the Insurance Bureau of Canada (IBC), 13 percent of all property crime in Canada is related to auto theft. Although the national property-crime rate decreased 26.1 percent between 1993 and 2003, the rate of car theft essentially remained static. In 2005, over 160,000 incidents of motor vehicle theft were reported to police—an average of 438 vehicles a day—constituting an almost billion-dollar-a-year problem for Canada if you include the cost to repair and replace cars (about $600 million plus) as well as police, health-care, court and correctional services costs ($300 million plus). Like the crime of break and enter, auto theft is associated mainly with youth. About 40 percent of all persons charged with auto theft are aged twelve to seventeen years, and in some cities—such as Winnipeg and Regina, which boast some of the highest auto theft rates in North America—youth are responsible for more than 75 percent of all auto theft.

Recovery rates are a good indicator of the primary type of auto theft being committed. In cities such as Winnipeg, Regina, Calgary and Windsor (Ontario), the recovery rates are as high as 90 percent, suggesting that the crimes are largely a problem of so-called theft for transportation: stolen cars are used for joyriding and to assist in the commission of crimes. Alternatively, lower recovery rates in major port cities such as Halifax, Montreal and Toronto suggest theft for profit, in which cars are chopped up for parts or are illegally exported overseas. While there is no shortage of cars being stolen by street gangs and other organized criminal groups to facilitate crimes such as robbery and drive-by shootings (gunmen in the shooting that left Toronto mother of three Louise Russo paralyzed from the waist down were driving a stolen minivan), the theft of cars for profit is increasingly a means by which street gangs raise money.

The risk–reward proposition of auto theft is increasingly attractive compared to selling drugs. As in insurance fraud, the chance of capture is low, since police agencies do not deploy many resources against auto theft because they are already overtaxed dealing with the many crimes against persons. As well, automobiles are, of course, mobile, and they are remarkably easy to steal. If you are skilled in the art, it is a relatively simple proposition to make a car disappear into a waiting shipping container.

Today's most popular vehicles, SUVs, are expensive vehicles and in high demand around the world, and the "commission" for stealing a car destined for illegal export is attractive. Insofar as theft for profit is concerned, law enforcement officials concede that the leaders of this underground economy are various ethnic organized crime syndicates, groups that cannot properly be considered street gangs. However, recognizing that street gangs are growing and that their members are both hungry for cash and tolerant of danger, these syndicates are recruiting younger street-gang members to do their dirty work and secure the cars their overseas counterparts demand.

Consider the steal-to-order auto theft ring. In emerging world economies and those experiencing socio-political tumult, the demand for high-end makes such as Lexus, Mercedes-Benz, BMW and Porsche is high. Import duties for these vehicles, plus the cost of the vehicle itself, mean that acquiring the car by legitimate means is an extremely expensive proposition, a situation often compounded by the restricted inventory allotted by marquee brand manufacturers to these non-traditional markets. A growing underground economy has therefore sprung up to supply individuals and auto dealers with stolen cars at a discount to local prices, but still as much as 200 percent higher than our domestic prices. Orders for late-model cars are taken—a gold Lexus LS 470, a black BMW M3, a red Porsche Carrera coupe, a silver Mercedes S-class sedan—and payment in cash is received in advance, then sent by an offshore criminal ring to local counterparts with whom they have a relationship. The desired cars are located, stolen and loaded into a shipping container, a popular form of transportation. The economics are compelling. Take a $50,000 SUV: the actual thief gets about $500 in hard cash and the onshore ringleader gets roughly $2,500; overseas shipping costs an additional $3,000; ultimately the car will sell for $100,000—total profit: $94,000.

Ironically, the advent of new auto theft prevention technologies has given rise to the involvement of street gangs in this steal-to-order market. Ten years ago, criminal rings wishing to steal a specific car would simply scout the market and locate their car. Armed with only a slim jim (a thin, ruler-sized piece of metal with a notch cut in the bottom), the thief would slide the device down between the driver's door window and the door frame, jiggle it around until he located the door-lock mechanism, then pull the device up sharply, unlocking the door. Entrance gained, starting the car was a simple matter: hot-wire it or break the ignition lock, insert a screwdriver and start the car. The time required for a reasonably competent auto thief to complete this transaction would be as little as 40 to 60 seconds (hence the title of a movie starring Nicolas Cage, *Gone in Sixty Seconds*)—shocking, given the value of the automobile. While auto theft devices such as alarms and steering wheel locks could slow him down, they were never enough to discourage a motivated thief. But pressure from the IBC, government-owned insurers and other bodies, such as Auto 21 and the National Committee to Reduce Auto Theft, changed that, and the immobilizer has since made its way into most new cars.

Crime-reduction specialists consider electronic immobilizers to be the best defence for preventing drive-away auto thefts. Consisting of a small computer installed behind the dash and integrated with the vehicle's wiring, the immobilizer will permit the car to be started only if it receives an encrypted signal from a transponder embedded in the vehicle's key. Cars at every price point are still remarkably easy to get into, but most mid- to high-end cars now include immobilizers, making the key absolutely essential if you want to steal them. Here's where car theft rings have increasingly recruited street-gang members to do the heavy lifting. Now once a car on the ring's wish list is located, the gang member or thief waits until the owner approaches or enters the car, keys in hand (as in the opening scene of Paul Haggis's film *Crash*), or knocks on the door of the owner of the desired car, thrusts a gun in his or her face and demands the keys, or breaks into the house and collect the keys, which in most homes are in plain sight within feet of the front door. If you think these scenarios are urban fiction, I encourage you to survey the wealthy homeowners of Toronto's Rosedale and Forest Hill districts—virtually everyone knows of someone whose car was stolen in one of these ways. The level of intimidation necessary to get someone to hand over their keys, plus the prospect of resistance from some car owners, makes the street-gang member an ideal foot soldier for the steal-to-order auto theft ring.

THE MANY FACES OF FRAUD

Debit card fraud is a fast-growth business that is also attracting street gangs and other criminal rings. Canadians are among the world's most active users of debit cards. We hold 35 million of them, and they can be used at more than 625,000 point-of-sale locations and another 51,000-plus automated banking machines, or ATMs, the latter processing almost 1.1 billion transactions in 2005 alone. Despite their financial convenience, the only thing that separates your money from a thief is your PIN (personal identification number) and a bit of data encoded onto the card's magnetic stripe. Unfortunately, both of these pieces of data are remarkably easy for thieves to capture. By installing a tiny video camera on an ATM (to capture your PIN) and a fake-front card-swipe device (which captures your account access information), a crook can get all the information he needs to create a new debit card and clean out your account. Interac, Canada's sole debit card network, estimated this kind of fraud to be a $70.4 million problem in 2005 alone. One fifty-eight-member Eastern European gang was busted last year after siphoning more than $10 million from Canadian accounts. If the banking and payment industry were only to employ new "smart card" chip technologies, much of this fraud would disappear. But they have been reluctant to assume the estimated cost of $500 million or more, again treating fraud as the cost of doing business.

The business of fraud is indeed diverse. Every day, fraudsters are dreaming up ways to separate you from your hard-earned money. Recently a gang ring in Ontario preyed on a large retailer's lax returns policy. Gang members bought inexpensive barbeques for under $200, then printed up UPC bar codes for a higher-priced unit and affixed them to the boxes. When they returned the barbeque, claiming they had lost their receipt, the gang members received a store credit for the larger amount. To complete the scam, they either bought merchandise using the credit and resold it at a discount or sold the store credit itself, also at a discount to its actual value. For the small cost of a computer and some digital technology, the fraudsters could literally print money.

According to police reports, a Toronto-based street gang called the Malvern Crew, which was the subject of a 2004 gang sweep, ran a lucrative fraud business to augment their drug-dealing revenue streams. The gang operated a variant of a multi-million dollar telemarketing scam well-known to crooks that police sources estimate generates some $50 million a year in Canada. In the Malvern Crew example, members operated several "boiler room" call centres throughout Toronto that accepted toll-free responses to phony loan advertisements placed in American newspapers. To qualify for the loans, the mostly elderly callers were asked to provide personal information that typically accompanies any loan request, such as driver's licence number, social security number, banking information, date of birth and the like. Later a gang member would call the applicant back and approve the fake loan with the condition that they prepay a "loan default" insurance premium, ranging from a few hundred dollars to more than $10,000, by wiring funds to a local Western Union office. Once the transfer was made, low-level gang runners would attempt to collect the funds at the Western Union location. In addition, armed with the applicant's personal details, the gang would also attempt to take out credit cards or obtain loans or cellphones in the victim's name. According to a *Toronto Star* report, detectives with the Toronto fraud squad, commenting on the Malvern Crew case, confirmed that fraud was on the increase because of huge profits and light jail sentences. As Detective Jim White of the squad said in reference to court sanctions, "If you get done for a fraud, you get a kiss from the courts."

Our vaunted health-care system is also rife with fraud, more and more of it perpetrated by increasingly sophisticated street gangs and small criminal syndicates. I was the author and research director of the 2004 Canadian Health Care Fraud Survey, which was conducted in conjunction with the Canadian Health Care Anti-Fraud Association. This survey of organizations that processed health-care claims found that fully 95 percent had been victims of claims fraud, with a majority (54 percent) suggesting that from 3 to 9 percent of *all* claims their organizations paid were in some way fraudulent. If we accept the mid-point of this estimate—6 percent—and assume total health-care spending of $130 billion annually in Canada, then it is conceivable that some $8 billion of Canadian taxpayers' money is being fraudulently drained from our health-care system every year. This would be enough to drastically reduce waiting times for heart surgery, put MRI machines in every hospital and clinic in the country and make good on those increasingly empty proclamations that Canada has the world's finest health-care system.

Expressed in total dollar terms, just how large is the fraud problem in Canada? As I mentioned earlier, if it were treated as a corporation's annual revenues, fraud would be one of Canada's biggest enterprises. Last year the P&C insurance industry paid out $20 billion in claims; with premeditated fraud estimated at about 15 percent of all claims, that's a theft of $3 billion a year. Add to this the billion dollars a year associated with auto theft, $8 billion in health-care frauds, $70 million in debit card frauds, $280 million in credit card frauds and, conservatively speaking, perhaps another $2 billion in other financial frauds (mortgage, retail, telephone, telemarketing and offshore finance, for example). These, and other fraud schemes that are constantly being conceived, tested and refined by entrepreneurial fraudsters and street gangsters, represent the illegal diversion from our economy of $13 billion plus every year—equivalent to the annual sales of Canada's largest retail giant, Wal-Mart. However, unlike Wal-Mart, which, like most retailers, operates with very slim profit margins, our Fraud Canada, Inc. would be Canada's most profitable enterprise by far, as the cost and effort involved in separating people from their money fraudulently are remarkably insignificant.

Together, the massive enterprise of fraud and the even more profitable trade in illicit drugs create a magnetic force for youth who are at risk of street-gang involvement and who sincerely believe that legitimate economic opportunities are beyond their grasp. With so many billions there for the taking by anyone willing to assume the risks of being a street gangster, one might think it difficult, if not impossible, to tackle the gang problem in any meaningful way. This may seem a reasonable perspective, but it is a decidedly defeatist one. As you will discover in Part 2 of this book, there is much we can do—in the form of intelligent gang suppression and prevention strategies, legislative reforms and, indeed, effective parenting—to render street gangs but a minor inconvenience, a mere blemish on our country.

PART 2:
Confronting and Controlling Street Gangs

6: ON THE FRONT LINES

How Police Can Investigate and Suppress Street Gangs

A whole new lexicon has entered our language as far as street gangs are concerned, offering some impressive words to describe our collective response to their growth. Prevention, diversion, intervention, community mobilization, suppression—all embody a measure of hope that, when these responses are applied, we can somehow stem the tide of gangs and insulate ourselves from their dangers.

For aware Canadians who live in cities with an emerging gang problem (virtually every medium to large community in the country), *suppression* is perhaps the top-of-mind word. Accustomed to the relative safety and security of the traditional Canadian urban experience, we simply want gangs and their brazen violence *stopped*, and quickly. Most of us intuitively understand that, in the long term, the old adage "An ounce of prevention is worth a pound of cure" is probably the best bet for any social ill. But when it comes to street gangs, the prevailing approach seems to be "Prevention, intervention and diversion be damned—let's just suppress the immediate problem, take stock and then think about a long-term, sustainable solution to a problem that is likely to percolate for years to come."

Street-gang suppression is largely seen as a police job consisting of aggressive action to curtail, overpower and control gangs and their violence. But this is a decidedly narrow view, and a dangerous one, because the police are just one piece of the puzzle. The police, the courts and the corrections and parole system work together, theoretically at least, to reduce the impact of gangs and keep us safe. Think of it this way: what if the local constabulary swept through town and arrested all the gangsters in a frenzy of suppression, then discovered that the courts couldn't process them efficiently? The result would be dropped charges and angry, police-hating gangsters back on the streets. If we judge by police statistics only—that is, arrests—we may perceive that suppression is working; judged in the broader view, it's simply an illusion.

You are going to hear more about suppression in the coming years as street gangs attempt to expand their sphere of influence in Canada. Your local police force will become increasingly vocal, demanding more funds to enhance its gang-suppression capacity. You'll hear elected officials increasingly trying to justify why more of your tax dollars must go to the police, courts and corrections system, and why more laws and tougher sentences are required. Your fellow citizens will demand with greater frequency, "Enough is enough—just get these troublemakers off the street by whatever legal measures you can." And you'll probably wonder whether we are on the right path as far as gang suppression is concerned.

A healthy dose of skepticism is indeed warranted. We may fall (or may have fallen already) into the same pitfalls of gang suppression that Americans have over the past three decades. Unlike many of life's mistakes that simply force us to try again without serious ramifications, gang-suppression mistakes tend to produce a larger gang problem than would have otherwise been the case (just ask the Americans, whose success in curtailing the growth of gangs is dismal at best). Therefore we need to pay attention and to hold our public servants to account for the gang-suppression strategies to which your community will be increasingly subjected.

:::

According to the latest Statistics Canada data, overall spending on justice in Canada was just over $11 billion dollars in 2001, of which almost $7 billion was allocated to policing, $2.5 billion to corrections and the balance to a combination of the courts, prosecution and legal aid plans. Police expenditures are most visible to us, of course. In 2005, municipal, provincial and national police agencies employed some 84,441 Canadians, of whom 61,000 were sworn officers and the balance civilian personnel. This represents a ratio of one sworn police officer to every 528 Canadians, an improvement from 2001, when one police officer served 544. With new funding stemming from Prime Minister Harper's "tough on crime" agenda, expect police hiring to increase as gang rivalries continue.

The number of police does not tell us much about the quality of policing we receive in this country. Measuring quality is a subjective exercise, and for most of us our scant (if any) interactions with police (generally a good thing!) give us little capacity to judge the quality of services rendered. By international standards, however, Canadian policing is very good. We are reasonably well protected as far as officer-to-population ratios are concerned (in contrast, the United States has a 1:435 ratio, but a much higher per capita crime rate). Notwithstanding the 2004 Toronto drug unit scandal, the Ipperwash affair and various controversies involving the RCMP (such as the Maher Arar case and the 1997 Vancouver APEC summit), Canadian police agencies have been relatively free of the contentious incidents and charges of police brutality that have plagued U.S. forces, especially the Los Angeles Police Department (LAPD). Police screening, recruitment, training and continuing education programs in Canada are first-rate, and we boast some of the most skilled police chiefs in the world. Our police agencies have worked to increase the diversity of their workforces and to implement the forward-thinking and effective enforcement style known as problem-oriented or community policing. And notwithstanding that most Canadians would like to see more police on the street (even though violent crime is on the decline), Statistics Canada surveys of Canadians' feelings about community safety generally demonstrate that we feel quite secure and protected.

When it comes to gangs, three groups of officers bring their talents to bear on the problem. Each group sits at a different point on a continuum of response that is reactive on one end and proactive on the other. At the reactive end of the continuum are the plainclothes detectives who spring into action when a possibly gang-related crime, such as an assault or murder, is committed. Take, for instance, the Ace Crew case, in which major-crimes detective Patty Lowell of the Ottawa Police Service ran the investigation and managed this massive case, from the moment he appeared at the crime scene all the way to its conclusion, which resulted in thirty-nine successful convictions. Because they react to crimes that have already taken place, these officers play a very minor role in suppression and therefore are less important to our enquiry.

The second group of officers is the new breed of specialist gang cops—the "gang hunters," as it were—who occupy the proactive end of the continuum. Singularly entrusted with the task of suppression, gang cops work to understand the nature and scope of the community's problem through information gathering and intelligence procedures, including interviewing existing and reformed gangsters, developing confidential informants, participating in wiretaps and "Web taps." Their efforts generally culminate in arrests targeted to incapacitate gang leaders and the most violent gang members and associates, as well as high-profile and increasingly common "gang sweeps," which I describe later in this chapter.

The third group is the rank-and-file uniformed officers who patrol our streets every day. They can be thought of as occupying the middle ground of the response continuum, as they both respond first to emergency calls and—if they are carrying out active, visible, true community policing—proactively deter crime through their presence alone. With the recent dusting off and increasing acceptance of "Broken Windows"–style policing (see pages 141–146), uniformed officers can be thought of as playing an active role in the suppression of more serious crimes, including gangsterism.

A NEW AND MORE EFFECTIVE FORM OF POLICING

Perhaps the biggest change in policing has come in the past thirty years, with the move from incident-based "professional policing" to the more interactive and effective mode of "community policing." Professional policing is reactive policing. It consists of random patrols combined with a rapid response to all calls for service, with the focus on laying charges and maintaining law and order through a visible, authoritative police presence. This style of incident-based policing, unfortunately, has been shown time and time again to be ineffective for the needs of a growing city. As critics have wryly suggested, random police patrols make about as much sense as having fire trucks drive around looking for fires.

Because of its general ineffectiveness in large urban areas, throughout Canada professional policing has given way to what we now generally refer to as community policing, a sensible and more sensitive philosophy in which the police are seen as active members of the community rather than just its hired protectors. It embodies a greater sense of partnership, quality of service, critical thinking, empathy and problem solving. The police, including rank-and-file uniformed patrol officers, work with broader social actors (schools, business, social service agencies and citizens) to identify problems, determine their causes and develop proactive, crime-preventing solutions, all the while maintaining order. This approach promotes a different style of deployment where cops get away from police headquarters, out of their cars and onto the streets, walking the beat and working from community offices where they are more accessible and approachable. It also suggests a more active role for citizens in crime prevention and the policing of their communities, theoretically lubricated by their enhanced relationships with police officers whom they know and trust.

Viewed through the lens of street-gang suppression, community policing makes eminent sense. Gang violence is generally the outcome of festering gang rivalries and ongoing gang activities, which are perpetually in a state of flux. Rather than responding after the fact, by employing community policing practices and working in close partnership with administrators of schools, malls, city-run recreation facilities and transit systems (places where gang members tend to congregate, recruit and generally cause trouble), police increase their chances of forestalling gang crimes, thereby enhancing community safety. If a uniformed officer who patrols and perhaps lives in an area becomes aware of a growing street-gang problem through his work in the community, he is empowered, theoretically at least, to build a multifaceted solution to address it. His tactics might include organizing sports and recreation programs, initiating graffiti removal, participating in a school resource officer (SRO) program (where cops maintain a presence in secondary schools), encouraging business to step up with jobs and mentors, getting the faith community involved to teach life skills and prosocial values, and calling for a more visible police presence.

Few would argue against the logic of community policing, and it is the key guiding principle of every Canadian police force. The big problem with it, however, is acculturation, even twenty-five years after the philosophy was adopted. While it is perhaps too broad a generalization, those who choose policing as a career do so for the authority and sense of power the position confers. The opportunity to be part of a unified, codified group (some would call it a state-sanctioned gang) with a "thin blue line" mentality, which demands that they protect innocent civilians from criminal marauders, is a powerful elixir to many. Regardless of community policing's enviable tenets, the enduring belief among many police officers, and those who aspire to the position, is that their job is not crime prevention but rather the "acquisition" of criminals to be dealt with by judges, juries and jails. In other words, policing as a rule does not generally attract the "touchy-feely," empathetic, analytical, problem-solving types that the community policing paradigm requires. This is not to say that no cops have these characteristics or believe that community policing is the way to go; rather, the natural default position of police is, quite simply, to *police*—to admonish, regulate, control and react, not to prevent or suppress crime on a proactive, forward-thinking basis. This is reinforced by the military ethos of policing: the unrelenting environment of peer pressure and competition for rank among police officers forces them to be strong, brave, macho, tough and tactically proficient, not caring, compassionate and sensitive—qualities that are perceived as weaknesses, especially in new recruits.

An example demonstrates this durable gulf between community policing theory and practice. Back in 1990 the Ottawa Police Service established the Ottawa Police Youth Centre in response to serious crime problems that included a rampant drug trade and the shooting of an officer in the Debra Dynes low-income housing community in south Ottawa. Located in an abandoned fire hall near the troubled community, it seemed to be held together by duct tape and binder twine and contained a dog's breakfast of well-used sports equipment, games and other equipment. The centre offered prosocial diversionary programs to youth including a broad selection of sports leagues, recreation activities and counselling opportunities, to name just a few, to get kids off the street and help establish better relationships between the police and the community at large. Children aged six to eighteen were the primary target of the outreach activities, and by the late 1990s the youth centre boasted more than 1,100 young members. It was internationally acclaimed as an innovative police- and community-led youth-crime-prevention program, with delegates visiting from around the world to see the centre in action. More important, police calls for service plummeted in the area, and charges against youth under the age of eighteen dropped by almost half between 1991 and 1996.

By any measure the youth centre was a smashing success. Anyone who visited it on a weekday after school was shocked to see how lively and jam-packed with kids the place was, and many of them would freely attest that the youth centre had helped turn around their troubled lives. Youth centre staff, community volunteers and business leaders, headed by Constable Claude Turgeon of the Ottawa police, who rarely dressed in his standard-issue uniform in order to remain approachable, were equally engaged as mentors and program leaders, demonstrating the power of the idea that engaging at-risk youth often meant the difference between a life of crime and a life of promise. However, despite its many successes and a setting ready-made for community policing, it was next to impossible to get officers to work a shift at the centre or volunteer for many of its wonderful programs (summer adventure camps, midnight basketball leagues, computer camps), despite constant requests from Turgeon and then police chief Brian Ford. Save for a young, black, breakdancing constable who was immensely popular with the children, police rank and file missed a huge opportunity to give meaning to community policing and further the larger goal of prevention and suppression. Later I would learn the reason why: officers weren't motivated to join the "empty-holstered" Turgeon because they were too focused on the job of being a police officer.

BROKEN WINDOWS, BROKEN PROMISES?

Community policing in many respects goes against the grain of traditional policing, but there is renewed interest in what is popularly known as the "Broken Windows" theory of crime suppression and prevention. This interest is so acute that an evolving concept of community policing now embodies the community revitalization, "taking back the streets" approach that is fundamental to the Broken Windows theory.

Faced with growing demands from citizens to deal with street gangs, gun crimes and other violent crime in our big cities, and perhaps a growing impatience with the apparent softness of the community policing model, Canadian police have naturally looked to the Americans for guidance, since they have been dealing with these issues for years. Engage in any debate on street gangs in Canada and you are bound to hear about the value of and need for Broken Windows approaches to policing. You will also hear case studies demonstrating how New York, Boston and other large U.S. cities, faced with spiralling street crime and gang activity, turned their situation around remarkably through the application of this style of policing by uniformed officers. However, before embracing Broken Windows policing techniques to deal with our gang situation, we must first assess the veracity of its proponents' claims, as well as their applicability within a Canadian context.

The Broken Windows theory first appeared in the March 1982 edition of *The Atlantic Monthly* in an article written by James Q. Wilson and Harvard University researcher George L. Kelling. In the article the authors wrote that "if a window in a building is broken and is left unrepaired, all of the rest of the windows will soon be broken . . . one unrepaired window is a signal that no one cares, and so breaking more windows costs nothing."[26] According to the theory, the key to preventing vandalism and other anti-social behaviour is to fix problems—broken windows, graffiti, panhandling, prostitution, littering—when they are small so that they do not escalate, and thus respectable residents do not flee a neighbourhood. Through Broken Windows policing, it was further theorized, major crime would be suppressed. In other words, the theory endorsed the belief that crime is the result of lax police efforts and that stricter law enforcement policy is the primary ingredient to promoting safer communities.

Wilson and Kelling's work perhaps derives from the work of world-renowned Stanford psychologist Philip Zimbardo, who conducted an ingenious experiment on human behaviour in 1969. Zimbardo parked a car on a street in Palo Alto, California, and an identical car in a comparable Bronx, New York, neighbourhood, the only difference being that the plates of the latter were removed and its hood was propped open. Within a day the Bronx car was stripped, but the Palo Alto car remained untouched for a week. To test his emerging "broken windows" theory, Zimbardo smashed one of the Palo Alto car's windows with a sledgehammer. Within a few hours that car too was destroyed, allowing Zimbardo to make the point that disorder begets even more disorder and that a small deviation from the norm can set into motion a cascade of vandalism and criminality.

The renewed Broken Windows theory as espoused by Kelling and Catherine M. Coles quickly became gospel among the media and politicians in the United States. It also helped foment an ideological debate about the effectiveness of twenty-five years' worth of liberal "root cause" thinking and civil rights policies that had failed to maintain urban peace. Broken Windows theories supported police tactics such as foot patrols and re-emphasized community policing. Inherent also in the approach was stern punishment—a cracking of the whip—of criminal "wannabes" for the relatively marginal offences they committed. Doing so would deter the wannabes from future crimes and, since they had "important information about who was dealing drugs from where; about who carries weapons and when," they would snitch and strike a deal, thus short-circuiting further criminality in their neighbourhood.[11] And while the authors conceded that the wannabes needed education, opportunity and jobs, they first needed to be controlled and imprisoned, offering four types of social benefits: retribution, deterrence, rehabilitation and, of course, incapacitation.

In 1984 Kelling was hired as a consultant by the New York Transit Authority to put Broken Windows theory into practice. From 1984 to 1990 subway graffiti was targeted and removed to the tune of $250 million, and in 1990 the new Transit Authority police chief, William J. Bratton, implemented a zero-tolerance policy for fare dodgers, backed by new approaches to processing and background-checking arrestees. In 1993 Rudolph Giuliani was elected as mayor of New York City and stepped up the Broken Windows approach under the rubric "quality of life." Bratton was appointed commissioner of the NYPD in 1994 and added seven thousand new officers to the payroll, introduced a new police intelligence database called CompStat, cleared more than fifty thousand outstanding warrants, promoted stop-and-frisk policing (more than a million incidents in ten years) and showed zero tolerance for vagrancy, public intoxication, public urination and just about every other petty offence. When George Pataki was elected governor in 1994, he also supported Broken Windows policing, moving to introduce new DNA technologies and "Jenna's Law," which ended parole for violent felons.

A decade later New York City boasted a police force of more than 40,000 (a 45 percent increase over ten years), representing one cop per 202 people. Police staff levels in 2002 were four times those of Los Angeles (one cop per 380 people) and eight times Toronto's total uniform strength of 5,100 (one per 512 people). Compelling crime statistics strengthened the resolve of Broken Windows proponents: a 50 percent reduction in reported violent crime in a decade and a reduction in murders from 30.7 per 100,000 people in 1990 to 8.4 per 100,000 people in 2000 (a reduction of 73.6 percent). Other proponents, mostly from the political right, argued that between 1988 and 1998 more than sixty thousand crimes were *not* committed. Today New York City, statistically speaking, is the safest big city in America, with a crime rate of 2,800 per 100,000 people—in contrast to 9,000 in Dallas, 7,900 in Detroit and 7,400 in Phoenix. For many, New York's rapid drop in crime has indeed been a miracle, and the declining rates catapulted Mayor Giuliani into the national spotlight, as his policies seemed to confirm the assumptions of conservative commentators and law enforcement advocates.

People clamour for quick fixes to seemingly intractable problems, and it is hard to deny the attractiveness of Broken Windows policies. To average citizens the theory resonates well—who among us does not want quick restoration of order and the reclaiming of our streets? After all, today's graffiti artist may be tomorrow's gangster murderer, so it's better to take hard, decisive action now rather than risk spiralling crime. If people are faced with a choice between more cops on the streets snuffing out crime of every kind and root-cause prevention and intervention efforts that may take years to pay dividends (if at all), Broken Windows usually takes the prize. More than one Canadian media outlet has advocated for Giuliani-inspired Broken Windows approaches, but the New York crime decline begs the question, What role did the theory actually play? When one begins to examine the numbers carefully, the true impact of Broken Windows becomes cloudy. We should critically assess the extent to which the theory holds promise in the Canadian context insofar as street gangs are concerned.

In his exhaustively researched book *New York Murder Mystery: The True Story Behind the Crime Crash of the 1990s,* criminologist Andrew Karmen accords respect to Giuliani and Bratton for some of their moves (such as a robust intelligence database), but suggests that New York was a skewed model. The police force, through massive hiring, was twice the per capita size of those in other major cities; more police, rather than innovative policing strategies, had led to the crime reductions. Moreover, Karmen suggests that while the data showed that street murders declined, it also demonstrated that murders committed behind closed doors (for example, in domestic disputes) dropped as well—locales that were presumably not subject to the NYPD's prying eyes and influence. And Karmen correctly points out that the drop in violent crime began in 1990—four years before Giuliani assumed power—and that by 1993 the rate of property and violent crimes, including homicide, had dropped by 20 percent.

During the time that New York City was being heralded as a national model, similar crime rate declines were occurring in other cities around the country, including cities that did not apply Broken Windows policies. Perhaps the most notable antithesis to New York City was San Francisco, which adopted less stringent law enforcement policies such as community involvement and alternative sentencing. Labelled by conservative critics like Giuliani as "soft on crime" and its tactics ineffective, San Francisco registered reductions in crime that equalled or exceeded comparable cities and jurisdictions—including New York. According to data from the Federal Bureau of Investigation, the United States Census Bureau, the California Criminal Justice Statistics Center, the California Youth Authority and the California Department of Corrections, San Francisco demonstrated a greater reduction in violent crime than an index of comparable cities deemed by the U.S. Department of Justice to be "models of effective crime policy," including Boston, Charlotte, Chicago, Dallas, Denver, Jacksonville, New Orleans, New York City, Phoenix and Washington, DC.

In the period from 1995 to 1998—the heyday of aggressive Broken Windows policing in New York City—San Francisco's violent crime rate dropped by 33 percent versus New York's decline of 26 percent. For virtually every violent offence, including rape, murder, aggravated assault and robbery, San Francisco bettered New York, with no Broken Windows policing and not a scrap of national media attention. Even Los Angeles, a city long derided for its poor police practices and scandals, showed a similar decrease in crime if you adjust for the probable impact of New York's massive hiring binge.

A case can also be made that the machinations of the crack cocaine market also had much to do with New York's crime decline. In the early 1990s New Yorkers grew increasingly revolted by the crack epidemic and began to take back the streets. *New York Times* columnist Bob Herbert, who was astonished by the drop in crime, noted that "young New Yorkers have gotten too little credit for the changes in their behavior that have contributed to the curtailment of crime in the city."[28] A 1997 Department of Justice study also suggested that the most important reason for the decline in crime may have been the waning of the crack cocaine epidemic.

A more common-sense argument is rooted in economics, however. In the 1980s, the early days of crack cocaine in New York, demand was high and supply was scarce. The early drug dealers who brought crack to market became demonstrably rich very quickly, stimulating more gangsters to join the ranks of street-level pushers. Competition for drug turf and customers spiked massively, and violence increased in lockstep, making crack dealing one of the most dangerous professions around. Over time the drug's potency and addictiveness sent demand through the roof. This stimulated supplies from offshore, and dealers who wished to maintain their income streams began to undercut each other on price, reducing profits accordingly. With profit margins being competed away but no corresponding decline in violence, many gangsters simply gave up on the business of moving crack as the risk–reward proposition became untenable, ultimately driving down violent crime rates.

To be fair, New York's reduced crime rate is laudable, and Giuliani, Pataki, Bratton et al. made good moves in ensuring tougher gun laws, longer prison sentences for violent crime, and a more robust police presence. Travel today down a major New York street such as Fifth Avenue or Broadway and the sight of uniformed officers standing on street corners among the citizenry is indeed comforting to many of us, since New York's previous reputation as a dangerous city still casts a long shadow. However, if Canadian crime-fighting leaders model their tactics on the New York experience, they ought to ensure that our expectations remain in check. Toronto, Montreal and Vancouver are not New York City, and some of the conditions that may have given rise to New York's crime decline (demographics and declining profits in the drug trade, for instance) may not be relevant here.

Broken Windows is not a panacea for suppression of crime or street gangs, and I worry that its application in Canada will take us farther away from the promise of the community policing model, which in many respects has not been fully realized. Broken Windows does get cops out of their cars and into the community, which is desirable, but in my opinion it is more about traditional policing, but in proactive clothing: making arrests and keeping the bad guys away from the passive and easily victimized citizenry. Broken Windows inexorably leads to burgeoning police forces and renewed licence to bust heads at the expense of real prevention efforts, which rarely see the light of day in our country as far as street gangs are concerned. Before we embrace it wholeheartedly as a way of suppressing crime, including street-gang activity, we need to fully think through the ramifications of Broken Windows.

THE GANG COP: A NEW BREED OF OFFICER

Uniformed officers patrolling the streets in their cars, on bikes or on foot remain the first responders to life's legal travails and are therefore not typically the ones who directly chase gang members on a day-to-day basis. This job is increasingly being left to a new breed of cop, the "gang cop": a plainclothes officer who, unlike the homicide detectives and undercover drug cops popularized by Hollywood, we know little about yet who plays an increasingly important role in ensuring our overall safety.

The position of gang cop pays no more or less than any other position of similar rank in a major Canadian police agency. The conditions of the job—the hours, the nature of the criminals pursued, the lack of co-operation among those who witness crimes, and the inherent personal danger to both practitioners and their families—perhaps make it even less desirable. However, the role is highly sought after and contested, for it confers admission into a brotherhood of peace officer "soldiers" who are fighting a highly challenging guerrilla war daily on our urban streets against an elusive home-grown enemy whom we fear: the street gangster.

Gang cops, and the specialized gang units that are increasingly coalescing around them, are a unique breed of officer, tasked with the job of suppressing gang crime and dealing with immediate and acute gang issues.[29] Guided informally by a "hit the gangsters as hard as you can" approach—and, some would say, an "intimidate those who intimidate" orientation—gang units and their members tend to display a militaristic flair, attracting Type A, cocksure, aggressive and sometimes secretive cops who enjoy the thrill of the chase. Described to me by other police service members as most often the cops "with the biggest balls"—*cojones,* as my Spanish mother would say—gang cops need all the bravado they can muster against violent young male thugs.

The logo of Canada's largest gang-suppression unit, the Toronto Police Guns and Gangs Task Force, is perhaps emblematic of this ethic of confident state-sanctioned aggression. Adorning golf shirts and other popular swag sold at Task Force presentations to other gang cops and police service members, the striking logo features a muscular cartoon-like bulldog, its teeth clenched and its eyes shaded by wraparound sunglasses, holding a massive machine gun. Wearing a muscle shirt with the Toronto police logo, the dog has massive arms that feature a red bandana around the left biceps and a blue one around the right—perhaps a "taking of the flag" sign of victory against some indeterminate Blood or Crip gang set. The logo is as menacing as the targets of the Task Force members themselves.

Cops entrusted with the task of gang suppression must understand the nature and scope of a community's gang problem and develop strategies to incapacitate gang leaders and their most violent members and associates. In contrast to prevention and intervention strategies, which demand early and broader community involvement, gang suppression brings the full weight of the law, led by the police, to deterring, dissolving and incarcerating gangs. Gang cops focus the majority of their time on intelligence activities, studying their prey through important preparatory work such as twenty-four-hour surveillance of suspected gangsters, carrying out wiretaps, accessing cellphone records, developing confidential informants, "working" gangs and their members for information, and using database and analytics technologies to establish links between people, places, property and crime incidents. All these intelligence activities are undertaken in support of the actual act of suppression, which for gang cops generally takes three forms: the targeted arrest of a gang member suspected of a crime; the broader gang "sting" operation in which a small number of gangsters are set up by undercover operatives (for example, a staged gun or drug deal) and then arrested; and finally, the increasingly common massive gang sweep, in which thousands of hours of police work result in entire gangs being arrested and yanked out of the community.

The job of a gang cop is a tough one. His prey does not play by any reasonable facsimile of rules and there is constant danger of violent confrontation with gangsters, some of them fatalists who feel they have nothing to lose and are willing to die for their cause. Gang cops face personal dangers that extend to their families and face the constant risk of infiltration by gangsters who wish to send a message of intimidation. Fearing reprisals from gangsters, witnesses to gang crimes seldom step forward, greatly complicating the gathering of intelligence and the building of cases against suspected criminals. Because of the relatively recent emergence of more widespread street gangsterism in Canada, gang cops are still in the process of marshalling sufficient resources to combat the gangs, including obtaining the necessary technical tools (such as regional or province-wide databases shared among police agencies) to enhance the intelligence-gathering process. Because of a shortage of formal training, many gang cops are forced to learn on the job or derive their how-tos from several conferences offered throughout North America. These meetings, while offering delegates useable information, are usually structured to deal with another city's gang problem, which may differ substantially from our own. Perhaps the greatest contributor that makes the job of gang cop difficult is the sheer weight of expectations, the pressure to perform when gang violence takes its ugly toll.

THE ADVENT OF THE GANG SWEEP

With Canadians' collective anxiety about gangs at an all-time high and the police wishing to allay public concern and build confidence, massive gang sweeps, which were virtually unknown in Canada just a few years ago, are bound to become more commonplace. Attracting massive media attention, sweeps are multimillion-dollar police operations that can make or break careers and, if successful, render a street gang impotent.

Or can they? Because of the size and prominence of modern gang sweeps, they are a great focus for assessing the efficacy of gang suppression. Arguably we can link the increasing use of gang sweeps to Canada's previous war on bikers, which gave Canadian law enforcement agencies new legislative powers to apply against street gangsters. Between 1994 and 2001 the province of Quebec witnessed a bloody battle between the Hell's Angels and the Rock Machine/Bandidos motorcycle gangs for control of the lucrative Quebec drug market. In 1997 Parliament tabled a "gangsterism" bill that finally became law in 2001. In Section 467 of the Criminal Code of Canada, it sets out broad penalties for participating in a "criminal organization"—a.k.a. a gang.

Under the gangsterism provisions, a criminal organization means a group composed of three or more persons that has as its main purpose the facilitation or commission of serious offences that result in the direct or indirect receipt of benefits, including money, by the group or by any of the persons who belong to the group. The law adds three tiers of involvement, with associated penalties, for gangsters considered sympathizers, participants and leaders. Those who act to enhance the ability of a criminal organization to facilitate or commit an indictable offence under Canada's laws ("sympathizers"), or who participate in or contribute to any activity of that criminal organization, will be found guilty of an indictable offence and liable to imprisonment for a term not exceeding five years. Those persons who actually commit an indictable offence under Canada's laws for the benefit of, at the direction of, or in association with a criminal organization ("participants") will be found guilty of an indictable offence and liable to imprisonment for a term not exceeding fourteen years. And every person who belongs to a criminal organization and knowingly instructs any person to commit an offence under the laws of Canada for the benefit of, at the direction of or in association with the criminal organization ("leaders") will be found guilty of an indictable offence and liable to imprisonment for life. Given the breadth and teeth of the anti-gang laws, police now have incentive to carefully build a case against an entire gang and attempt to take it out in one fell swoop through the gang sweep.

Consider some recent Canadian examples. At dawn on May 18, 2006, more than six hundred cops led by the Toronto Police Service executed more than ninety search warrants in an attempt to take out the core of the Jamestown Crew, which was based in the Rexdale area north of Toronto and long considered one of the region's most violent street gangs. In what was dubbed Project XXX, more than 125 people—mostly fourteen to twenty-five years old—were arrested on more than a thousand charges of gangsterism, drugs and weapons trafficking, obstruction of justice and murder. With "military precision," police sources said, the cops simultaneously raided seventy-two homes and twenty-six other locations, including vehicles, in Toronto, Brampton, Montreal and elsewhere, and seized more than twenty firearms, fifteen kilos of cocaine, thousands of dollars in cash and several vehicles. After the raid, Toronto police chief William Blair boasted, "The leadership of the Jamestown Crew has been surgically removed from the community . . . [they] are no longer able to intimidate and threaten the lives and safety of people of our community and in particular the lives and safety of the people of Jamestown."

This raid followed a similar one in September 2005, also in Toronto, in which several dozen suspected members of the Ardwick Blood Crew were arrested in a series of early-morning raids involving three hundred officers in an operation dubbed Project Flicker. Officers executed more than forty search warrants in the raids and laid more than a thousand criminal charges (including ninety-nine against one seventeen-year-old alone), including attempted murder, armed robbery, conspiracy to traffic narcotics, firearms trafficking and fraud; key players were also prosecuted under federal gangsterism legislation. In May 2004, as part of Project Pathfinder, police arrested sixty-four people suspected of involvement in the Malvern Crew, which specialized in drugs, guns and telemarketing scams. Another large-scale Toronto police operation, Project Impact, led to the arrests of many members of the Galloway Boys, a gang that was terrorizing residents of Scarborough, and over five hundred charges. "Street gangs are cancers that, left unchecked, consume and destroy our communities," then Toronto police chief Julian Fantino told reporters later, as he detailed the seizure of five firearms, over a kilogram of the amphetamine crystal meth and a hundred thousand hits of ecstasy, along with quantities of marijuana, cocaine and hashish. Included in the more than five hundred charges were eighty-two counts of participation in a criminal organization and twenty-five charges of commission of offences for criminal organizations under Canada's anti-gang laws.

In contrast to the lengthy undercover investigations that resulted in those sensational one-day raids, Winnipeg police have taken a different approach. In November 2005 they launched a forty-person mobile task force named Operation Clean Sweep, which was designed to combat rampant crime, especially in the city's west end. The task force used aggressive enforcement and a highly visible police presence to suppress general street violence and disorder, including gang-, drug- and prostitution-related offences. In the six-month period up to the end of May 2006, Operation Clean Sweep claimed 803 arrests and 69 apprehensions; 633 offences notices were made and more than $925,000 was seized.

GANG SWEEPS CHOKE THE JUSTICE SYSTEM

The list of sweeps goes on and on, each with its associated media frenzy and collective sigh of relief from the community. But rarely is any critical examination made of their short- and long-term effects. I am all for taking dangerous gangsters off the street as fast as possible, but the manner in which we implement suppression techniques must be informed not by what sells newspapers and makes people feel better, but by what actually works. Effectiveness, not expediency, is the most important gang-suppression measure of which we must be mindful. We need to tread carefully as far as gang sweeps are concerned and use this tool in moderation. I liken these sweeps to the destructive fishing practice of bottom trawling, in which enormous "factory" fishing boats use advanced technology to locate large schools of fish, then drag massive nets weighted with chains across the bottom of the sea floor. Not only does this damage the sea floor, it is the least selective of fishing methods: everything is captured in the net and much of it is useless and must therefore be disposed of. Gang sweeps work in a similar way. Informed by ample intelligence and motivated by anti-gang laws that produce lengthy sentences upon conviction, police cast the biggest possible net and drag in dozens of gangsters in the hope that (a) they have captured the ones they really wanted and (b) they are sending a message to fringe and wannabe gangsters that the police are close and they should leave.

I admit to the visceral appeal of gang sweeps, perhaps law enforcement's most manifest example of a tough approach on gangs. They are often breathtaking in scope and dimension and the stuff of dreams as far as six o'clock news directors are concerned. The stolid police chief standing in front of a table full of seized guns, cash and drugs, quoting dramatic numbers of gangsters arrested and charges made, makes us feel good and reaffirms our faith in our men and women in blue. Our community begins to feel safer, especially those freed from the marauding gangsters, and we believe somehow that we are surely winning the war on gangs. For our intrepid cops, successful gang sweeps signal the victory of will, smarts and dogged determination over muscle and guts, and go a long way to improving morale in what is generally a pretty thankless job.

While the optics are attractive, the real cost and impact are rarely understood. Major gang sweeps are pricey—well into millions of dollars in terms of direct police expenditures such as salaries, overtime, surveillance equipment and remuneration for confidential informants, as well as the associated judicial system costs, including Crown attorney salaries and overtime, court costs and legal aid costs. Aside from the hard costs, one must also take into account the real and ever-present opportunity costs. Allocating a dozen specialist investigators to piece together the genome of an individual gang over six months means those dozen investigators cannot investigate new or emerging gang threats that have not yet reached critical mass. In cities as diverse as Montreal, Toronto and Vancouver, with their gang situation percolating steadily beneath the surface, this preference for gang sweeps allocates scarce resources disproportionately to one particularly egregious and troublesome gang, giving to others the conditions they need to flourish. I liken this to trying to put out a forest fire by dumping a load of water on its hot spot but ignoring all the emerging hotspots that will surely cause an even bigger fire.

Just as problematic, gang sweeps create an almost indigestible "pig in the python" as far as the judicial system is concerned. It is one thing to charge dozens of gangsters with hundreds of crimes, but our crowded criminal justice system cannot now—and for many years into the future—handle this flood of defendants, even if we build new courts, appoint new judges and hire scores of Crown attorneys tomorrow. The rules of evidence being as stringent as they are—and defence lawyers are some of the most skilled and savvy legal practitioners around—gang cases must be rock solid; otherwise prosecutors risk wasting their time. A resource-constrained Crown attorney's office, faced with a massive roster of accused, a thousand-plus charges and literally tens of thousands of pages of technical evidence and first-person witness accounts—some of them so complex, unreliable and/or convoluted that the average jury member could never comprehend—will naturally cherry-pick the strongest cases, those they are confident about getting through the system in a timely manner (as is a defendant's constitutional right), and either drop or plea bargain the rest. This is the reality when a six-lane police system, with its growing inventory of resources to crack down on a growing inventory of gangsters, attempts to merge with a two-lane court system: accidents and slowdowns will occur. This is the pig-in-the-python dilemma of gang sweeps: the snake (the cops), always eager to consume, can certainly get the pig started down its alimentary canal, but can the rest of the body (the criminal justice system) process it? In many cases they cannot, so what gets mistaken for good policing is really just good public relations.

Gang-sweep investigations are complex, and the police, of course, don't always get it right. This bottom trawling often results in arrests of marginal significance and sometimes serves only to inflame the community, drive gangsters deeper underground or, most problematically, create better gangsters. In the Project XXX case, one week after the Jamestown sweep twenty-three people were granted bail, including a woman who worked at a bank who was accused of telling her boyfriend how he could rob the bank (she faces a penalty of up to five years for this indiscretion). The court-prepared summary of charges associated with Project XXX proves the truism that not all gangsters are the same. They range from a twenty-one-year-old alleged gang member facing the relatively minor charge of possession of a controlled substance to a twenty-seven-year-old alleged member facing a hundred charges, including ninety firearms-possession charges alone. With respect to Project Impact, to date only a handful of convictions has been obtained under the anti-gang charge "participation in a criminal organization." Many of the accused are still in custody and proceeding through lengthy and expensive trials.

Often the community experiences a loss of faith when it learns later that many of those arrested in the multi-month, multimillion-dollar gang sweep have been released from remand, have had their cases dropped or plea bargained to virtually nothing, or are back in the community on bail. We write letters to the editor and complain to our member of Parliament that the courts and "liberal judges" have failed us and that bad men are now free. But this is not quite the case—the court system actually works pretty much as intended. It is simply that massive gang sweeps put additional pressure on an already overtaxed system.

To be sure, big gang sweeps can destabilize a major gang, or at least render it comatose for a while. In their aftermath, however, gang sweeps also destabilize the victimized community—something we rarely consider but should, because community destabilization can mitigate the benefits produced by the sweep in the first place. The housing status of many blameless residents is threatened because many adult male breadwinners are now behind bars. The "whack-a-mole" principle also applies: the leadership void naturally creates more elbow room for gangsters and wannabes who were not caught in the sweep to continue with their gangster ways. And while we may have swept up some of the most active gangsters, little has been done to change the real and ever-present socio-economic conditions that helped give rise to gangsterism in the first place. It's like ridding your lawn of dandelions by snipping off their heads. If you don't remove the roots, those persistent little yellow weeds will inevitably return.

My biggest criticism of gang sweeps is that, in their haste to ultimately incarcerate gangsters regardless of their individual threat, we end up producing better, more seasoned gangsters and thus perpetuate the cycle, but in ever widening arcs. As you will read in Chapter 7, Canadian prisons are ideal finishing schools—"Gang U," as it were—for gangsters. Despite what you may think or what the learned Correctional Service of Canada officials in Ottawa assert, prison does not rehabilitate gangsters or reform their criminal behaviour. These institutions actually help many gang members learn new skills and money-making schemes; they build and reinforce social networks that will enhance their gangsterism when they are released. Dangerous gang leaders should do lots of time—hard time, indeed. As we will one day discover, however, incarcerating increasing numbers of marginal gangsters collected via more and more sweeps, rather than finding ways to divert their illegal behaviour, is tantamount to pumping athletes full of steroids, enforcing rigorous training and equipping them with the very best teachers, then later wondering how they manage to achieve remarkable results in their chosen sport.

Of course, what happens in prison is not the responsibility of the police, but I predict that it will be added to their list of concerns as time goes by. The failure of the prison system to make good on its promise of rehabilitation will become a constant source of police frustration and cynicism. Police will feel that they did their part—they fed the system with gangsters—but gang activity did not abate and the streets got no safer, because prison only hardened them. The most regrettable outcome of this reasoning will be a plethora of excuses from police and little acceptance of their responsibility for the growth of gangs that resulted, in part, from their aggressive sweeps and crime-fighter mentality. "We did our job, but the rest of the system failed us. So look elsewhere for reform," will become the common refrain. This abdication of responsibility will be truly unfortunate and will further mask the real solution, which, I believe, is prevention supported by intelligent suppression and intervention.

A RACE AGAINST TIME

The biggest challenge for Canadian police agencies today as far as gang suppression is concerned is perhaps the inexorable impact of demographics. The front-line officer patrolling Canada's increasingly gang-infested streets is more and more an inexperienced one, and the street gangs know this.

Being a microcosm of the larger society, police agencies are subject to the same demographic shifts. Sometimes referred to as a simultaneous greening and greying, the demographic changes that are affecting our police protectors have huge implications for major case investigation generally and gang investigations specifically. Depending on the police agency in question—for example, the venerable RCMP—as many as 50 percent of sworn officers are set to retire within the next five years, and many of them have thirty or thirty-five years of experience under their belts. Charted on a graph, police service demographics are rendered as a shallow V, with ample distribution at the younger and older ends, but less in between.

Visit a major Canadian police agency and you'll discover where all the grey-haired, slightly overweight, often divorced once or twice, overworked *veteranos* toil—either in staff and unit management positions (staff sergeants, staff inspectors, inspectors and the like) or in premier detective postings, including homicide, sexual assault and other major crimes. When the Patty Lowells of Canadian policing begin to enjoy their well-deserved retirement, out the door with them goes an irreplaceable font of knowledge.

Much has been made recently about new government funding to put more cops on the street. This is welcome news to most Canadians, as they equate more cops with more safety. However, many of these new officers are being recruited and trained simply to deal with the attrition that is thinning out the senior, experienced ranks of their agency's talent pool, rather than adding significant new capacity to the corps of front-line police. Even if the level of hiring exceeds the level of attrition due to retirement, we may not be any better off in the short or medium term. When police officers are hired, they must first complete a police training program (such as the six-month, $7,500 intensive program offered by the Ontario Police College) before they see active front-line duty. Once they complete their police college education, newly minted officers will likely spend time in training programs offered by their employer, such as firearms training, classes in deportment, police service policies and procedures, and interviewing skills, before they are assigned to "grunt duty"—front-line patrol in a car. Officers may also receive additional training in the form of mentorship by a more experienced "coach officer." Today a new officer is likely to be deployed for patrol duty for as little as one to three years before taking on specialty work that values young, eager cops, such as the drug unit or the gang task force.

Today the police officers who pull you over for speeding or running a red light are likely to be quite raw, with as little as two or three years of active service under their belt. A decade or two ago the same infractions would have brought you face-to-face with a cop who had more than six or eight years of service. What has happened, of course, is that, as the police force has greyed and veterans have retired from the desirable specialty positions, younger officers who show promise have been fast-tracked.

Most of the cops I know—and I have gotten to know many of every stripe—tell me that the job is a tough one and that it took them years to feel comfortable in the role. Sure, a studious mind can learn the ins and outs of the Criminal Code of Canada and absorb an agency's policies and procedures manual in relatively short order, but it is the rest of policing that is the hard part. Cops are constantly scrutinized by their superiors, by the public at large (which has always been concerned about restraining the power of the state) and by internal affairs departments, which investigate major police incidents such as the shooting of a civilian by an officer. Officers spend a large part of their week completing paperwork at the expense of front-line policing. Many front-line officers say that they spend half their time looking for trouble and half their time staying out of trouble—by completing forms, incident reports and other mandated paperwork—which speaks to an increasing "cover your ass" mentality. Police officers work in perhaps the most competitive workplaces in the country, where the rank system means that you are always distracted by competition against your peers for positions of increasing importance, prestige and pay. For investigative officers, learning the subtleties of human behaviour and body language—the "nose" or intuition for the job—can take many years. And crime is never static: criminals are always devising new ways to commit crimes and hide existing ones, forcing the front-line officer to be constantly innovating.

Patrol officers are the first to respond to a 911 or crime-in-progress calls, and their limited experience and presence of mind, which often takes years to develop, may mean a poorer-quality response in terms of crowd control, offender pursuit and securing the crime scene, including protection of evidence. Don't get me wrong—front-line officers are among the hardest-working and most underpaid civil servants in the country. But their lack of experience is statistically obvious, and it affects the way we are managing our growing street-gang problem.

More than that, however, demographics are affecting major case management; as far as I am concerned, this is where the rubber hits the road as far as prosecuting gang members is concerned. Major case management, especially as it pertains to complex cases under Canada's gangsterism laws, involves complex investigative activities that include leading team members in a pressure-filled, information-rich environment. The job of heading up a gang investigation is challenging. Lead investigators must ensure that their responsibilities and those of their peers are carried out efficiently and effectively, that all necessary information is collected and that ethical investigative standards are upheld. Witnesses must be found and interviewed and their testimony secured, which is easier said than done, since witness intimidation is a big issue today. In large gang sweeps such as the 2006 Jamestown Crew crackdown, the volume of evidence is massive and sometimes complex, and it all must be managed and prepared so as to ensure that dozens, if not hundreds, of charges stick. If a major case manager is unable to carry out these varied responsibilities, the result can be a failed investigation, resulting in exclusion of evidence collected improperly, charges of wrongful arrest, and collapse of the prosecution. The complexities of major case management demand that experienced officers play these roles, but with levels of experience in decline, the challenge of managing cases is mounting.

RETHINKING THE ROLE OF POLICE

Winston Churchill once said, "Criticism may not be agreeable, but it is necessary. It fulfils the same function as pain in the human body. It calls attention to an unhealthy state of things." I feel mixed emotions when I criticize our police officers, as I count many among my dearest friends. I personally could not, and would not, do the job of a gang cop, a role that I believe is dangerous, grossly underpaid and, frankly, less and less likely to produce "spiritual remuneration" as our gang situation continues to worsen. To criticize those who are doing their best in a difficult situation, their faces "marred by dust, sweat and blood," as Theodore Roosevelt wrote, is difficult for me, yet never more important. I believe completely that we as a society need a better way of suppressing gang activity—beyond Broken Windows and sweeps.

We first need to rethink the role of police in Canada generally and of gang cops specifically. For the police "doing their job" means operating the front end of what we refer to as the criminal justice "system." In this model police capture criminals, prosecutors convict, judges sentence and prisons deter, punish and rehabilitate. Crime is therefore prevented through primary deterrence (the criminal fears being caught), secondary deterrence (potential criminals see others being caught), incarceration and rehabilitation. Under this system it is not the particular job of police or anyone else to prevent crime, as this laudable goal is supposed to be achieved by the system as a whole. Unfortunately the system isn't working very well, especially as it pertains to street gangs.

A change in perspective is needed to rectify part of the problem that affects our criminal justice system. What if police saw their role not as feeders of the system but as barriers to it? I believe that police agencies must recommit to the notion of community policing, problem-oriented policing or whatever you choose to call it, and give it a fair shake. While the idea of being a crime fighter is perhaps more compelling to most cops than being a peacekeeper, we need to do everything possible to ensure that a cultural shift takes place in Canadian policing, so that cops become primary agents of crime prevention by being visible and active in the communities they serve. With regard to street gangs, this means working the beat in troubled communities, working with youth one-on-one and in groups as positive role models to help develop their life skills and ameliorate anti-social attitudes. It means building bridges between at-risk youth and their families to the supportive programs they need to cope. And it means using their considerable influence to motivate businesses, educators, families and others in the community to get engaged in keeping the streets safe.

Notice that I do not say the police should write more tickets and make more arrests as part of their approach to so-called quality-of-life issues. I think we need to resist the temptation to employ broad Broken Windows tactics, which only serve to anchor the "feed the system" mentality. Indeed, some argue that the success of Broken Windows in New York and other U.S. cities has been confused with an underlying phenomenon that few have mentioned: the people living in the community had simply had enough and were no longer prepared to tolerate the level of criminality they were experiencing. In other words, they got engaged in the process of crime prevention themselves, with support from the police. And this is the way it should be. In safe and orderly neighbourhoods, the citizens, not police, are the prime keepers of the peace. As Jane Jacobs wrote, "The first thing to understand is that the public peace—the sidewalk and street peace—of cities is not kept primarily by the police, necessary as police are. It is kept primarily by an intricate, almost unconscious, network of voluntary control and standards among the people themselves, and enforced by the people themselves."

I am not suggesting that police should be soft on crime but rather that they need to think more about peacekeeping, in collaboration with the community and its citizens, who feel crime most acutely. This of course means that we must also become engaged as citizens rather than let the cops do our dirty work. Police also must be motivated, skilled and empowered enough to achieve an outcome that is truly in the best interests of the community and the somewhat elusive goal of crime prevention. Not every gangster is the same: some are the worst of the worst, but many are just stupid kids who have gotten in with the wrong crowd for a variety of reasons. It is this latter group we fail by hitting them with gangsterism charges and five years in prison, only to see them come out as more skilled and dangerous gangsters. Al Valdez, author of the book *Gangs: A Guide to Understanding Street Gangs,* correctly says that we cannot ever arrest our way out of the gang problem. Gang intelligence should remain a preoccupation of gang cops, and that should lead to selective culling of the most dangerous and active gang members. Then we can deploy the resources saved (court costs, legal aid fees, prison costs) towards prevention, diversion and intervention.

Let me return to the Jamestown sweep, Project XXX. As I noted earlier, two of the alleged gang members demonstrate, on their charge sheets at least, vastly different levels of criminality. Perhaps the Toronto police were simply unable to make a stronger case against the twenty-one-year-old man charged with a single count of possession of a controlled substance, but my guess is that he was a fringe member or recent addition to the gang, while the twenty-seven-year-old man with a hundred charges against him was a gang leader or established member with a much more prominent role. If the Crown attorneys can make their cases stick, under Section 467 the twenty-one-year-old may get up to five years in a federal penitentiary, and the twenty-seven-year-old may receive fourteen years, or even life, in prison. If the latter was indeed a shot-caller for the gang, responsible for importing and distributing guns on the street, as his lengthy charge sheet would suggest, then few among us would have issue with the severity of his sentence, even a life sentence (meaning he would be back on the street in about sixteen years). But if the younger man was a fringe member, caught up in gang life because of stupid decisions made in his late teens or challenging life circumstances, are we as a society best served by incarcerating him for five years? About $76,000 per year to keep him in a medium-security federal prison might see him come out a hardened gangster. By investing that $380,000 in intensive rehabilitation, counselling and job training, perhaps he could be set on a more productive course, with no further gang affiliation. For the same financial investment we can produce two vastly different outcomes, but we tend to lose this nuance when we focus on sweeps. You might say, "He deserves it for joining the gang. Let five years in prison straighten him out." That may be a comforting thought, but, rest assured, prison will not reform his ways. If he went in a fringe member, he will likely come out a real member, and then what have we accomplished?

I am not advocating for the young man with the single charge caught up in the Project XXX sweep, far from it. I do not know him or the circumstances of his alleged crime. If he is proven to have been running with a dangerous and violent gang, he ought to be held accountable for his decisions and actions, however ill-informed they were. If our goal is to ensure a reduction in gang activity now and well into the future, we need to intelligently use the many tools provided by our criminal justice system, rather than just its most serious sanctions. These are tough decisions to make, as we must sometimes resist our initial inclination ("Throw him away!") in order to decide what might be the best long-term course of action. Think of it this way: are there overachievers in your workplace sitting alongside people who are slacking off while they wait for a better opportunity to come along? Do some children in your family pull their weight more than others, simply because they are "programmed" that way? Are there elite performers on your sports team who are responsible for the lion's share of the team's success, supported by a cast of rather ordinary players? In virtually every group of people the diversity of human capital will be immense. My belief is that, when dealing with people who are part of a group, we ought to deal with them *equitably* (fairly) rather than *equally* (the same)—there is a world of difference between these two concepts. In other words, to deal productively with people it is okay to discriminate—in a good sense—by dealing with them in a manner consistent with their unique characteristics, behaviours and attitudes.

An important lesson we can learn from the U.S. experience with street gangs is that massive sweeps, while seemingly expedient and politically popular, are not as effective as the art of "working" gangs. America has been dealing with street gangs for decades and the country is teeming with gang cops. One of the top gang cops in the States, if not the world, is my friend and associate Tony Moreno of the Los Angeles Police Department. Now a thirty-one-year veteran of the LAPD, Tony has seen it all as far as gangs are concerned, because Los Angeles has been and always will be the street gang capital of the world.[30] Tony has pursued gangsters throughout L.A., including the notorious South Central area, and was stationed for a time with the L.A. County Jail's gang unit, where he spent his days investigating gangs by working with the most violent members of various Crip and Blood sets. Tony has seen virtually every kind of police suppression tactic, including notorious gang sweeps such as Operation Hammer. That operation was conducted by the LAPD's infamous CRASH (Community Resources Against Street Hoodlums) gang-suppression unit, which was later caught up in the Rampart scandal, in which a few members of the unit covered up the beating and asphyxiation of an 18th Street gang member. If you ask Tony to describe what he believes made him so successful, he will say that he did not get caught up in the militarism of the gang sweep but rather learned how to "work" gangs better than any one of his counterparts.

What exactly is meant by working a gang? For Tony it means taking a measured, intelligent and patient approach rather than just swooping down on gangsters, busting heads and throwing them in jail. He believes also that not all gangsters are the same and that the job of the gang cop is to try to take out the worst ones—the most violent ones, the most admired ones, the ones who create most of the problems in the community—rather than try (most often unsuccessfully) to take 'em all out. To work a gang is to get to know it and its members intimately: who they are, where they live, what their habits are, who they are related to and even what their nicknames are. Moreno does this by working both sides of the street. To learn about Gang X, he gets to know members of rival Gang Y, impressing upon them that their biggest threat in terms of death and injury is not the police but the other gang, so they ought to tell him as much as he needs to know to take out their biggest players. And he does the same thing in reverse, a carefully calculated cat-and-mouse game of infiltration and deception that allows him to compile a compelling dossier on both gangs. This knowledge is also helpful in determining which members are disenfranchised and possibly at risk of flight—they make ideal paid informants who can provide a deep insider's view of the anatomy of a gang.

There is a logic to Moreno's approach of working gangs from the inside out, something that is hard to do if you sweep them all up in the hope of incarcerating them. The other notable feature of Moreno's approach is that he is relatively non-confrontational with the gangsters. He is low-key and calm; he jokes with them and asks about their families; he calls them by their nicknames (which tells them Moreno is in the know), and they in turn call him by the nickname bestowed upon him by other gang members: Pac-Man. He doesn't try to intimidate them with his badge or the power it conveys. Rather, he "respects" that they have a job to do as gangsters, and this in turn earns him the respect of the gangsters, who understand that he too is just doing his job, even when he arrests them. Through this approach he gets their co-operation and the information he needs to catch the worst of the worst, something at which he excels (Moreno heads a special LAPD unit that hunts down fugitive gangsters wanted in connection with violent crimes). Through this process he also learns who is at the margins of the gang and who can possibly be influenced to take a different path.

In his internationally acclaimed book *Lessons from a Gang Cop* (which I edited), Moreno proposes a new vision of gang policing that is consistent with a prevention perspective. Since it never closes, he sees a community's police department as the ideal vehicle for solutions to community problems that are largely not criminal but nonetheless often give rise to criminal behaviour. In his ideal police force, officers would be required to enforce the laws but also to issue written citations—referrals, as it were—to people in need. Citizens would be referred to screened and sanctioned social service agencies in the community for the help they needed, whether it be food, housing, skills training or tattoo removal. The citizen, the social service agency and the police department would each receive a copy of the citation to facilitate proper follow-up. To ensure the new approach takes root, Moreno proposes that police performance be judged not just on the basis of arrests and successful responses to calls for service, but also on the basis of citations made and people served. This should also be supported by training at police college about the root causes of criminal behaviour, so that they are equipped at the outset of their career to think in a problem-solving mode. Through this model Moreno believes that police could be in the vanguard of gang prevention and suppression, and that gang violence would, as a result, slowly but inexorably decline.

For most Canadians who are concerned about gangs, this approach challenges our notion of what police should do. We want the police to do our dirty work, to chase down and cuff the bad guys as fast as possible to render our streets as safe as possible. The idea of a savvy gang cop poking, prodding, advancing, retreating and slowly building a strong dossier before the cuffs come out seems anathema in a time of extreme anxiety. But this is exactly the kind of policing we need if our goal is to undercut the growth of gangs. Selective culling now, when the gang situation is not yet out of control, will be more effective than a clear-cut approach—assuming, of course, that we redeploy the saved costs into intervention, diversion and prevention.

7: GLADIATOR SCHOOL

Gangs and the Canadian Correctional System

They had no name, no colours, no hand signs, no standard-issue tattoo and no specific turf to claim as their own, but Steve and the dozen or so teenaged buddies he hung out with were every bit a part of a street gang.[31] Back then, stuck in an eastern Ontario industrial town in the mid-1980s, there wasn't much for young men approaching manhood to do with their time. Described by Steve as "not your front-of-the-classroom guys," he and his gang-mates did poorly in school but excelled on the street, showing promise in stealing cars, wheeling dope, dispensing black eyes and broken noses, committing petty crimes and generally sparking trouble. With ample "negative police contacts," to borrow today's phraseology, but no convictions or police record of any sort, Steve's shenanigans were his sport, his gang involvement a temporary way station in life before he grudgingly went down the traditional path for many men in his town, shift work in a factory.

By the late 1980s, on the edge of Ontario's impending recession, Steve had been laid off from his factory job, and he was forced to consider his options outside of manufacturing. Since he had had the pleasure of meeting so many police officers in his past, he thought that law enforcement would be a good career path, although his previous activities and reputation precluded any hope of getting on either the local police force or one in a nearby city. He also considered the fire department and the military for the job security they conferred, but eventually decided to try school again, this time a course in corrections offered by the local community college.

For the first time in his life school came easily to Steve, who earned A's in every one of his classes. He had experienced no overnight conversion in terms of study habits or academic discipline—he just understood the material, because his previous street-gang ways had taught him to readily understand the workings of the criminal mind. Soon after graduation Steve was interviewed for a corrections officer job with the Correctional Service of Canada (CSC). He was struck by the simplicity of the interview process. For more than an hour he and the interviewer talked about football and other sports, and then, for about three minutes, the interviewer spoke of the "last stop" nature of the federal prison system—last stop for inmates because they did "very bad things" indeed. The only question he could remember fielding that was of any direct relevance to the job of prison guard was, "Do you think you will have any problem fighting inmates?" Big, muscular, athletic, eager and toughened by more street fights than he could remember, Steve gave an unequivocal no. He got the job and a first posting in a medium-security Kingston prison.

Steve took to the job immediately, as he felt comfortable working around cons. Since many of them were affiliated with street gangs and involved in widespread gang activity in the prison, he understood their world and their life of crime. Because he had been involved in so many of them himself, he was adept at catching "plays" in the prison ranges: hand-offs of drugs, conspiratorial body language, meetings between people who otherwise would never deal with one another. He showed skill in finding contraband, such as drugs, weapons and prison-made brew, because he too had learned, at a young age, how to hide things from his nosy parents. And because he knew the street lingo he was good at interacting with prisoners to find snitches—cons who would trade information about prison life and other inmate activity for protection or other valuable currency.

In the late 1980s the first on-the-job responsibility of rookie guards was to prove themselves to their more experienced counterparts, to "make their bones" and confirm that they were worthy of the posting and capable of watching others' backs. In many respects this would manifest itself in a rookie's willingness to mix it up with inmates if the situation arose. Steve embraced this role wholeheartedly and tried to be first to respond to a prison alarm or inmate uprising. Challenged physically by a con known to be tough and murderous, Steve never backed down and would, if necessary, go toe-to-toe in a fight. He had to earn the respect of not only his fellow guards but the inmate population as well, demonstrating that he was a strong, stand-up guy who could withstand pressure. Inmates who were disrespectful to staff or broke prison rules earned a visit to solitary confinement ("the hole"). If they refused to go, most often the young guards were sent in to do the cell extraction, which was always a violent encounter.[32] Always protective of their image on the prison range, cons had to fight during extractions to keep face, so when the guards popped the inmate's cell door, they always came out swinging. One guard went high, one went low, and they hoped for the best until the con was securely handcuffed, after which he usually offered them a simple apology: "Sorry, guys, I was just doing my job."

Steve thoroughly enjoyed his work. It provided steady employment, a pension and other union benefits. Netting pay of less than $400 a week, though, he was barely able to cover his monthly living expenses and the rent for his tiny apartment. Nonetheless, he derived other, valuable remuneration from the camaraderie of his peers and even his unionized supervisors, who had come up through the ranks of guards. It was the kind of brothers-in-arms bond that is created and cemented by stress and shared experiences that go well beyond the ordinary. He, his fellow guards and their overseers, most of them hands-on, rough-and-tumble men, drank a lot, partied a lot and revelled in their unique boys' club, in part to escape the constant stress of their jobs and the secondary stress of crumbling family lives, and also because the alternative—life in a dead-end factory job—was nowhere as appealing.

Ironically, Steve also embraced the job because it had a certain simplicity, if not predictability, to it. Notwithstanding the potential for occasional inmate violence, prison was not an environment of constant prisoner–guard disrespect. Cons knew that if they got too hot with guards they could be locked down, which would make it impossible for them to continue making money by selling drugs or operating other criminal enterprises within the confines of the jail. When a guard squared off against an inmate, the incident stayed inside the walls of the prison and life went on as usual. There was a certain decorum between guards and their cons, embodied in mutually understood rules of the jungle. For instance, a key tenet of the jungle was that if a guard did not screw with the cons' lives by restricting or cancelling their personal visits and conjugal-visit trailer time, they would not screw with his by having his loved ones attacked or stalked. Once mutual respect and day-to-day order were established, the prison usually "ran cold" and people went about their business—cons being cons, guards being guards—leaving personalities out of it.

There was a certain ethnic and racial predictability to gang activity within prison: blacks dealt only with blacks, Asians with Asians, Natives with Natives and whites (bikers) with whites, largely for control and protection of the trade in drugs and other valuable commodities. This predictability enhanced the guards' abilities to sniff out when something big was going down—usually when people who did not normally deal with one another were all of a sudden huddling in prison corners. Gangsters too carried on their activities with a certain deportment towards the guards. One time, after a gang-involved con tried to hit Steve over the head with a metal pipe, the con apologized, saying, "Nothing personal, boss," and admitted that he had been involved in a drug deal gone bad and needed a visit to the hole to let things cool down. Not wanting to ask for protective custody, which would tell others he was weak, the only way he could get that transfer in a face-saving manner was to attack a guard—any guard.

Job stability and intrinsic satisfaction aside, guards like Steve pay a steep price—stress. If you worked in an environment where around any corner you could be attacked by a professional criminal, you'd be stressed too. In just under twenty years of service Steve conservatively estimates that he has been involved in hundreds of physical altercations—fistfights, wrestling matches and wild cell extractions. But it is not just personal attacks or threats thereof that cause stress for a guard. It is also what they see and hear. One of Steve's best friends held another guard in his arms—a man with thirty years of service and close to retirement—as he quickly bled out and died, unable to staunch the blood flowing from a jugular sliced by a disgruntled gangster inmate. Responding to a prisoner's suicide attempt, Steve entered a cell that had so much congealing blood on the floor he can still hear the sucking sound of his workboots as he walked across the tiny space to attend to the con. Then there's having to bear witness to inmate-on-inmate violence stimulated by gang rivalries. Pent-up aggression and the need to make others stand up and take notice mean that con violence is extreme. Cons may be stabbed dozens of times by gangs of ten, twenty or more during riots as blood cast-off from homemade weapons drips from the ceilings. Heavy weightlifting bars can cause considerable damage, and Steve has seen more than one dead inmate with his face utterly destroyed by hundreds of blows, as if he had been in a massive head-on automobile accident. Some murdered inmates suffer the final indignity of having their rectum forced or cut open to reveal illicit drugs concealed there. As old guards are fond of saying, you are paid not so much for what you do as for what you might have to do, and the memories that you have to live with.

Steve estimates that of guards with more than five years of service, at least 80 percent suffer from post-traumatic stress disorder (PTSD). After being attacked by five inmates intent on killing him, Steve spent three months battling his own PTSD, but the demons never really went away. His body just adapted and for the sake of his mental health he learned to live with them. He knows of guards in their late thirties and early forties who have been married and divorced three times and are battling booze and drugs, incapable of maintaining loving relationships because of the deadening hatred and stress to which they are exposed daily.

Today, as Steve benefits from a new union contract that raised his annual salary to $63,000, some things have remained the same in his work, but much has changed. When he was a rookie, the guards and their union-brother supervisors controlled the prisons and the prison experience. Today, Steve asserts unequivocally, the prisoners—or, more correctly, prison gangs and their leaders—now pull the levers of power. He contends that this situation stems from the faulty thinking of CSC masters in Ottawa, an unabashed granting of rights and privileges to purportedly hard-done-by prisoners, massive layers of cover-your-ass bureaucracy that have neutered the guards' ability to act and make decisions in the prison setting, and the growth of gangs.

According to Steve, prison supervisors are no longer range-wise former guards. They are now civil servants, many of them transferred from other government departments, without a scrap of front-line experience. They are committed more to making nice with their Ottawa bosses and accommodating the demands of inmates than to supporting the CSC's most tasked employees, the guards. "At one time we had a range composed entirely of white bikers that we tried to keep apart from the black Jamaican posses they fought with for control of the lucrative drug trade inside the prison," says Steve. "But prison management, wanting a melting-pot approach based on orders from Ottawa, added two posse members to the biker range. Pissed off by the decision because they were their rivals and they were considered obnoxiously loud, a biker gang heavy took me aside and said, 'Your quota is two. We're gonna charge them rent, but if you add any more to the range, the rest go out the back door in body bags.'"

Again highlighting who calls the shots inside, Steve tells of another time when the CSC tried to sneak a sex offender into his prison, which does not house them, by "bleaching" his files. The inmates got wind and told Steve, "We know he's a hound, so you have until lunchtime to take him off the range alive, and if you don't, you can come back later and take him off dead."

Cons know how to work the system, suggests Steve. "If I start breathing too hard down the neck of a gangster who we all know is bringing in drugs, they'll file a complaint with the unit manager. Since they don't want the extra work in dealing with the situation, they'll ask me to give the con a break and stand down. Or, if there is a situation where I have a consistent issue with a con, management will move me off the range, not the inmate, which only reinforces to them that they run the show." The seizing of control is insidious, he adds. "Years ago, if a con lipped off he was sent to the hole to think about it. If a con was late for 8:00 p.m. count, he also went to the hole. Today we start doing our count at 7:45 and still have cons ambling in at 8:15 and later, because they know they can get away with it." The effect of the power switch, Steve contends, is more and more demoralized corrections officers caught in a "damned if you do, damned if you don't" dilemma. "We're more hands-off now. If we see a play on the strip it is sometimes not worth the hassle to pursue it, as we don't have the backing of our managers and we risk investigation, fines or both. So we give cons a wider berth, implementing the least invasive form of control we can that still maintains a reasonable sense of order."

The biggest difference Steve sees now is the extent of gangsterism and the unique brand of violence that comes with it. While there have always been gangs in prison, they are different now. "They don't show their colours or advertise their gang affiliations as much, since it attracts unwanted attention. And they don't just stick with their own kind anymore," says Steve. "If they see there is money to be made, they will co-operate with each other, which makes it more difficult for us to catch plays. They are also more violent, with young twenty-something street gangsters, who barely look like they can shave and have grown up fighting and killing for control of a street corner or battling other inmates in YO [young offender] jails, prepared to shank anyone at the drop of a hat or because of a wrong look, because they know that first murder that got them there was expensive, but all the rest of them are free." Steve notes that even the grizzled old cons, some of whom have served twenty or thirty-plus years of their lives in jail and were prison heavies in their prime, are spooked by the new street gangsters and are seeking protective custody to sidestep their volatility.

Today the can-do attitude of Steve's rookie days has been replaced by resigned apathy. "I used to love going to work, but now it's just a job that pays the mortgage, feeds the family and provides for my retirement—no more, no less. I often wake up and say to myself, 'I can't stand dealing with these cons anymore,' but the only thing that keeps me coming back are the guys I work with, because we've been to hell and back, and we need to stick together."

But the gangs are never far from his mind, nor the changes that he believes are afoot. With the gang sweeps going on in Toronto, Ottawa and elsewhere, Steve knows that, absent any real prison reform and restoration of power for corrections officers, it is just a matter of time before things get much worse. "Once the provincial 'buckets' fill up or judges tire of issuing provincial sentences and start sending hard-core, volatile street gangsters to fed pens, things are going to get insane in here—a real zoo, a fucking bloodbath," he predicts matter-of-factly. "New gangsters, with access to cheaper drugs on the outside, rapidly destabilize a prison. Someone has to control the drug trade, and the gangbangers will fight the bikers and the other established gangs until blood flows in the ranges." But, in his characteristically stoic and fearless way, hardened as he is by almost twenty years of working in what is undeniably our country's most violent and stressful workplace, and with a hint of the passion that once possessed his soul, he says he's prepared to meet the challenges head on.

:::

Federal prisons are essentially the last stop for an incarcerated criminal, and provincial prisons are their feeder system. One such prison is the Ottawa Regional Detention Centre, located just a few miles from Parliament Hill. In contrast to federal penitentiaries, which house convicted criminals serving sentences of more than two years, provincially run institutions such as Ottawa's detention centre are home to an incredible diversity of inmates, from people who have been remanded into custody while awaiting trial or sentencing for serious crimes such as murder, to those serving sentences of two years less a day, to young offenders convicted of various offences.

A prominent feature of the centre is its new maximum-security wing, built during the days of the Mike Harris regime. Octagonal in shape, the facility features an elevated central security monitoring station at the hub with a 360-degree view. It's chock full of technology, including several computer monitors and state-of-the-art ventilation controls that can, in the event of a riot, cool, heat or douse inmates with water to quell the disturbance. Separated by a narrow hallway, encircling the security station, are seven separate glass-enclosed, pie-shaped prisoner pods, each capable of holding a couple of dozen orange-jumpsuit-clad inmates, who can be grouped according to type of offence committed, personality style, justice-system status and even possible gang affiliation. Bathed in ultra-bright fluorescent lighting, the pods are entirely self-contained. They feature a main floor consisting of bolted-down tables and chairs, at which inmates eat their prisoner-prepared meals, and washroom facilities, in addition to cells with solid doors on an overlooking mezzanine accessed via a metal staircase. Inmates spend up to twenty-three hours a day in their pods, more if they are not permitted to use the tiny adjoining exercise yard.

Corrections officers assigned to this new high-tech wing are justifiably proud of it, as it stands in stark contrast to the rundown and overcrowded remainder of the facility, built decades ago, that houses inmates considered to be less dangerous. Conditions in the new wing may be considered stark but modern, but the rest of the facility is downright deplorable. In 2004, Ontario Justice Denis Power, during the sentencing of a man convicted of a domestic dispute who had spent ten months in the facility, commented that overcrowding and staff shortages at the Ottawa Regional Detention Centre were so appalling that they brought the administration of justice into disrepute. Among other things, the court heard that the cells, measuring eighty square feet and meant to house two inmates, were being used for three or more, with new inmates sleeping on floor mattresses until a bunk became available—which is to say that they spent a long time on the floor. Inmates were forced to eat in their cells inches from open toilets, clean clothes were issued infrequently and showers were limited to one or two a week. Scheduled visits were often cancelled at the last minute, and raw sewage seeped into cells from the young offenders' unit. Sometimes too few guards were on duty to permit daily outings in the yard and virtually no activities were available to prisoners, including rehabilitation programs to attempt to quash recidivist behaviour. The conditions were so bad that Justice Power, instead of the customary two-for-one credit for time already served, gave the inmate a three-for-one credit, a move that has since been repeated in other cases.

Now some of you will no doubt be thinking, "Who cares? They're criminals who have hurt others, so they deserve to suffer." The retributionist in me sheds few tears when I hear of a man who has been convicted of beating and raping his wife or brutally assaulting another person for no good reason having to withstand crowded cells, dirty sheets, human filth and quite possibly a sexual predator wanting to victimize him. Prison is not meant to be a pleasant experience. This is especially important if the experience is to produce two of its intended aims: general and specific deterrence. However, if we are to make good on a prisoner's statutory right to rehabilitation and, much more important, if we are to improve public safety by avoiding a situation in which inmates become more hardened and dangerous from their prison experience, then perhaps we ought to be concerned about the state of Canadian prisons, both federal and provincial. And if those arguments don't sway you, perhaps you are disturbed, as am I, that prisoners are getting enhanced credit for time served because of the conditions they must endure, thereby putting them back on the streets perhaps sooner than they should be.

In 2004 I spent a day in the facility as part of the street-gang training program I created with Tony Moreno, which was being delivered to about twenty of the detention centre's off-duty corrections officers. During our lunch break (inmate-prepared coffee and finger sandwiches were offered that no one, not surprisingly, wished to consume), several guards lamented the deplorable conditions in which they were forced to work. They also remarked on the increasing level of violence among the inmates and towards staff, as well as what they saw as the changing composition of inmates from non-gang-involved to those with gang affiliations, which was being accelerated by inmates joining gangs while in prison for the obvious protection benefit. Perhaps their biggest critique was levelled at prison management and the broader judicial system; it failed to inform them ahead of time of incoming gang-affiliated inmates so they could properly prepare for their arrival, by segregating them from rivals and implementing more stringent surveillance to watch for drug dealing and other criminal enterprises.

HOW MANY GANGSTERS ARE IN PRISON?

At the training session I asked participants what percentage of inmates were likely gang involved. Not a single guard could offer a definite number, only a general estimate of "lots." Obtaining reliable figures on gang-affiliated inmates in Canadian federal or provincial prisons seems to be a difficult task for government bureaucrats. One CSC study done over the ten-year period from January 1993 to October 2003, *A Profile and Examination of Gang Affiliation within the Federally Sentenced Offender Population*, examined 1,955 male offenders identified in the Offender Management System (OMS) as being gang members or gang affiliates. The study focused on five different types of gang members and/or affiliates: motorcycle, traditional organized crime, prison, street and Asian gangs. It found that gang-affiliated inmate admissions showed a gradual increase, from 2.9 percent in 1996 to 5 percent in 2003. Motorcycle, traditional and prison gang affiliates were typically Caucasian, while street-gang affiliates were most often African-Canadian.

In general the study found that gang affiliates were younger than non-affiliates at the time of sentencing and that gang affiliates received longer sentences for their offences than non-affiliates. When compared to a matched sample of non-gang-affiliates, gang affiliates were more likely to have committed violent, weapons or drug trafficking offences, whereas gang affiliates were significantly less likely than non-affiliates to have committed a sexual offence. Moreover, gang affiliates were rated as having lower motivation levels and lower reintegration potential, and were likely to have more previous youth court convictions than those with no gang affiliations. The analysis further revealed that gang affiliates were more likely than non-affiliated offenders to be directly involved in assaults on other inmates, assaults on staff and narcotics seizures. Upon release, street-gang affiliates were more likely to reoffend, and were especially likely to commit drug trafficking and weapons-related offences.

But what can be said of prisoner gang-affiliation numbers after their admission? According to a senior Correctional Service official I met who wished to remain anonymous, the proportion of federally incarcerated inmates affiliated with a "criminal organization" (gang) in Canada is approximately 15 percent. This includes traditional organized crime groups, which cannot properly be considered street gangs. With federal penitentiaries now boasting a population of just under 13,000 inmates, this suggests that there are perhaps 2,000 gang-affiliated inmates in federal Canadian prisons. In the October 2005 *Let's Talk* magazine (an official CSC publication), the number of members or affiliates of "organized criminal groups" was quoted as 1,700. Of these, the publication suggested that Aboriginal gangs constituted 32 percent, outlaw motorcycle gangs 31 percent, street gangs 15 percent, Mafia-style gangs 12 percent, Asian gangs 4 percent, and other gangs (including terrorist organizations) 6 percent. As previously reported by Sun Media, 2003 documents obtained from the CSC through access-to-information provisions reveal that some fifty-one different gangs are operating behind bars, from white supremacist, Asian, Aboriginal and cult gangs to motorcycle, Mob and terrorist groups. Assuming that the 8 to 15 percent estimate is a reliable one, and based on a total provincial inmate population of just under 20,000, we can assume that there are another 1,500 to 3,000 gang-affiliated inmates stowed in provincial jails and detention centres, for a national total that likely exceeds 5,000.

So fertile are the conditions for street gangsterism inside prison that the number of gangsters inexorably increases in size as previously non-gang-involved inmates, wishing to avoid extortion, rape, serious injury or even death, join gangs for self-protection. "Victim or victimizer" could be an appropriate slogan for new Canadian prisoners, and gangs are growing as a result. CSC officials naturally contend that few offenders join gangs after they have been incarcerated. To admit to the contrary would suggest that they are not firmly in control of the prison setting (they're not, but more on this later). Sylvain Martel, national president of the Union of Canadian Correctional Officers, rebuffs such claims, insisting that more and more inmates are joining soon after their entrance to prison for status, privileges and, most important, survival. Surrounded by crime, violence and volatile gang rivalries, much of it induced by the trade and consumption of psychotropic drugs and homemade brew, inmates have to make a choice in terms of their life inside. Many of them sidestep gang activity and try to keep their noses clean, choosing to behave and to rehabilitate themselves with a view to as early a release as possible, but that is easier said than done in an environment where predation and violence go hand in hand.

Does the CSC's estimate of the proportion of gangsters and its assertion that few new inmates join gangs stand the sniff test of guards? The front-line personnel are, after all, best able to judge the extent of gang membership. The answer to that question depends largely on the nature of the institution. If the frame of reference is Canadian-minimum security prisons such as Rockwood in Manitoba, Beavercreek in Ontario or Westmorland in New Brunswick, which are home to some of Canada's 2,400 or so non-violent inmates, the answer is that their estimate is likely reasonable, if not slightly overstated. But if the frame of reference is Canada's twenty-six medium- and maximum-security institutions such as Collins Bay in Ontario, Drummond in Quebec or Matsqui in British Columbia, corrections officers answer the question with a chuckle and a somewhat derisive "Are you kidding me?" expression.

According to the guards whom I informally surveyed (on condition of anonymity, as they are forbidden by their contract to speak to anyone outside the CSC about their work), the estimated number of gang-affiliated inmates ranges from a low of 50 percent to a high of *85 percent*. If they are indeed correct, there may be as many as eight or nine thousand gang-affiliated inmates in Canada's more secure federal prisons. Granted, some of these inmates may be "situationally" involved in a prison gang, that is, they join out of necessity for protection while in prison but do not carry forward their affiliation once released. The fact remains that prisons are chock full of gangsters and, ergo, gangster activity. These variances in estimates suggest that Canadian corrections executives are simply unaware of the magnitude of the problem in their own institutions—or are reticent to admit to the full scale and scope of the prison gang problem.

THE IMPACT OF GANGS IN PRISON

There is a general desire across the county to crack down on the growing street-gang problem in Canada through an undeclared, but nonetheless real, "war on gangs." The resulting effect of gang members on the daily operations of federal and provincial institutions has been a growing concern for prison administrators, especially front-line officers, who are far removed from the safe confines of Ottawa. The presence of gangs changes the way you do business in a prison. They constantly test the bounds of power and control, and they complicate things because gang rivalries can explode at a moment's notice. Gangs participate in criminal activities and they continue recruiting both inside and outside institutions. Incoming gang members, especially those with power on the outside, rapidly destabilize an institution as they vie for standing and control of inside criminal activities. They sometimes even continue to participate in gang activities outside the prison, and they are significantly more likely to be involved in assaults on inmates and staff. Intimidation of staff is a constant issue, and gang members have been known to try to corrupt officials to make their stay in the "bucket" more palatable.

Prison is not designed to be a pleasant place. Take several hundred violent men, many of whom have a fatalistic view of life, a Grade 7 or 8 education at most and prior criminal records, force them into a box and subject them to constant surveillance, a mundane daily routine of meals, counts and contrived activities, and lock them up every night in a cage for sleep time, and tensions will obviously run high. Perhaps the greatest contributors to violence, crime and the rampant gang problem in Canada's federal prisons are illicit drugs and alcohol, combined with a shift in power from the guards to the prisoners they are so poorly paid to watch.

Officially the Correctional Service of Canada adheres to a "zero-tolerance" drug strategy, which was promulgated in its Commissioner's Directive 585 in January 1996. The directive's statement of objectives declares that the CSC "will not tolerate drug or alcohol use or the trafficking of drugs in federal institutions" and that "a safe, drug-free institutional environment is a fundamental condition for the success of the reintegration of inmates into society as law-abiding citizens." Every inmate's correctional plan, which the prisoner must review and affirm in writing, contains a clause specifying that he or she is expected to remain "drug and alcohol free" for the duration of the incarceration. Breaches of these provisions, according to the directive, will result in either "administrative sanctions"—denial of family visits, suspension from a prison job that lets the inmate move around the facility, denial of a conditional release such as parole—or a "disciplinary sanction" such as removal of recreation privileges.

Most corrections officers will tell you that Commissioner's Directive 585 is the CSC's biggest fabrication, one that makes a mockery of the bureaucracy's mission to successfully remake inmates into law-abiding citizens. Indeed, in Canada's fifty-four federal penitentiaries, virtually all the drugs sought after on the street are readily available to inmates who wish to purchase them, including crack cocaine, heroin, marijuana, morphine, ecstasy, crystal meth, "hillbilly heroin" (the painkiller OxyContin), steroids and much more. Added to this volatile mix of drugs is inmate "brew." Each year inmates produce and consume hundreds of gallons of powerful cell-concocted alcohol made from whatever ingredients the industrious brewmasters can get their hands on, including potatoes, rice, bread, sugar, yeast and fruit.

As you can imagine, serving a sentence in a federal penitentiary means years of boredom and deadening routine punctuated by brief periods of sheer terror. The illicit drug and alcohol market alleviates the boredom of doing time, offering an escape through the thrill of the high, which dulls pain and improves one's conscious perceptions, but also through the thrill of the chase—acquiring or making, hiding, dealing or trafficking illicit substances under the prying eyes of prison officials. More than that, however, drugs and alcohol offer the inmate a powerful currency that can be traded for protection, power and privilege. So ubiquitous are drugs and alcohol in Canada's federal prisons that some estimates peg their use at more than 80 percent of the inmate population.

Pardon the pun, but prison inmates are a captive audience, so street gangs on the outside, facilitated by their incarcerated brethren, compete to supply drugs to them. The laws of supply and demand ensure stiff competition. Drugs inside a prison can command as much as 300 to 500 percent more than equivalent street prices, and it's paid for largely with drug deal money previously earned and sitting safely in outside bank accounts. According to Steve, one dealer affiliated with a street gang who was about to complete his three-year sentence told him, "Boss, my friends inside provincial told me I would make a lot of money while I was in here, but I never expected to make what I made," estimating that he cleared more than a quarter of a million dollars.

While drugs are available, it takes a modicum of planning and subterfuge to get them inside prison walls. With supply restricted and demand assured (with 80 percent of the inmate population using, customers number into the hundreds), a prison can quickly become a gang's most profitable sales territory. Before former solicitor general Lawrence MacAuley ordered new anti-drug initiatives instituted in every medium- and maximum-security prison in 2000, including drug-sniffing dogs and expensive ion scanners, approximately 75 percent of drugs, money and other contraband came through the front doors of prisons, smuggled in gifts, food, body cavities, baby diapers and other means by inmates' friends and family members. Typically this happened through open, or "contact," visits, where the family member and prisoner do not have a physical barrier between them; through private family visits (PFVs) when families can spend up to seventy-two hours with an inmate in a self-contained home on prison property; or through periodic inmate socials. As well, escorted temporary absences (ETAs), when prisoners were allowed to leave for eight hours a month under escort, were another opportunity for inmates to smuggle drugs. The other 25 percent of drugs came through the back door, smuggled in by the hundreds of suppliers, contractors and workers who go in and out of prison every week.

With the advent of new screening apparatus, drug suppliers and inmates' friends and families (spouses are often coerced into transporting contraband) have shown remarkable creativity when trying to deliver the goods to those on the inside. "Hooping" is a method of hiding drugs that attempts to evade the detection capabilities of both dogs and scanners. Drugs are enclosed in either a tied latex condom or a two-part Kinder Surprise plastic egg, to which is attached a length of dental floss. The floss is then looped around one of the drug mule's molars and the condom or egg is swallowed. To retrieve the drugs from the carrier's stomach one need only pull on the floss. My prison contacts suggest that drugs have also been hidden in tennis balls or dead birds thrown over prison walls; archers have attached drugs (or other contraband such as cellphone parts, which, when reconstituted, allow an inmate to carry on with outside business activities) to an arrow and then shot it into an outdoor common area, to be retrieved later by the intended inmate. Inmates also prey on unhappy, needy female volunteers from various prisoners' rights groups, such as the John Howard Society, who pay them regular visits. It is not uncommon for a young woman who has volunteered to work with cons to quit, then show up later on a con's visitors list, perhaps becoming a source of drugs. And, most troubling, the CSC suggests that inmate traffickers are bribing and corrupting disaffected corrections personnel who, while officially subject to "routine non-intrusive" searches as they enter the prison, are not scrutinized that closely and therefore make ideal drug smugglers.

Presumably the zero-tolerance provisions of Commissioner's Directive 585 should come into full force when the drugs are surreptitiously smuggled inside. In a pitiful case of "good in theory, poor in practice," the CSC essentially allows illicit drug use to continue. Unarmed corrections officers doing their rounds can readily smell marijuana smoke or identify an inmate hopped up on brew or heroin, but they are often instructed by management—off the record, of course—to let the offenders sleep it off rather than risk a confrontation with surly inmates. Penalties for drug trafficking in Canadian prisons are trifling compared to the potential profits to be made. Searches of cells and common areas, when they occur, are cursory, taking a mere five to ten minutes, when a thorough search should rightfully take several hours. Inmates with nothing but time on their hands are remarkably ingenious at hiding contraband, especially in their cells, since they are already so cluttered with permitted personal effects.

So ignored is Directive 585 that the CSC has made methadone available to inmates; this synthetic narcotic is used to detoxify those addicted to opiates such as heroin, morphine and codeine. The CSC has formally adopted a "harm reduction" strategy of issuing bleach kits to intravenous drug users, in large part as a way of combating the rampant spread of hepatitis and HIV through the sharing of needles.[33] Since heroin is often cut with strychnine or sodium cyanide—similar-looking but cheaper (and highly toxic) white powders—some prison wardens have resorted to issuing warnings to inmates about the poisoning risk. Guards told me that management is reluctant to crack down on drugs—they are not interested in dealing with the effects of mass withdrawals, which would likely grip the institution in further violence, if not a full-scale riot.

While the complementary Commissioner's Directive 566–10 calls for random samples of inmates' urine to be tested for drugs, that testing is limited at any one time to just 5 percent of the inmate population, which is essentially useless if more than 75 or 80 percent are using. Ironically, the introduction of random urinalysis has created a massive unintended consequence: a switch to more powerful drugs such as heroin and cocaine. Tetrahydrocannabinol, commonly known as THC, is the main psychoactive substance found in marijuana. THC is fat-soluble, storing itself in the fatty lipid tissues of the body. It has a half-life of about seven days, meaning that half of the THC ingested or inhaled stays in brain and body tissue for seven days. For a regular user, traces of THC can be detected in the urine a month after last use, or as long as twelve weeks for habitual users, depending on the strength consumed. Contrast this to the detectability of harder drugs, which are soluble in water and therefore have a much shorter half-life—heroin: one to four days; morphine: four days; opium: two days; LSD: three days; and cocaine: two to three days. Since a positive drug test will result in an administrative or disciplinary sanction, offenders will often switch from marijuana and use the harder drugs simply because they're less detectable. So random drug testing, which is more for show than effect anyway, has created more danger, more gangsterism and more addiction in Canada's penitentiaries.

The widespread existence and use of drugs in prisons polarizes public opinion and generates competing moral arguments. On the one hand, some wonder what the fuss is about regarding inmates consuming drugs and alcohol in prison. So what if they shoot heroin with a dirty needle and contract HIV or hepatitis C? So what if the powdered drugs they consume are cut with cyanide and can produce rapid cardiac arrest? As long as they are locked up, some would say, if an inmate passes his time stoned or drunk, what happens behind bars is of little consequence to the average citizen. On the other hand, others would say that doing time should be hard, bereft of the benefits of living outside prison walls, which includes the use of recreational drugs and alcohol; make them pound rocks, dig ditches and manufacture licence plates rather than escape in a purple haze in "Club Fed."

Moral arguments may challenge us intellectually, but they have very little value in helping to address the core issues associated with rampant drug and alcohol use in prisons. All prisoners are paid similarly while in captivity: under ten dollars per day, the amount depending on the extent to which an inmate actively participates in his rehabilitation. However, not all prisoners are equal in terms of drug-trafficking entrepreneurialism or the cash reserves they hold in outside bank accounts—for some inmates, tens of thousands of dollars. This imbalance in the ability to acquire, pay for, traffic and consume black-market drugs, combined with their massive use and consequent inmate addiction, creates drug debts. This is what destabilizes an institution and leads to a constant level of violence.

Drugs are a portable, convertible and powerful currency, and dealing drugs confers obvious clout. A result of the CSC's inability to enforce Commissioner's Directive 585 is that power tends to become concentrated in those most adept at dealing drugs—usually Jamaican, Chinese,

Southeast Asian, Aboriginal and African-Canadian street-gang members who cut their teeth selling drugs on the streets. These individuals continue to maintain their drug networks despite their incarceration. "Birds of a feather flock together" holds true even here, because gang members in prison invariably coalesce to form gangs similar to their outside counterparts in order to compete with other gangs for control of drug trafficking inside the prison.

According to CSC reports, there is mounting evidence that prison-gang rivalries have spilled over to the rest of the prison population, and beyond their primary preoccupation with drugs. Gangs in medium- and maximum-security prisons engage in arson and strong-arm robbery and protection rackets. Prison gangsters have been known to manage prostitution rings in which inmates are forced to provide homosexual sex for money or other valuable goods or prostitution services are provided through private family visits. Slavery, murder for hire, pornography distribution and rape are some of the businesses that prison gang sets operate. Extortion is alive and well inside prisons, and even a shower can cost inmates in some maximum-security institutions several packs of cigarettes—also a valued prison currency that can be traded in turn for drugs, brew and other commodities. As one of my guard contacts, an individual who has worked at Collins Bay, Millhaven and the 172-year-old Kingston Pen, says, any criminal activity that takes place in broader society takes place in Canadian prisons as well.

With blatant violence and crime an ever-present reality for virtually every provincial and federal inmate, what's a con to do but protect himself? Combining the virtually inexhaustible raw ingredients of ample time, constant danger, forced creativity, hard materials and underground how-to instructions, inmates have been known to fashion deadly armaments from just about any material available to them. In the netherworld of violence that characterizes today's prison, a weapon may be a convict's only means of holding predators at bay and sending the message that, if attacked, the inmate will fight to the end, inflicting as much reciprocal damage as possible. The presence of weapons ensures some semblance of order in the jungle—akin to the mutual deterrence achieved through building up nuclear stockpiles in the Cold War—the principal difference being that prison weapons actually get used.

GANGS CONTROL OUR PRISONS

You may be wondering what all the guards are doing while inmates are making weapons and dealing drugs. This is a fair question, but unfortunately largely misplaced. Of the CSC's 15,900 employees, approximately 6,000 are unionized corrections officers who are essentially classified as "peace officers," equivalent in status to sworn members of federal, provincial or municipal police services. The least visible of our justice system's peace officers, corrections officers cannot carry firearms within the perimeter of the prison, with the exception of some special circumstances. Official CSC policy—which is grossly misguided, I would suggest—is to avoid "ostentatious show of force" to prisoners, further justified by the assumption that, if guards carry guns, they will be attacked and their weapons seized by the inmates.

The Canadian Charter of Rights and Freedoms has (ironically) stimulated demands from various prisoners' rights groups for better conditions for hard-done-by criminals. Since the Charter's inception in 1982, several cases have made their way into the courts. Some have sought to expand prisoners' rights, including the right to vote and the right to enjoy conjugal visits with non-spouses, and others have sought to reduce the powers of the CSC, including restricting widespread urinalysis to detect drug use and strip searches for drugs (today consent from the inmate must be obtained, under Commissioner's Directive 566–7). A decade or so of judicial pronouncements laid the foundation for a massive increase in prisoners' rights that were eventually incorporated into the 1992 Corrections and Conditional Release Act.

Added to the mix were overcrowding of prisons and budget constraints in the late 1980s, which initiated a shift to more liberal policies under the direction of commissioner Ole Ingstrup, creating "softer" and more cost-effective alternative approaches to sentencing such as community service, probation, victim–offender reconciliation and the like. These developments thinned the ranks of corrections officers but not those of the increasingly bloated CSC bureaucracy, and indeed led to the introduction of Club Fed–style changes in the way prisons were operated.

The death of twenty-three-year-old inmate Robert "Tex" Gentles of Hamilton in October 1993 did not help matters. Gentles, an African-Canadian, was serving thirty-one months in the Kingston Pen for sexual assault. A founding member of the Prison Violence Project, a prisoner-based group that was documenting human rights violations in Canadian prisons, Gentles was protesting the inmates' lack of supper during a twenty-four-hour lockdown and had refused guards' repeated requests to turn down the music in his cell. When he maintained his intransigence, six white guards initiated a cell extraction: they entered his cell, sprayed him with mace and allegedly held him face down on the bed for over ten minutes, causing him to suffocate. The guards were originally charged with manslaughter, but the charges were later dropped and a coroner's inquiry further acquitted them of any wrongdoing. Amid continued public accusations of racism and officer brutality, the coroner issued an exhaustive list of seventy-four recommendations in June 1999, addressing such issues as cell extraction procedures, the use of chemical agents and inflammatory sprays, institutional lockdowns, correctional staff training, correctional officer stress, management accountability and increased independent civilian oversight of the Correctional Service.

Around the same time, proposals from the influential April 1996 Arbour Commission report (chaired by then Madame Justice Louise Arbour, now United Nations High Commissioner for Human Rights) were released. They stemmed from the April 1994 cell extraction, shackling and strip-searching of eight women at Kingston's Prison for Women (P4W). Commenting on the use of "administrative segregation," a confinement tool that prison wardens can order when inmates act, attempt to act or intend to act in a manner that jeopardizes the security of the penitentiary or the safety of any person, including themselves, Arbour concluded that "prolonged segregation is a devastating experience" and that it is a "deprivation of liberty." Moreover, Madame Justice Arbour recommended the development of a "culture of rights" within the correctional system and that administrative segregation be placed under the control and supervision of the courts. In a particularly stinging indictment of prison officials' management of their institutions, she wrote, "There is little hope that the Rule of Law will implant itself within the correctional culture without assistance and control from Parliament and the courts."

These developments and others remarkably changed both the balance of power in prisons and the severity of doing time. The new talk was about Arbour's culture of rights for prisoners, rather than their obligations to society or to their keepers. Wardens, with their decision-making authority hamstrung by their CSC masters, had to constrain the situational decision-making powers of their front-line staff. Cognizant of their new rights and mindful of the sensitivities aroused by the Gentles and P4W incidents, inmates have taken full advantage of the situation, and the treatment of guards has deteriorated. Behaviour from their incarcerated charges that would likely result in arrest or other sanctions in the outside world—threatening death, offering bribes to facilitate the smuggling of contraband, ordering illegal surveillance of family members by outside accomplices, throwing of urine and feces—must often be tolerated by the guards. Fiercely protective of their visiting privileges, since they are the obvious pipeline to drugs, prisoners threaten reprisals (work stoppages, riots and such) if prison officials enforce too stringently the various search and seizure provisions. The list goes on and on, and the effect has been an erosion of security in Canada's fifty-four penitentiaries and only tenuous appeasement of emboldened inmates. For all intents and purposes, we have ceded control of our prisons to inmates generally and, more problematically, to prison gangs specifically.

PRISONS AS GANGSTER FACTORIES

In practical terms, whether you like it or not, what happens inside a Canadian prison today affects all of us tomorrow. The presence of black-market drugs, homemade weapons, acute gangsterism, declining respect and constant violence greatly diminishes, if not eliminates, any chance that a gang-involved, drug-addicted offender will successfully integrate back into society upon release. The current state of our prisons makes a myth of the CSC's mission to contribute "to the protection of society by actively encouraging and assisting offenders to become law-abiding citizens" and makes a mockery of CSC management's claims that rehabilitation actually occurs in prison. Prison—a.k.a. Crime University or Gladiator School (the actual inmate alumni's name for Collins Bay Pen)—produces better, more skilled and harder criminals and helps inmates forge and solidify criminal social networks that can last a lifetime. This is not just my opinion or that of the guards; the police leadership believe it as well. Former Ottawa police chief Vince Bevan says simply that prisons are "advanced education for existing gangsters."

But the problem is much more than that. Prison creates new gangsters. Most new inmates are preyed upon from day one: a veteran inmate will order a rookie to hand over his shoes, irrespective of their condition or quality, as a test of his will and guts. If the rookie doesn't treat his shoes as if they were made from solid platinum, and complies with the request, the demands only increase, and then they come from other inmates as well, who hear through the prison grapevine that the new guy on the range is a patsy. A demand for shoes will morph into a demand for watch, money, television, stereo or for the use of his mouth or anus. Only by fighting back, risking death or serious injury for a pair of smelly shoes—or by joining a gang for protection—can an inmate retain his dignity and maintain his standing in the prison jungle.

Every decision a new inmate makes is watched and provides an opportunity for gang-involved inmates to extort more power and recruit more members. Take something as seemingly benign as a prisoner visit. Especially for young inmates, the first few weeks of the stay in a federal penitentiary are far and away the most traumatic as they struggle to find their place in the established order. Visits from family and loved ones are for many a godsend, allowing a connection, however tenuous, to the unshackled world left behind. Established gangsters in the ranges pay particular attention to new inmates who receive regular visits, monitoring who comes and how often the new con enjoys time with a loved one. "Before they know it, a new con will be cornered by two or three drug-dealing gangsters and told that their wife, girlfriend or mother must be at this place at this time and that they will be given a package that they must attempt to smuggle in," says Steve. Compliance is assured by the threat of being stabbed, piped or killed in the showers. As Steve notes, everyone in prison has a job to do, so the smaller and weaker guys comply and turn their family members into drug runners, "a better outcome than becoming the range whore." In this way new inmates quickly become implicated in working for the gang, and their involvement grows through time.

So, while we may congratulate ourselves and our police protectors over the coming years for throwing hundreds of street gangsters into federal prisons for increasingly lengthy sentences, we rarely consider that prison is simply finishing school for criminals, and the end product is likely to be more dangerous than the gangster punks who entered in the first place. Like the breeder nuclear reactor that produces more fissionable material than it consumes, in the coming decade our prisons will produce more gangsters than went into them in the first place.

THE EFFECTS OF NEW JUSTICE REFORMS

So what are we to expect from recently proposed criminal justice reforms, including mandatory minimum sentences for a variety of serious crimes, the elimination of house arrest, the raising of the age of consent for sexual relations and the hiring of over a thousand new police officers? The most obvious effect of the proposed changes will of course be a large influx of prisoners. Using 2004 numbers, 12,641 adult prisoners were confined in federal institutions that had an official capacity of 14,155, representing an occupancy rate of about 90 percent. Provincially and territorially, 19,366 prisoners were being housed in institutions with an official capacity of 21,398, again a 90 percent occupancy rate. Government officials have suggested that the reforms will add approximately three or four hundred inmates to the system at any given time, at a cost of about $50 million per year. Our prisons, we are led to believe, have sufficient capacity to accommodate these new inmates with no further investment in facilities. That's a good thing, as a prison designed to house approximately a thousand inmates, even a no-frills version, costs about $80 million to $100 million to construct, and many more millions to staff, maintain and operate.

However, I believe that for political reasons these numbers have been grossly understated and fail to reflect the full impact on our provincial jails and detention centres. The elimination of house arrest for a variety of crimes, including drug offences and those involving violence alone, will put an additional six thousand offenders behind bars every year if the incidence of those crimes continues at their present pace. If these convicts are housed in a provincial jail for just one year at the average cost of approximately $52,000 (compared to $1,600 a year to supervise a criminal under house arrest), this legislative amendment alone will cost our country an extra $300 million.

Moreover, the new minimum mandatory sentences will further clog provincial jails and materially increase the costs associated with the trial process, because defendants will no longer have an incentive to plead guilty and will therefore opt to go down kicking and screaming via a protracted and expensive jury trial. Under the current regime, defence lawyers and Crown attorneys have the latitude to negotiate plea bargains to ensure that cases are dispensed with in a relatively timely manner, and judges have the flexibility they need to render appropriate sentencing decisions (including prison time, conditional sentences and the like) that will ensure that justice is achieved under the circumstances presented of the case. This flexibility is important in large cases where dozens of charges are laid or when the evidence is exceedingly complex—such as recent gang-sweep charges laid under the gangsterism provisions. All of those accused will now be remanded into custody in provincial jails, further exacerbating an already dismal situation.

It would be folly to believe that within a year our provincial jails will readily be able to accommodate an influx of prisoners totalling fully a third of their existing capacity without major problems such as drugs, overcrowding, violence and gang activity, thus overwhelming prison management. Canadians are generally quite content for our men and women in blue to capture gangsters and other bad people so they can enjoy a well-deserved time out in prison, but the government's new anti-crime efforts force us to consider whether jamming the jails full of new prisoners—without implementing corresponding reforms in our corrections system—is actually the best long-term solution to reducing crime. Our prisons are already bursting at the seams, a situation that will only be exacerbated by the changes that are afoot. Warehousing thousands of new inmates in already crowded jails, which will soon fill to beyond their official capacity, will not make you or me or our children any safer.

8: STEMMING THE TIDE

Preventing Future Gang Activity

Ogijita pimatiswin kinamatwin—Ojibway for "warrior spirit"—denotes not an ethic of violent confrontation but the traditional Aboriginal recognition that we all, as members of a community, have a role to play in ensuring its health and fighting for its well-being, a role governed by the unique skills and attributes with which we are endowed at birth and with which we must endow our community before we depart. Ogijita Pimatiswin Kinamatwin, or OPK for short, also happens to be the name of a program run by Winnipeg's Larry Morrissette. It is designed to give meaning and direction to some of the city's many Aboriginal youth involved in the Indian Posse gang, which operates in what is known (often unaffectionately) as the North End.

Virtually every reasonably sized city in Canada has its own version of "the other side of the tracks": an area known for its crime, violence and poverty. For many Winnipeg natives the Salter Street bridge holds the distinction of being the crossing point into the poverty-stricken North End and Indian Posse territory, an area with a long history of suffering. At the beginning of the twentieth century, Eastern European immigrant workers flooded into the area to take advantage of the city's manufacturing boom. Housing developers snapped up the cheap and plentiful land, cut it up into tiny unserviced lots and constructed homes of poor quality, thus generating large profits. After the Second World War many of the North End's original settlers and their descendents fled to larger properties that were emerging in the suburbs, along with their social support networks and the businesses they worked for, leaving the woebegone community to others, including absentee landlords who did little to maintain their newly acquired assets.

Attracted by the inexpensive housing, a new wave of people descended on the area in the 1960s and '70s, especially Aboriginals from rural and northern communities. Ill-prepared for urban life, with limited education or paid work experience, damaged by colonialism and faced with constant discrimination, lack of jobs and little social support, the area's young Aboriginal population fell into the racialized poverty for which it is well-known today and likely will be for decades to come. Both the city and the province are well aware of the inner-city blight that is the North End; in 2000 the non-profit North End Housing Project (NEHP) was established to acquire and rehabilitate rundown North End homes—eventually as many as two thousand of them—which would then be leased under five-year lease-to-purchase agreements or operated as long-term rentals for low-income families.

Larry Morrissette, a fifty-year-old Aboriginal man, grew up in the North End; more than thirty years earlier he had run with groups that could be considered "gangs with no names"—"We all had to, for survival and companionship." Larry was trusted in Winnipeg's Aboriginal community because he had been working with at-risk youth since his 1986 graduation from the University of Manitoba with a social work degree. Soon after the inception of the NEHP, he was approached by a group of leaders of the Indian Posse street gang (then and now one of the largest in the region), who asked for his help in becoming "legit." Complaining that no one would touch them, including many individuals from the Aboriginal community who had long since disavowed their gangster ways, the Posse leaders expressed their desire to end the cycle of incarceration that plagued their young community and to provide meaningful employment opportunities for their members being released from jail. Considering the virtually inexhaustible inventory of houses that the NEHP needed to rehabilitate, as well as the organization's success in obtaining grants well into seven figures, Larry struck upon the idea of creating OPK, also known as the Aboriginal Youth Housing Renovation Project.

Through OPK Larry seeks to reconnect Posse ex-offenders with the mainstream community, as well as with the traditional Aboriginal values of non-violence and mutual respect, by teaching them essential life and employment skills through home renovation work. In partnership with the NEHP, OPK is assigned a newly acquired home and Larry is responsible for deploying his crew of a dozen men to renovate the house according to the NEHP's requirements. The team comprises ten former gang members, average age about twenty-four, with a collective hundred years of time behind bars—"citizens," as they prefer to be referred to now—along with two experienced Aboriginal elder tradesmen who act as mentors. They are paid only nine dollars an hour for what is usually a tough and unglamorous task, so Larry has no illusions that the work will enrich his men financially. But with a steady job that teaches them discipline and marketable skills, the mentorship of Native elders and a range of other social supports (including Larry's on-call ear, available twenty-four hours a day, seven days a week, to deal with any emergencies), Larry is convinced that his young men's principal remuneration will come in the form of spiritual and ethical development and a path to the treasured status of being "legit" for both themselves and their family members. Now about five years old and with an annual budget of less than $250,000 cobbled together from government grants and donations, OPK boasts several completed homes, a waiting list of gang members who wish to participate and, perhaps most significantly, all ten of Larry's current staff enrolled in classes at the University of Manitoba.

I met Larry one hot, humid afternoon in August 2006. Over some bad coffee he told me about his program and shared with me his well-reasoned perspective on the rampant Winnipeg street-gang situation, which he attributed concisely to loss of Aboriginal culture, poor socio-economics and lasting discrimination. Justifiably proud of the work his meagrely funded group was doing and wanting to ensure that I saw for myself the degradation of the community he has called home since birth, Larry insisted we go for a drive through some of the most gang-infested areas of Winnipeg, including the notorious North End and West End, and past the parking lot where seventeen-year-old Philippe Haiart was the unintended victim of a gang sniper's bullet in 2005.

I admit that I had a fleeting moment of hesitation and a quick internal debate as to the value and safety of his offer. Originally referred to Larry by a complete stranger—Rachel Charette, head of the local John Howard Society—I had met him only two hours earlier. Despite our shared interest in Winnipeg street gangs and their impact on the young Aboriginal community, we were otherwise complete strangers with little in common. About to be escorted to ground zero of Winnipeg's gang problem, there I was, a white man regrettably clad in a golf shirt embroidered with "Toronto Police" in large letters, a label that would surely enrage any hardcore gang member we might encounter along the way. It's not that

I'd never been escorted into gang slums before, but it had always been in the presence of police officers, such as when Tony Moreno drove me through bleak South Central Los Angeles one bright Sunday morning in a fully equipped unmarked police car. I'd always had the protection of people who provided an assurance of confidence that, even if all hell broke loose, I would somehow be safe. But hearing about an acute social issue, even when described in rich detail by a person with first-hand knowledge, pales in comparison to actually witnessing the issue yourself. In order to derive a personal understanding, you must see, feel and hear for yourself and allow those sensory inputs to be filtered by your life experiences and world view. Sensing an uncommon authenticity of soul and humble spirit—*kinamatwin,* as Larry might say—and wanting to see for myself the Winnipeg slums he described so starkly, I discarded my concerns, and Larry and I set out on our journey.

Departing the Delta Winnipeg Hotel, we walked around the corner to Larry's car, which was parked on Carlton Street, and he apologized for its lack of air conditioning on such a stifling day. His dusty and dilapidated Dodge Neon, once bright red but now bleached to a mottled magenta, was so badly in need of mechanical attention that I thought it might not be capable of the intended trip. After he coaxed the vehicle to life we proceeded south to Broadway, then west past the beautiful grounds of the Manitoba Legislature to the Spence district. Heading north up Maryland and across Portage Avenue, Larry described how this area—the West End—had been home to mostly poor Aboriginal Canadians and their street gangs. Lately, however, immigration had changed the complexion of the community to include ample numbers of newcomers from the Philippines, Sierra Leone, Ethiopia and Somalia, among others. They in turn have produced their own gangs battling for a place in the urban jungle, such as the violent Mad Cowz and the African Mafia.

As we continued north up Maryland Street, the streetscape became increasingly shabby and grim, with all manner of businesses whose futures looked bleak indeed. Clearly, the choices were slim when it came to where they could afford to set up shop, and business looked anything but brisk. Larry drove a bit farther and stopped briefly on McGee, a residential street, in front of a ramshackle white structure with plywood-clad windows that looked as if it were waiting for a hurricane. This was the crack house from which the deadly bullet destined for Philippe Haiart had emanated. Larry spoke for a while about his recollections of that tragic event. Then we continued the tour, weaving slowly east and north through several streets in what Larry casually mentioned was turf of the Native Syndicate gang, the Indian Posse's primary rival.

The streets feature dense urban housing characteristic of the 1920s, with deep, narrow lots. The fronts of the tall and mostly neglected homes and low-rise apartments stand close to the sidewalk just a few yards away, while mature trees provide a verdant leafy canopy over the crumbling asphalt below. Since the buildings here are pushed to the front of their lots, their garages are at the rear, opening onto a narrow laneway that separates the lots from their rear neighbours. Hidden from view from the street, these back lanes are the roving grounds of gangs, their crack-addicted customers and other miscreants, as evidenced by remnants of bonfires, gang graffiti, abandoned autos, filthy discarded mattresses, shards of glass, hypodermic needles and even the odd intact crack pipe. I couldn't help but imagine that these streets, now fouled by neglect, despair and persistent gang rivalries, had decades earlier offered sanctuary to people filled with the unbridled hope and sense of possibility that recent immigrants and rural émigrés bring to new urban endeavours.

As we were leaving Syndicate territory and waiting for a light to change, I saw a well-tanned white man—the deep and dirty kind of tan earned by toiling under the hot sun—push a grocery cart half-full of aluminum beer cans into the pedestrian crosswalk. "A good day," Larry muttered. Perhaps in his mid-thirties, the man was tall and extremely slight, his shirtless torso revealing his rib cage pressing taut against the skin. Dressed only in tattered jeans and mismatched shoes, he pushed the wobbly cart halfway across the intersection, then looked over his shoulder and said gently, "C'mon, son, we gotta hurry." A young boy with a blond crewcut, no more than five or six years old and equally sun-kissed and shirtless, ambled across the intersection, paying rapt attention to the small ice cream cone he held tightly in his hands.

The components of this scene struck me hard. Here was a man who, by choice or necessity, searched the hardscrabble streets of inner-city Winnipeg—likely for hours on end—for cans he could redeem somewhere for a few meagre dollars. Despite the massive imbalance between effort and reward, the humbleness of the enterprise and the many better uses for the money he made from his metallic quarry, the enduring love of parent for child had led him to reward his son with the simple pleasure of an ice cream cone on a hot August day. The juxtaposition of the innocent child enjoying his cone, not fully aware of his limited (and undeserved) station in life, and his father working in stifling heat at whatever he could to survive was as poignant as the slums Larry had shown me moments earlier.

Past the intersection we turned right and drove north across the Salter Street bridge, which crosses over a large railway yard. Despite its chequered history, Larry perked up as we crested the high bridge and declared, almost proudly, that this was his home—the place where he had spent most of his childhood and where he now toiled to improve the lives of gang members through his project. Turning right onto Dufferin, we toured the Lord Selkirk Park Housing Development, known simply as "the development," which was built in the 1960s. We also passed through a square mile or so that featured a mishmash of neglected public housing apartments, rent-geared-to-income townhouse units, single-family homes and various commercial buildings, including a school and an Aboriginal community centre; the last was the only bright spot in the neighbourhood because of its striking Douglas fir construction. Like a papa proud of his successful progeny, Larry showed me several of the homes his organization had gutted and renovated, as well as their current project, a decrepit two-storey white house of perhaps 1930s vintage that rightfully should have seen the business end of a bulldozer rather than $60,000 worth of $9-an-hour Posse labour.

As we drove deeper into the neighbourhood, away from the main roads, the true complexion of the community began to reveal itself. On one tree-lined street we passed a small group of BMX bike–riding youngsters dealing crack in plain view on the sidewalk. Larry mentioned that he knew them and that they were all eight years old, a common occurrence, he said, because often entire Aboriginal families were gang-involved in some way—as full-patch Posse members, as strykers (new initiates) or as young wannabes. Stopping at the next street corner, in what could only be deemed an Aboriginal ghetto, Larry yelled to a young man peering through an open window in an end-unit townhouse to ask "John"—one of his Indian Posse workers seeking to become legit—to come down and talk to us. Waiting for John to appear, Larry told me that he detested the police, so I should somehow hide the logo on my golf shirt; I dutifully bunched the fabric and wedged it into my armpit, forcing the shirt ridiculously askew.

A few moments later John, who was twenty-one years old and slightly built, emerged and limped across the street to Larry's open window. As I sat there, shirt in armpit, the two men exchanged a few pleasantries. Larry then asked what had happened to his leg and when was he coming back to work, as he was needed for the gruelling job of hand-digging a foot and a half of compacted dirt and crushed stone from the basement of their current project. John indicated that he had had a run-in with a woman and her friend who had attacked him for "no good reason," and he, of course, had defended himself. The word on the street was that she had pressed charges against him. Because he had many previous convictions and outstanding parole conditions, he was expecting the cops to pick him up and return him to custody at any moment, likely precluding him from basement-digging duties. John seemed entirely nonplussed by the prospect. His repeated comments, "I'm not sure where the cops are—they should be here by now. They know where I live," were as matter-of-fact as if you or I were wondering where the taxi was that we had ordered. The thought of being picked up by the police and escorted immediately to jail would likely frighten us, but for John and many of his young Indian Posse brethren it seemed routine in a life full of deadly risk and frequent encounters with the criminal justice system.

After John had hobbled back to his residence we rounded a corner onto a small street. Ahead of us we saw a light blue late-model Acura, utterly out of place in this community of last resort. It pulled over to the curb in front of what Larry said was an abused women's shelter. As we slowly drew near, a pretty, petite, bottle-blond young woman of perhaps seventeen or eighteen emerged from the car wearing exaggerated makeup, a tight white tank top and a too-short denim skirt. She reached back into the car to accept something from the driver—perhaps payment for a hastily rendered blowjob—slammed the door and made a beeline for the shelter. The driver, a heavy-set white man of about forty, made his own hasty exit towards the next intersection. Larry, pissed off by a transaction he has witnessed hundreds of time in his community—middle-class white men buying sex for twenty dollars a pop—accelerated as if to catch up with the driver and admonish him for despoiling his neighbourhood and exacerbating the problems he and others were working so hard to solve. He was, however, foiled by his car's ever-diminishing capabilities. The brief pursuit brought us to a street corner and another young girl, this time an Aboriginal female of no more than twelve or thirteen, unkempt but dressed just as enticingly, with the dark, vacant look of quiet desperation complemented by the characteristic restless twitchiness of crack addition. Larry said simply, "These are my people." He then surprised me by accelerating again in pursuit of a late-model coupe, this one owned by a higher-up in the Indian Posse who also worked in Larry's ragtag crew of home renovators, because he needed to confirm whether he too would be at work the next day.

This is Larry's life. Governed by an indefatigable spirit, a non-judgmental approach to young people who have done "bad things, very bad things" and a resolute conviction that he can somehow improve his bedraggled but beloved community one life at a time, one day at a time, he forges ahead, cajoling reformed gangsters wherever and whenever he sees them to come to work. Old habits die hard, however, and the lure of the gang and all that it offers, especially in a setting that one aspires only to leave, remains strong, ensuring that Larry will never be out of work.

In a scant sliver of time I witnessed all this and so much more—the wellspring of Winnipeg's Aboriginal gang activity. No violent video games were evident; boom boxes did not blare gangsta rap inciting impressionable youth to recreate the MC'ed narratives; American influences, however they might be defined, were nowhere to be seen. Just unimaginable poverty, crumbling communities, decades of accumulated despair and unfulfilled potential, the ravages of crack cocaine—all foisted upon the once proud people who first settled our great country. One cannot tour this or any other of Canada's many urban slums and feel no shame or some sense of responsibility for what we—yes, we—have largely created and allowed to continue in one of the world's richest countries. If you steadfastly believe that street gangs have been thrust upon us from the outside, that lazy youth are doing it just for the money and the thrills, or that the optimum solution is to arrest our way out of the problem and fill the jails to capacity, I encourage you to call Larry and arrange for your own personal guided tour of Winnipeg's North End—just one of Canada's many shameful little secrets. It will cost you nothing, you will enjoy the company and you will never see the street-gang issue the same way again.

:::

Is an ounce of prevention worth a pound of cure, or simply a pound of uncertainty? I suppose the answer depends on the subject. When it comes to health outcomes, most would agree that primary prevention is a worthwhile endeavour. While many of us for a host of reasons fail to take the necessary steps to avoid later serious illness ("I'm too busy"; "I'll start tomorrow"; "I've got lots of time to get healthy"), we still believe in the core truth of the old saying. But when it comes to youth-crime prevention we seem far less committed to the proposition, even though a large international body of evidence suggests that every dollar spent on crime-prevention programs that focus on children saves seven dollars of judicial and other ancillary costs.[34]

As far as street gangs are concerned, prevention is the poor trailer-park-dwelling cousin of our preferred approach, suppression. Especially in what I would call emerging gang cities—where material gang activity began only in the past five or ten years—prevention is given short shrift. In those cities, just as in Toronto, Winnipeg, Edmonton, Ottawa and Calgary, public anxiety about the issue is increasing. Political leaders are navigating through this problem without a practical, scientific approach, trying a little bit of short-term this and a lot of get-tough that, in an attempt to mollify a rather ill-informed populace. Seeing gang behaviour as largely the product of individual choices and deficiencies rather than one of social disorganization, we opt for a "cut the head off the serpent" suppression approach in an effort to control the problem. Operating with little regard for everything we already know about youth-crime prevention, and never giving it the chance it deserves (because it bears fruit very slowly), we continue to repeat the mistakes of those who went before us. Our current preoccupation with suppression is overwhelming a feeble prevention response consisting of stand-alone and one-off programs that fail to recognize the complexity of the conditions that give rise to gangs; the strategies to prevent them must be just as complex. As more and more suppression-funding announcements are made, we defer prevention approaches until some later date. But that time seldom comes, and if and when it does, the measures are too small to make a real difference.

Let me give you some numbers to demonstrate my thesis that we do not take gang prevention specifically, or youth-crime prevention generally, very seriously. In Toronto, in the two-year period between 2003 and 2005, when the impact of street gangs was felt throughout the region, some $16 million of provincial and city funding was allocated to "enhance community safety and target youth crime." Numbers from the Solicitor General's Office show that, of this money, only $43,967 (less than 0.33 percent) went towards prevention programming, including $18,740 for the Serious Teen Offender Program (STOP) and $15,630 to produce a video on recognizing the signs of street-gang activity. In contrast, almost the entire balance went to hiring 251 new police officers, none of whom were assigned to the Youth Services unit that handles anti-gang community initiatives.

More recently, in January 2006 Ontario premier Dalton McGuinty announced a $51 million package of initiatives designed to help Toronto police and prosecutors get criminals with guns off the streets, including funding for new cops and Crown prosecutors, a new major crimes court and, at the cost of $26 million, a new state-of-the-art operations centre for the Toronto Police Service's Guns and Gangs Task Force. The official news release from the premier, which contained a long list of details of the $51 million investment, ended simply, "And we will have more to say on prevention in the weeks and months to come." In February the premier launched the $15 million Youth Challenge Fund, which targeted thirteen troubled Toronto neighbourhoods. Chaired by football great Mike "Pinball" Clemons, the fund is designed to support local programs, training and jobs for at-risk youth, although no specific plan or approach was unveiled with the funding announcement. In April the premier announced a $3 million commitment to Toronto's "Down with Guns" program. So crime prevention in Toronto got $18 million, while suppression received three times that amount, with the extra $51 million being added to an already existing hundreds of millions of dollars' worth of annual funding. It is interesting to note that in February the premier also announced that $70 million (more money than gang prevention and new suppression funding combined) was to be refunded to forestry firms for stumpage fees paid in 2005. I have no quarrel with investing in improving the gang-suppression capabilities of police (assuming that we are targeting and processing the right gangsters), but I find troublesome what is in effect a $70 million subsidy to huge forestry firms when a paltry $18 million is set aside to keep our young people engaged and out of trouble.

On a national level, consider the budget allocation for the National Crime Prevention Centre (NCPC), the federal responsibility centre for crime-prevention policy and programs, that reports jointly to the minister of justice and the Solicitor General. The objective of the NCPC is to increase individual and community safety by providing the knowledge, skills and resources needed to enhance crime prevention by dealing with the root causes of crime. The agency administers a number of grant programs, the most significant being the Community Mobilization Program, which helps Canadian communities develop, implement and evaluate community-based crime-prevention demonstration programs. The NCPC seems to have a weighty mandate indeed, but when you consider that its paltry base funding is about $33 million per year, you might wonder how much impact the organization can have in the face of a growing street-gang problem.

Why does crime prevention take a back seat to crime suppression? Time is perhaps its biggest enemy. A principal characteristic of crime prevention—especially "crime prevention through social development," which consists of efforts to promote the well-being of youth through social, health and educational measures—is that the benefits of these programs are typically not seen until many years later. A truly comprehensive, well-reasoned crime-prevention program for a given community could very well cost millions of dollars, with few demonstrable results in the short or even the medium term. This lag between investment and results, sometimes ten years in duration, troubles our increasing impatience and need for instant gratification, as we tend to prefer rapid and visible return on a given investment. That's why crime suppression is so alluring and comforting to some people. When we can see more cops on the street we feel safer, and the metrics associated with massive gang sweeps (numbers of arrests and charges, extent of contraband seized) produce a false sense of return on investment and a false sense of confidence that we are beating the gang problem. To me it's like a sugar fix—empty, ill-conceived and producing no lasting benefit.

Prevention is also a second-string strategy because to do good prevention means attacking causes, not symptoms. The politically favoured suppression approach is all about attacking the symptoms and sweeping under the rug the things that gave rise to a problem in the first place. So we go the quick-fix cosmetic route and sweep the gangsters off the street, but we do little to address the possible causes of gangsterism—racism, lack of affordable housing, diminishing recreation and economic opportunities for youth—because to address and fix those things takes real effort, real money and real commitment. Then, to justify our actions, we say that gangsters are just bad, deficient, psychopathic folks (and some are) who deserve severe punishment rather than youth who set out on the wrong path years ago and made some bad decisions along the way, but may otherwise be salvageable.

To be fair, prevention doesn't play second fiddle only because of our desire for rapid results in the face of a growing problem. A lot of prevention programs are poorly conceived "feel-good" efforts whose presumed efficacy rests more on blind faith than on proven fact. As well, like any industry, the social services sector contains lots of well-meaning people but few true innovators who are capable of superb organizational management and the delivery of excellent programs that stand the test of time. Most large cities have dozens of crime-prevention programs in place, but their poor coordination means they are relegated to being stop-gap measures. If it is not supported by the right programs and staff, building a youth centre in a troubled community won't make a difference in crime rates, nor will lecturing kids in school about the evils of gangs, drugs or any other high-risk activity. We have also done a poor job of measuring the effectiveness of crime-prevention initiatives through rigorous process and impact and cost-effectiveness evaluation: the body of research on what works or doesn't work in gang prevention is embarrassingly small compared to the scope of the problem.

If we are to make a dent in street gangs in the coming ten years, we must assess our fundamental attitudes about what influences gang behaviour. If you are convinced that the young gangster is basically a psychopath who was influenced to become a gangster solely by video games, hip hop culture or today's allegedly slothful and materialistic attitudes, there is probably not much I can say to change your mind. Likewise if you are convinced that society can arrest its way out of the street-gang problem through sweeps and blanket Broken Windows policing, as many communities in the United States have tried (unsuccessfully) to do. But if you will allow for the possibility that numerous factors can contribute to street-gang behaviour, many of which can be readily addressed through thoughtful planning and careful execution, then perhaps you will be open to the idea that in the long term, a heavy dose of prevention plus intelligent use of suppression, among other key ingredients, is the only way we are going to win this battle. Allow me to make the case.

IS MY CHILD AT RISK?

Research clearly shows that no single so-called risk factor (one that has a proven causal relationship to a problem) by itself causes violent and criminal behaviour. Poverty on its own, for example, no more causes gangsterism alone than do female-headed, single-parent households, a lack of good jobs, violent video games, the availability of guns in a community or parental child abuse. Most children who live for years in such settings never consider a gang as a viable option. No one could ever say unequivocally, "One thing—(you fill in the blank)—causes a youth to join a gang." This is important to understand, because those who believe in root causes often get shouted down by critics who say, "Yeah, but the majority of poor kids don't join gangs, so poverty doesn't cause gangs," perhaps as a way of sidestepping the need to address systemic poverty in our society. It is the impact of a *range* of risk factors, operating at various strengths and in differing measures, and offset by certain "protective factors" that build resistance to the risk factors, that ultimately determines whether an adolescent engages in anti-social behaviours such as gang involvement. Risk factors and protective factors are neither causes nor cures; they are simply statistical predictors.

An analogy may be helpful, so let's think of this issue in terms of heart disease. Assume that you enjoy consuming high-fat foods such as spaghetti carbonara, southern fried chicken and (my personal favourite) bone-in rib steak with garlic mashed potatoes—foods deemed to be a risk factor for heart disease. Most cardiologists would probably agree that eating these delicious foods in moderation is okay, as long as they're balanced by proven heart-disease protective factors such as exercise, regular check-ups and maintaining a healthy weight and appropriate cholesterol levels. But if all you did was eat, sleep, smoke, watch TV and then eat some more, this accumulation of risk factors would definitely increase your chances of a heart attack. The same principle applies for gang behaviour: if the risk factors outweigh the protective factors, the potential for gang involvement is greatly enhanced.

It makes sense, then, that development of effective street-gang prevention strategies should take into consideration the interrelationship of both types of factors, as well as the context in which those factors exist. A good way to understand the dynamic between risk factors and protective factors is to view them in an ecological framework, one that recognizes that each person functions within a complex system of environmental, community, family and individual contexts that influence their capacity to avoid risk. The table below summarizes some of the risk and protective factors associated with street-gang activity across different contexts.

Context	Risk Factors	Protective Factors
Environmental	Poverty Disenfranchised youth Tolerance of gang activity Lack of economic opportunities	Crime-prevention programs Presence of caring relationships Meaningful jobs
Community	Access to guns Access to drugs Street-gang activity Community deterioration Lack of education and recreation opportunities	Strong community infrastructure Sports and recreation programs Prosocial mentors Problem-oriented policing
Family	Lack of parental involvement Gang-involved relatives Single-parent household Inadequate youth supervision Substance abuse at home Child abuse and neglect Poor parenting skills Lack of male role model	Nurturing parenting style Presence of extended families Non-kin support network Enforced structure and rules
Individual	Mental health disorders Poor academic achievement Early aggressive behaviour Substance abuse School expulsion	Commitment to education Presence of positive role models Strong life skills Marketable job skills

Every piece of research I have reviewed in respect to the risk factors associated with street gangs, including the results of interviews with dozens of reformed or incarcerated gang members, shows that multiple factors most often influence the decision to participate in the gang subculture. These people will tell you about many things that perhaps contributed to their decision to get involved in a gang, and they generally span the range of risk factors noted above: "I was poor and had no opportunities"; "I was kicked out of school"; "I was abused as a child"; "I was addicted to drugs and needed cash"; "Gangs were active in my community and I needed protection"; "My brother was running with a gang"; "I was taught early on that violence was an okay way to settle disputes." This is why stand-alone, single-factor gang-prevention interventions are never enough, which contributes to a general sense that suppression—the default position—is the only tenable solution.

The belief in simple solutions to complex social problems persists. Thinking that if we do *this*, we'll prevent *that*, without concrete proof, seems to be one of the many paradoxes of modern society. When we face day-to-day decisions, we want good data to inform us. Buying a car? You want to know its gas mileage, its safety ratings, the cost of insurance. Buying a house? You'll want to find out what the property taxes are, whether property values are going up or down and how much it costs to heat. Selecting a school for your child? You'll investigate its provincial rating, its teacher-to-pupil ratio, the percentage of students who gain entrance to university. Taking a prescription drug? You'll check out how fast it works, its side effects, its contraindications. We spend our lives swimming in a sea of data that we feel is necessary for making our decisions, but when it comes to certain important investments that will keep us and our children safe—including police suppression or gang-prevention efforts funded by our hard-earned tax dollars—we rarely ask, "How do you know it works? And if so, what *makes* it work?" We hold auto manufacturers more accountable for their products than our government leaders for theirs, and that is just plain stupid.

My use of the heart disease analogy earlier was deliberate. I believe that the only way we can get a handle on street gangs—or any other youth-crime issue, for that matter—is to diligently apply the lessons learned in the public health domain. We have come a long way since the days of Hippocrates and the practice of phlebotomy, or "bloodletting," in which knives or leeches were used to remove some of the patient's blood in the hope of curing an ailment. This practice no doubt seemed logical when medical treatment was based on the four body humours of blood, phlegm, yellow bile and black bile. However, in the past few decades especially, mistaken beliefs and folklore have given way to science and a practical model of public health, and the outcomes have been remarkable. This model focuses on reducing risks and increasing resistance to problem behaviours. It follows a four-step procedure to identify problems and develop solutions for entire population groups: (1) define the nature of the problem, using data; (2) identify potential causes through analysis of risk and protective factors associated with the problem; (3) design, develop and evaluate interventions; and (4) disseminate successful models through education and outreach programs. Ironically, we often refer to street gangs as a cancer that requires immediate eradication. But while we use a disease metaphor to describe gangs, we don't use health lessons to deal with them. Primary prevention—curtailment of risk factors that give rise to the disease and evaluation of various approaches to handling it—is really the best course of action, not reactive eradication.

The ecological perspective and the interplay of risk and protective factors are essential for understanding what constitutes an intelligent and effective street-gang prevention program—which, unfortunately, I have rarely seen in ten years of working in this field. Few rigorous evaluations of gang-prevention programs have been conducted in Canada or the United States. One U.S. study, however, a careful five-year longitudinal evaluation of the Gang Resistance Education and Training (GREAT) program, demonstrates the need for a comprehensive preventive approach. In 1991 the GREAT program was developed through the combined efforts of the U.S. Bureau of Alcohol, Tobacco, Firearms and Explosives and the Phoenix Police Department. Similar in style and approach to the RCMP's Drug Awareness and Resistance Education (DARE) program, to which your Grade 5 or 6 child may have been exposed, GREAT sends uniformed police officers into middle-school classes to teach a thirteen-week curriculum. The program seeks to reduce youth's involvement in gangs and other delinquent behaviour, teach them the consequences of gang involvement and foster better relationships with law enforcers. Since its inception in 1991, more than eight thousand law enforcement officers have been certified as GREAT instructors and more than four million American students have graduated from the program. It is hard to pinpoint the total cost of GREAT, but including officer training (most complete an eighty-hour training program), delivery time and community grants to facilitate the program, it is surely well over $100 million by now.

A longitudinal study is one in which data is collected from subjects at several points in time. In the evaluation of GREAT, this meant collecting data about the Grade 7 students' attitudes and behaviours before and after the thirteen-week program, and then at one-year intervals from Grade 8 to 11. Results showed that GREAT produced modest improvements in attitudes related to several risk factors associated with delinquency, largely because of the program's encouragement of prosocial attitudes and peer relationships. The data show an improvement in attitudes about the police and an improvement in awareness of the dangers of gang involvement. Despite the program's success in addressing risk factors, however, no discernable differences were seen in actual gang membership or delinquent behaviour.

GREAT has generated a storm of debate about its value and efficacy. Proponents say that the program improved attitudes, and since ample research shows that negative attitudes are linked with delinquent behaviour, the program can be viewed as successful. Critics counter by saying that attitudes are not enough, that gang-prevention programs must reduce gang participation if they are to be judged a success. In a way, both camps are right. Awareness programs like GREAT must be viewed for what they are: just a piece of the gang-prevention picture, not the entire scene. We can improve children's attitudes about police and ensure they understand the ramifications of gang membership, but if they go home to abuse, gang-involved siblings, not enough food, few economic opportunities, crime-infested social housing and systemic racism (all risk factors), programs like GREAT will have only a modest effect at best.

THE NECESSARY CONDITIONS FOR SUCCESSFUL PREVENTION

So where should we go as far as prevention is concerned? How do we make good on the adage that an ounce of prevention is worth a pound of cure? I believe that three conditions are necessary for Canada to succeed in this area; I will refer to them as the three Ps of street-gang prevention.

The first P is a reasoned *perspective.* To get on the right path, one that will produce less actual gang activity in the future, rather than just the promise of such, we first need to get past viewing this issue on ideological grounds. Emotions run high on the issue of street gangs, and Canadian discourse is regrettably descending to the level of a fist fight between the Left (soft on criminals, prevention bias) and the Right (tough on crime, suppression bias). Our current political climate has inflamed this situation, and the real victim is the truth: our Conservative minority government is doing everything it can to distance itself from the previous

Liberals, including its stance on crime. Well, I believe you can be both tough on crime and big on prevention, and that we should leave the political labelling to the media and the folks on Parliament Hill.

Having a reasoned perspective also means that Canadians of every stripe must see this as a problem that affects us all. As I have suggested elsewhere, unless you have a child or other family member involved with or at risk of joining a gang, or you live in a part of town where gang activity is growing, the chances of your being directly affected by street-gang activity is low, notwithstanding the tragedies that befell the Creba and Haiart families, among others. While you may take comfort in living far from the mean streets of Spryfield, North Winnipeg, Gastown, Banff–Ledbury or Jamestown, complacency does not produce immunity for any of us. Gang activity is naturally expansive and respects no physical boundaries. Leaving this problem for the cops to suppress and expecting poor, struggling, most often immigrant inner-city families (yes, that is the predominant profile) to make do is just wrong. In spite of our country's incredible wealth and potential, this short-sighted view means that gang activity, allowed to fester, could affect us all in terms of property values, personal safety, civic pride and other quality-of-life dimensions. We—individuals, schools, businesses, social service agencies and the government—all need to do our proactive, preventive part rather than wait for the criminal justice system, in its usual reactive, suppressive manner, to spring into action later, when it may be too late.

Finally, perspective means that we need to invest in prevention, not just talk about it. Surely, with over $11 billion invested annually in the criminal justice system, we can reallocate a paltry few hundred million dollars to prevention strategies. Let me do the math. Assume that we arrest and incarcerate five hundred gangsters per year over the next five years in medium-security penitentiaries for sentences of five years each, as per Section 467.11 (the gangsterism provisions) of the Criminal Code of Canada. At an annual 2004 cost of $74,610 (this is just the prison cost and does not include trial or legal aid costs), this translates into a total five-year "investment" of $933 million dollars. The product of that expenditure would likely be 2,000-plus hardened, even more violent gangsters ready to perpetuate the cycle of violence. Ask yourself what we could do with almost a billion dollars dedicated to crime prevention through social development, with a specific focus on gang prevention (incidentally, that's the total cost of the previous Liberal government's gun registry). I suggest that an investment of $200 million a year over the next five years in comprehensive early intervention street-gang prevention—money that could be reallocated from other, wasteful programs—would produce massive results that would benefit us all.

The problem we face right now as far as street gangs are concerned is that we have inverted the pyramid that describes the recognized optimal approach to dealing with youth crime. Picture a triangle with prevention as the base upon which intervention and then suppression are placed. This pyramid indicates the optimal relative weighting of (and financial investment in) each strategy, with prevention being the important foundational element. Our current preoccupation with suppression places it on the bottom of the pyramid with prevention at the top, at the expense of what we know to be the best long-term approach to dealing with crime.

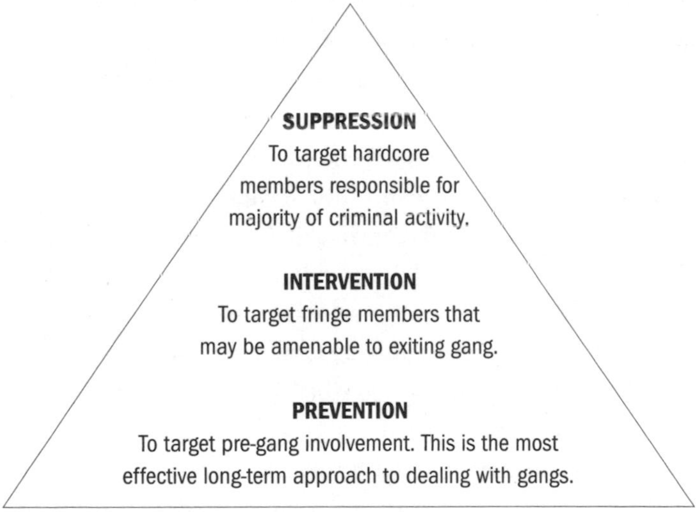

SUPPRESSION
To target hardcore members responsible for majority of criminal activity.

INTERVENTION
To target fringe members that may be amenable to exiting gang.

PREVENTION
To target pre-gang involvement. This is the most effective long-term approach to dealing with gangs.

The second P is *patience.* Prevention is decidedly the long, involved route, and it faces a constant battle against the culture of expediency that pervades our society. Just as prevention cannot work in my model without suppression, suppression cannot work without prevention. We need both in order to get on top of the growing problem with gangs, and so long as we give limited time and attention to prevention, we will surely be fighting a losing battle.

Perspective and patience are great, but without a *plan,* the third and perhaps most important P, it is all just good intentions. Despite some promising programs scattered about the country, there is no comprehensive street-gang prevention plan in Canada. However, formal evaluation of an approach from the United States shows it to hold promise for battling emerging and chronic street-gang problems. Known as the Comprehensive Gang Model—or the Spergel model, after its creator, U.S. street-gang expert Dr. Irving Spergel—it is based on the assumption that gang violence is a product of social disorganization in communities, where key organizations are inadequately integrated and not enough resources are available to target gang-involved and at-risk youth. The plan calls for community institutions—including law enforcement, social welfare agencies, parents, schools and grassroots organizations—to work together to achieve a more integrated, team-oriented approach. The model identifies five core strategies that communities should incorporate into their gang-prevention programs to achieve successful outcomes: (1) mobilization of the community to ensure an integrated approach; (2) social intervention in the form of counselling, treatment and training; (3) provision of social opportunities through outreach to engage youth in prosocial ways; (4) suppression tactics by police to hold youth accountable; and (5) organizational change to reallocate resources to the efforts showing the most promise.

Spergel's model was implemented in six communities in the United States from 1992 to 1999, and quasi-experimental evaluations demonstrated that, if implemented as intended, the model will work. A test of the model in Little Village Chicago, described in Dr. Spergel's book *Reducing Youth Gang Crime,* demonstrated a 40 percent reduction in serious violence for two hundred gang-involved youth, compared to an equivalent sample of non-served youth from the same gangs, over a five-year period. Another test in Riverside, California, showed that youth in the program were three times more likely to avoid becoming involved in violent crime than comparison youth not in the program.

A SIXTEEN-POINT GANG-PREVENTION PLAN

So far I have spoken only in generalities about prevention and its essential role in the fight against gangs. I am frequently asked what I would do if given the chance to design a good gang-prevention program for an at-risk community. This is tough to answer because the street-gang organism and the problems it creates are so complex, compounded by the fact that meaningful funding is rarely provided for prevention efforts. However, with a sufficient budget, a reasonable time frame in which to effect change, and supportive government policy in place (see Chapter 10), I think a readily transportable program could be created to reduce gang activity by 50 percent or more—though not to eliminate it entirely, as that would be impossible. For Canada and its emerging street-gang problem, I would merge the Spergel model with the standard public health model and add some important elements to create a new gang-prevention protocol. It is a decidedly community-focused approach, as crime prevention must begin with the people affected by crime, not far-removed policymakers in Ottawa or provincial capitals.

So here is my gang-prevention plan, an approach that cherry-picks from the fine work being done throughout North America by other committed crime preventionists. Each point that follows should not be considered a standalone initiative capable of solving gang problems. To be effective, a community faced with gang violence ought to incorporate all, or at least a majority, of the strategies noted below.

1. **Define the nature of the street-gang problem through good research.**
   First, each community needs to take stock of its situation and understand the unique characteristics of its street-gang problem before rushing off and doing prevention for prevention's sake. Qualitative police gang data of the kind contained in my national youth-gang surveys are a start, but the figures won't inform us about the qualitative characteristics of gang members (age, ethnicity, income, education) and the root causes of gang formation. Gangs in Winnipeg and Vancouver are not necessarily the gangs of Toronto and Montreal: good local data beget good local programs.

2. **Mobilize the community.**
   Gang prevention and suppression should not be the sole domain of well-meaning social service agencies and police services. Street gangs are not strictly a law enforcement problem or criminal justice problem, but a problem that must be addressed at the societal and

community level. If your community is to short-circuit a brewing problem, it must recruit all sectors of society, including government, business, schools and others, to enforce and reinforce broader social controls. Someone from your community must champion the cause and recruit others to join your gang-prevention initiative, including local school boards, politicians, business leaders and social service agencies.

A great example can be found in Edmonton. Faced with a growing gang problem, the Greater Edmonton Area responded intelligently by forming the Community Solution to Gang Violence (CSGV), comprising a diverse cross-section of private citizens, community organizations, the Edmonton Police Service and all levels of government. Established in 2003, the CSGV's mission is to implement a strategic community-wide approach to address the issue of gangs and gang violence through a focus on early intervention and youth social development. The community's response has already given rise to some promising anti-gang programs, including the award-winning Beat of Boyle Street, an inner-city program that lets at-risk youth in the tough Boyle–McCauley area express themselves through song and dance.

3. Focus on early intervention.

An effective anti-gang strategy starts when children are young, especially in the crucial age range of one to ten, when they are primarily socialized first by parents and then by schools. Teaching key life skills is essential during this period. To this end I would borrow the life-skills development program from Ottawa's Project Early Intervention, a multi-week interactive program targeted at youth aged six through nine. The program teaches, through discussion and role-playing, how to resist peer pressure, manage anger, resolve conflicts and so on. I would also borrow from the Child Development Centre (formerly the Earlscourt Child and Family Centre) of Toronto its highly successful Under 12 Outreach Project (ORP). This program was established in 1985 in conjunction with the Toronto Police Service to work with children under twelve who have had police contact or who are involved in activities that could lead to police contact. Combining social learning and cognitive behavioural perspectives, ORP interventions include decision-making training, victim restitution, home-based family counselling and tutoring, among other things. The involvement of trained staff skilled in the art of childhood development is essential. Life skills and morality education in particular are highly protective, and should be stressed (see Chapter 10 for more on this).

Another such program is the internationally acclaimed Montreal Preventive Treatment Program (also known as the Montreal Longitudinal Study or the Montreal Prevention Experiment). It was aimed at disruptive boys and their parents with the goal of reducing short- and long-term anti-social behaviour. Led by University of Montreal professor Dr. Richard E. Tremblay, the program targeted boys aged seven to nine from families low on the socio-economic scale who were assessed as having high levels of disruptive behaviour in kindergarten. The program provided training with the long-term goal of decreasing delinquency, substance abuse and gang involvement. For the subject boys, a school-based component promoted problem-solving skills, life skills, conflict resolution and self-control. The training was provided in small groups that included one or two disruptive boys and three to five peers who were identified by teachers as prosocial. Interactive learning methods and behavioural management techniques, such as coaching, peer modelling, self-instruction and role-playing to build skills, were used to promote positive change. Evaluations have demonstrated both short- and long-term gains for those who received the intervention. Three years afterwards, the treated boys were less likely to have committed minor offences such as trespassing and theft. At age fifteen, six years after the program, those who had received the intervention were less likely than untreated boys to report gang involvement.

4. Train and support parents.

How many times have you heard the saying, "Children don't come with an instruction manual"? Parenting is perhaps the most challenging job on Earth, yet many parents navigate blindly through their child-raising tasks with little instruction or support. For new parents, especially single parents, low-income Canadians and new

Canadians, a broader array of programs on parenting skills should be offered, focusing on things such as setting boundaries, how to discipline a child, how to teach life skills, how to teach morality lessons and, as important, how to be a good role model.

For example, in Tremblay's Montreal program, parents of subject boys received an average of seventeen sessions that concentrated on monitoring their children's behaviour, giving positive reinforcement for prosocial behaviour, using punishment effectively and managing family crises. Ottawa's Project Early Intervention included a robust parent support component designed to help parents understand the role of life-skills education so that they could reinforce the lessons their children learned in the program.

5. Provide after-school programs.

One of the riskiest times for many adolescents in terms of being victimized or running afoul of the law is between the hours of 3:00 and 7:00 p.m., between the end of the school day and when parents return from work. Research shows that this unsupervised time is a risk factor for substance abuse, gang behaviour and other juvenile delinquency. Supervised, high-quality, challenging after-school programs have been shown to be an effective buffer against delinquency and victimization and to benefit children greatly by improving their social skills, confidence, grades, range of interests and peer networks, as well as preventing the negative influences that lead to risky behaviours. After-school programs come in all shapes and sizes, but effective ones include athletic leagues, computer clubs, homework/tutoring clubs, arts and craft programs, employment preparation or training, volunteer and community service programs, language instruction (especially ESL), music clubs, youth leadership programs and community revitalization programs (graffiti removal, community cleanups), just to name a few. These programs do more than occupy a youth's time; they also provide an environment in which young people can test the life skills they are hopefully learning in other parts of my proposed plan. These programs are already everywhere across Canada, but their chronic underfunding renders them incapable of addressing our growing gang problem.

I think we all understand the value of keeping our children busy after school until we get home from work, rather than letting them fill the void with visits to the mall or by hanging out with other unsupervised youth. Unfortunately, the decisions we have made as parents (or have vicariously supported as unengaged voters) have eroded the availability of quality programs for our children and have made some of them prohibitively expensive. In the past decade school boards have been on the receiving end of massive funding cuts. This has forced schools—a staple of a healthy community—to eliminate many of the after-school programs they once offered (such as intramural sports) and has put the brakes on teachers' pay increases, which in turn increased the militancy of unions and reduced teachers' willingness to work late supervising after-school programs. Compounding this have been school board decisions to turn their facilities from a taxpayer-funded public good to a source of revenue in order to make up for budget shortfalls, increasing rental and maintenance charges for the community groups that usually use them.

With city governments also on the receiving end of provincial cutbacks, they too have raised rental rates for rinks, swimming pools, soccer pitches and libraries, thereby increasing registration costs for programs. Add our general apathy about youth-crime prevention to the mix and the net effect has been that after-school programs hosted in school or city facilities have been gutted, leaving more and more youth (especially low-income youth) to fend for themselves before Mom and Dad get home. If youth are unsupervised after school because their parents work (which describes the majority of lower-income families), if they are exposed to the dangers of gangs and if they are blocked from programs that can provide enjoyment, camaraderie, competition, acceptance and a sense of togetherness, they will most assuredly find some of those things in a gang.

Fortunately, a few city school boards are beginning to understand the ramifications of their revenue-seeking ways. Recently the Toronto District School Board (TDSB) extended a pilot project in which it offered free space for youth programs in schools in five communities. An evaluation of the pilot project found that greater availability of after-school programs kept more youth off the street and away from negative peers, trouble and crime. As well, with new funding from the Ontario Ministry of Education, the Toronto Catholic District School Board and the TDSB have made schools available to community groups at a considerable reduction in fees, which hopefully will stimulate new youth programs.

6. **Acquire or support a youth centre.**
At-risk youth need a home base, a place to call their own, that is accessible and staffed by caring counsellors. They need access to programs and services that will help keep them out of trouble. It need not be a fancy facility, it just has to be safe and accessible and fun. The internationally acclaimed Ottawa Police Youth Centre, now part of the Ottawa Boys and Girls Club, started in one room in an abandoned fire hall and grew to become the city's most lively youth centre, with more than 1,100 young members. Having spent considerable time in the centre, I can attest that it saved the adjacent Debra Dynes community from a downward spiral of crime and violence, because youth were engaged and in the presence of caring professionals. Because it was a physical space rather than simply a program hosted in a multipurpose city facility, the centre also attracted ample business support; corporations very much like to support "bricks and mortar" projects to which they can attach their name.

The good news is that many communities already have the infrastructure in place to achieve the goal of giving youth a home base. In Canada we have 104 Boys and Girls Clubs, local non-profit agencies that in 2006 served more than 178,000 youth from seven hundred locations. Some interesting statistics underscore the role of the clubs. Almost 60 percent of youth served were from low-income families, while 43 percent were from single-parent families. With a total staff complement of more than three thousand and an estimated fourteen thousand volunteers (a third of whom were themselves youth), the mission of the clubs is to provide safe, supportive places where children and youth can experience new opportunities, overcome barriers, build positive relationships and develop confidence and skills for life. Like most other social service agencies, however, local Boys and Girls Clubs face a constant struggle for financial survival, despite their powerful ability to help at-risk youth and to support communities in the fight against gangs. Wake up, Canada! If you want to play a small part in combating the growth of gangs, support your local Boys and Girls Club with your cash or your time.

7. **Create economic opportunities.**

The powerful business community must be engaged to help create meaningful economic opportunities for both at-risk and gang-involved youth. Employment and self-employment training programs would be offered in my model, along with job placement services and apprenticeship programs to teach youth high-demand (and increasingly lucrative) skills such as those in the building trades. The Council for Skilled Careers of Eastern Ontario, based in Ottawa, is one such program that needs our support. It is both assisting at-risk youth and helping our society keep pace with the demand for skilled professionals in the building trades by teaching young people to become carpenters and masons, including those who have served time in prison and are trying to reintegrate into society. As well, since many gangsters are fundamentally entrepreneurial in nature, I would create a micro-investment venture capital fund to which youth could apply to obtain seed funding for start-up businesses.

An interesting model to consider would be Homeboy Industries. Established in 1992 by Reverend Gregory Boyle in East Los Angeles, Homeboy is a $3-million-a-year non-profit organization that helps at-risk and former gang-involved youth become contributing members of their community. This is achieved by operating and working in several successful businesses, including a bakery, a silk-screening business, a landscaping and home services company, a merchandising firm and a café. Young people learn business skills such as budgeting, marketing, financial management and operations management. In addition, Homeboy further supports youth by offering free services such as counselling, education, tattoo removal, release transition services, job training and job placement.

In response to mounting gang violence, in March 2006 Canada's largest local chamber of commerce, the ten-thousand-member-strong Toronto Board of Trade, launched its Youth ONE campaign with the goal of creating, by September 2006, one thousand jobs and apprenticeship opportunities for at-risk youth in thirteen communities considered to be disadvantaged, including the Jane–Finch corridor, Jamestown and Malvern. As the campaign was managed by the City of Toronto's Youth Employment Partnership (YEP) program and sponsored by nine media outlets and large corporations such as the Royal Bank, PriceWaterhouseCoopers, Deloitte & Touche and Business Development Bank Canada, the thousand-job goal seemed quite reasonable. However, when the deadline came the Board of Trade claimed that only eighty-two jobs had been created by twenty participating firms, a shameful result and likely caused by the enduring stereotype of the target youth, especially young African-Canadian males, being criminally involved and therefore risky to hire. These partnerships are worthwhile to pursue, but their success ultimately comes down to the commitment, and willingness to act, of their participants.

More productively, the City of Toronto received half a million dollars in provincial funding for youth summer employment programs in four priority neighbourhoods: Malvern and Kingston–Galloway in Scarborough, Jane–Finch in North York and Jamestown in Etobicoke. Centennial College offered seven free summer skills-development programs for young people living in the Malvern community. Local 27 of the carpenters' union, the San Romanoway Revitalization Association, the YMCA and the city collaborated to offer Jane–Finch youth a nine-week pre-apprenticeship carpentry training program. The Get in Gear (GIG) project, funded by the city through Ontario Works Target Incentive Funds, helped 451 youth obtain training in a variety of fields; 332 individuals completed their training and 252 found employment. These are just a sample of some of the good things happening in the community.

8. Get serious about mentoring.

Defined as a relationship over a prolonged period between two or more people, where a caring older, more experienced individual helps a younger person in the journey through life, mentoring is one of the oldest and most effective forms of ensuring prosocial development. Perhaps the best-known example is Big Brothers

Big Sisters, a non-profit organization with chapters throughout the world that focus on providing mentors to children in need of additional positive adult support.

Formal and informal mentoring programs can support the development of healthy individuals by reducing risk factors and enhancing protective factors. A good mentor can provide a young person with supervision and guidance, a stable adult relationship, a sense of self-worth and affirmation, skills training and, perhaps most important, hope for the future. Research into mentorship programs demonstrates that at-risk youth who are involved with at least one caring adult are more likely to withstand negative influences than are peers who are not involved in a similar relationship, especially young men from single-parent female-headed families, since lack of a strong positive male role model may be a factor in increasing the chances of gang participation.

Despite their enduring power to help develop strong youth, good mentors are extremely scarce. People today are busy and the time commitment associated with effective one-on-one mentoring can be onerous for some. A new form of mentoring called group mentoring is on the rise, with groups as large as ten to thirty youth sharing one or two mentors. While more economical, group mentoring is not as effective as the one-on-one version, but it is a viable alternative nonetheless for youth who need strong role models.

9. Reach out to at-risk youth.

Using trained outreach workers to hit the streets and engage at-risk and gang-involved youth is an important element of my model. The gang issue is not going to be solved with a "build it and they will come" program approach. Young at-risk people need to be made aware of the existence of programs and what they offer in terms of features and benefits. Encouraging young people to drop in at a youth centre just to hang around and enjoy sports and recreation programs is often a good strategy to get them involved in more intensive and focused counselling programs in areas such as drug abuse and anger management.

Youth who are already involved with a gang should also be targeted with outreach. Time should be spent informing them how to leave a gang and the consequences of such an action (typically few). Programs should also be provided that may help in their transition, such as alternative schools, employment programs and tattoo removal.

10. Invest in alternative school programs.

In most Canadian provinces, elementary and secondary school governing bodies enforce some form of zero-tolerance policy for students' bad behaviour. Some, like Ontario, have brought into law specific "safe school" acts that provide greater latitude for educators to expel students for particularly egregious or consistent patterns of violence and misbehaviour. We all want our children to be safe at school, free from the deleterious and disruptive influence of bullies, drug dealers and gang recruiters. But however effective expulsion is in improving school life for kids who do behave, it can be disastrous for the expelled student and for broader society, especially if nothing is done for the expelled student during his or her time in purgatory.

Rather than expel a student from classes to roam the malls or take up with a gang (school expulsion and gang activity show a causal link), it may be advantageous to place that youth in an "alternative school," a specialized educational environment featuring small classes, individualized instruction, non-competitive performance assessments, prosocial skills training, parental involvement, a real-life learning-based curriculum and less structured classrooms. The purpose of these schools is to provide academic instruction to students who have been suspended or expelled for disruptive behaviour or weapons possession, or who are unable to succeed in the mainstream school environment.

11. Promote social marketing and public awareness.

Social marketing and public awareness programs have demonstrated their effectiveness in other domains such as drunk driving, smoking and HIV/AIDS prevention, and there is no reason to believe they would not also be effective for street gangs. Educating youth and broader society about gangs and their inherent dangers through creative social marketing programs will help support other aspects of this model. Messages from the criminal justice system that gang violence will not be tolerated and that gang leaders will be hunted down would also be important. Health Canada's efforts in building and promulgating the Business Case Against AIDS program were successful in getting corporate money and volunteers to assist with community programs.[35] We need to do the same for street gangs to encourage corporate involvement in the form of mentors, micro-investment loans for start-up businesses, and cash for worthwhile community projects.

Schools are an excellent forum for delivering information that encourages optimum outcomes for youth, including the avoidance of risky behaviours like substance abuse and gang involvement. Traditional prevention education in schools has been didactic in nature: concepts are taught through lectures and delivery of facts and figures by teachers or, in the case of the DARE drug prevention program, by police officers. However useful these approaches are for delivering information, they are not particularly effective in changing behaviours or attitudes. To be effective in school settings, prevention programs must incorporate several key elements. A corresponding promotion of social and emotional competencies through life-skills education has proven effective, as has a teaching style that incorporates smaller groups, ample interactivity (such as two-way discussions), role-playing and multimedia content, and outlets for creative expression.

12. Target suppression activities.

As I argued in Chapter 6, police need to target gang leaders and the most dangerous, active and volatile gangsters with their aggressive suppression tactics rather than go after all the gang members, regardless of their proclivities. This approach ensures that the main sources of gang tension are defused, that the rest of the criminal justice system does not become overtaxed and that "salvageable" youth are given another chance. Targeted suppression must be supported by aggressive enforcement of probation restrictions, promotion of zero tolerance of gangs through community messages and high-priority handling of gang cases in court, including reducing caseloads for Crown attorneys and providing additional investigative support and resources for assisting victims and protecting witnesses.

13. **Enhance community policing.**

In theory, community policing makes great sense. However, until there is a complete cultural shift in the way police officers see their jobs, community policing will remain an idealistic goal. One way we can hasten the impact of community policing and address front-line gang issues is by investing additional money in School Resource Officer (SRO) programs. An SRO is a sworn uniformed law enforcement officer deployed in a school setting, most typically in a high school. SROs play a number of important roles, including providing guidance to students, parents and teachers; participating as a resource person in classroom discussions, assemblies and meetings of parent groups; preventing delinquency through close contact with students and personnel; assisting with school safety assessments and crisis planning; acting as a positive role model and mentor for youth; and helping improve relations between youth and the local police service. Perhaps most important, through their presence SROs can play a key role in improving safety in schools, especially since street gangs often focus on schools for their drug sales and recruitment activities.

The thought of appropriately trained uniformed cops patrolling the high schools is probably comforting to parents and school administrators alike. However, SRO programs do not garner the budget support they deserve, nor do these positions necessarily attract many applicants—cops tend to prefer the more exciting street patrol or specialty investigative positions. It is not uncommon for SROs to have five or ten schools in their portfolio, thereby rendering their impact relatively minimal. In a perfect world each medium to large high school would have a dedicated SRO who would be equipped with the necessary resources to address the gang situation, including a life-skills program, gym time for after-school programming, awareness materials and so on. In Ontario the provincial government's new $51 million gang-suppression funding included money for a thousand new police officers. With 870 high schools in the province, this funding could have put an SRO in every school, a move that would have done more to address the growth of street gangs than simply deploying these new cops in patrol cars.

14. Revitalize social housing.

Poorly designed, geographically isolated and rapidly deteriorating Canadian social housing complexes—in St. Jamestown in Toronto, Banff–Ledbury in Ottawa, the Downtown Eastside in Vancouver, North-Central Regina and the North End of Winnipeg—are oftentimes hot spots for gang growth and activity. Immediate revitalization and remediation of these communities, through innovative partnerships between the private and public sectors, is required to further stem the growth of gangs.

There is no better Canadian example than Toronto's Regent Park, one of North America's oldest social housing communities. Located just a stone's throw from the downtown Toronto core, Regent Park's deteriorating and impoverished sixty-nine acres are occupied by 2,087 rent-geared-to-income housing units. They are set in an area devoid of through streets and mixed-use amenities such as shops, community centres, parks and businesses. Built in the 1940s and '50s, Regent Park is home to over eight thousand people, half of them immigrants, and approximately 70 percent live below Statistics Canada's low-income cut-off rate. The complex was originally designed as a transitional community, a place for new Canadians and those experiencing financial difficulties. This contributed to a low level of commitment to the community, which in turn led to the growth of various social ills, including crime.

Most civic planners agree that Regent Park's design is an obsolete one that makes it difficult to ensure a safe and healthy community. In 2006 the City of Toronto embarked on a sweeping twelve-year, $450 million revitalization plan that will see the entire site redeveloped to incorporate a mixed-use, environmentally sustainable neighbourhood containing 5,400 units of market and social housing, as well as shops, offices, parks, streets, and learning and recreation facilities. The plan has its critics, including those who suggest that the new Regent Park will further marginalize poor people by leading to the kind of gentrification that has affected other urban Toronto neighbourhoods such as Cabbagetown, South Parkdale, Kensington Market and Queen Street West, thus forcing the urban poor farther away from the city core. The project nonetheless demonstrates innovative thinking about how to build socio-economically diverse and healthy communities that may be more naturally protected against street gangs and other urban social problems.

15. Invest more in mental health services.

Many youthful offenders and gang members are behaviourally and emotionally challenged, with exceptional psychosocial needs that require mental health interventions. A large number of troubled youth were emotionally, physically or sexually abused when they were young, and specific counselling may be required to address the outcomes of this abuse. Moreover, it is reported that some 3 to 5 percent of the human population may be afflicted by the neurological condition called attention deficit hyperactivity disorder (ADHD), which is usually diagnosed in childhood and manifests itself in symptoms such as poor impulse control, distractibility, hyperactivity and forgetfulness. Thought to be caused by a number of factors including, among many, poor diet, maternal smoking during pregnancy, head trauma or hereditary dopamine deficiency, ADHD has no medical cure, so its symptoms must be addressed through drug or mental health care interventions.

Another disorder that requires mental health intervention is fetal alcohol spectrum disorder (FASD), a birth defect causing a range of symptoms that stems from maternal consumption of alcohol during pregnancy. The effects of FASD may include stunted emotional development, memory and attention deficits, poor impulse control, difficulty in distinguishing fantasy from reality, apparent lack of remorse, difficulty understanding the consequences of one's actions and an inability to get along with other people. An estimated 1 percent of Canadians are living with the syndrome, or more than 300,000, many of whom are from First Nations communities—which also happen to be challenged by street-gang issues. With no cure available, the symptoms of FASD can only be ameliorated by sometimes lifelong mental health and other supportive interventions.[36]

We need to put more resources into intensive community-based mental health services with a specific focus on conduct-disordered youth, rather than just increase the general stock of children's mental health services that are typically delivered in hospital settings. I would use as my model the Ottawa-based Roberts/Smart Centre, which offers crisis intervention, day treatment programs, residential care programs and even a young offenders' program that provides placements for youths in open custody under the Youth Criminal Justice Act. With more services like this available, police officers, for example, could refer youth for the care they need to attack the roots of their behavioural problems rather than try to effect a more traditional police response. This would give real meaning to the concept of problem-solving policing.

16. **Evaluate and disseminate.**
We need to commit to evaluation, even if it diverts funds from actual programs and into the hands of social science researchers. Programs should be established with proper evaluation protocols in mind so that we can determine what actually works. Programs that demonstrate success should be enhanced and disseminated broadly throughout the country, and those that do little or nothing should be dropped, leading to improvement in our gang strategy over time.

GOVERNMENT POLICY MUST SUPPORT THE COMMUNITY FIGHT AGAINST GANGS

As the above plan demonstrates, there is much a community can do to deal with gangs in a proactive, preventive fashion. However, communities can't do it alone. They need to be supported by provincial and national policies that assist in gang prevention. To the above plan I would add the following four supportive elements.

1. **Better support for new Canadians**
Immigration has benefited our country, but I am convinced that many of the problems we now face with street gangs can be attributed to our country not doing enough to smooth the transition for new Canadians. In particular, immigrants face the problems of

poor language skills; lack of recognition of their foreign credentials, which complicates finding suitable employment; lack of safe and affordable housing; and lack of kin or friendship networks. More robust ESL programs, encouraging the immigration of extended families, and proper prior learning assessments so that foreign credentials are accorded respect are just some of the ways we can better serve new Canadians.

2. **Intelligent application of diversion and alternative justice measures**

   We must apply diversion and alternative justice strategies on a case-by-case basis, especially for non-violent youth who run afoul of the law (possibly including actual gang members, who are not all gun-toting, drive-by-shooting maniacs). Alternative measures such as counselling, community service, restitution and victim–offender mediation may serve the community better than going for the hard-line five-year prison sentence provided under Section 467.11. Alternative measures provide some hope of remediating a young person's behaviour as compared to prison, which will only reinforce gang involvement. Fortunately, the often-criticized Youth Criminal Justice Act contains provisions for diversion and alternative measures, and we need to use them intelligently rather than ship all youthful offenders off to prison.

3. **Prison reform**

   Frankly, our prisons are factories and finishing schools for gangsters. For those who are sentenced to prison, we need to make good on the notion of rehabilitation by remaking the way we incarcerate prisoners. We need major prison reform in this country to put the power back into the hands of guards and prison administrators, especially now that suppression is cresting in popularity. If an offender is deemed to be conduct-disordered or capable of rehabilitation, participation must be made mandatory rather than optional, as it is now. Prisons must be made safe by reducing the extent of criminal behaviour inside prison walls, resulting in less gang activity. Related to this, we need to invest in reintegration programs such as Larry Morrissette's

OPK to help those who have served their time, especially the young ones, get started on a better path in life.

4. **A stronger National Crime Prevention Centre**
   Finally, we need a strong national body to advocate for crime prevention through social development practices, with a budget sufficient to provide seed financing and to evaluate and disseminate the results of new crime-prevention programs across the country. The existing framework of the National Crime Prevention Centre (NCPC) is sound, but it needs to be reinvigorated to fulfill its mandate. As long as the present government prefers the suppression approach, the NCPC is doomed to the status of mere window dressing. As part of a renewed NCPC I would also like to see a National Youth Gang Centre headed by a national gang "czar," similar to that in the United States, to specifically address our growing street-gang problem.

EXPERIMENT NOW OR REGRET LATER

We have before us the ideal conditions for evaluating new approaches in gang prevention. Throughout North America, especially in the United States, legislators and community leaders have largely been chasing their tails as far as gang prevention is concerned, employing a little bit of this and a little bit of that—with insufficient funding, I might add—in the hope that some strategy will prove itself effective. Growing anecdotal evidence suggests that the prevention approaches I advocate here work remarkably well if they are accorded the resources of time, money and attention. Of course, the tough-on-crime advocates (who often perform double duty as tough-on-prevention critics) respond that anecdotes mean little, and that it is their metrics (arrests, successful court cases, gangsters incarcerated) that demonstrate efficacy.

If we care about the long-term safety of our communities, then perhaps we should care enough to establish a legitimate experiment that will inform this ongoing debate, in the same way we test and evaluate drugs that purport to save lives. I would like to see us select three separate communities in three major cities (such as Toronto, Montreal and Vancouver) that are challenged by gang activity and that share characteristics in terms of size, density, ethnocultural composition, police presence, crime incidence and social service support networks, among other things. We would then measure a plethora of indicators to obtain the hard data we need to determine the baseline state of affairs. In Community 1 (our control group) let's continue to do what we do now in terms of preventing and suppressing gang activity, which is to say let's employ prevention haphazardly and use typical suppression tactics. In Community 2 (our first experimental group) let's allow the police to employ the tough-on-crime and Broken Windows approaches that have recently gained favour. And in Community 3 (our second experimental group) let's employ the model I advocate here: a balanced crime-fighting, prevention and intervention model led by community businesses, schools, parents, faith communities and police. Each community would be allocated the same budget and an independent evaluation team composed of social sciences experts. Let the experiment run for, say, ten years, and then measure the difference.

Regrettably, my ideal experiment will never occur, because people find ethical dilemmas in these kinds of human experiments. Heated criticism would centre on how we would be neglecting one community, treating its citizens as nothing more than a guinea pig control group, while others would be receiving the attention they deserved to fight gangs. But this is the price we must be willing to pay if our goal is to learn how to curtail the growth of street gangs, a lesson that America's thirty-year, multibillion-dollar get-tough war on gangs has failed to produce. I fear that, without this kind of experiment—finally bringing reason and logic head-to-head against emotion and supposition—we may never learn how to immunize our society against street gangs.

Experiments aside, gang prevention ultimately starts with all of us. The well-known West African proverb, "It takes a village to raise a child," has particular relevance when we address gangs, so we ought to ask ourselves what kind of future we want our children to have. And we must take steps now to ensure their safety by focusing on community-based street-gang prevention every bit as much as we focus on police-based street-gang suppression.

9: HOW TO STARVE GANGS OF OXYGEN

Drug Legalization and the Reduction of Street Gangs

Anecdotally and statistically, street gangs and the sale of illicit drugs are inextricably bound together. Where you find gangs, you will invariably find drugs. The vast majority of the violence directly and indirectly associated with street gangs in North America—the kind of violence that sometimes spills over into the general population—is directly attributable to the drug trade. So too is the bulk of criminal justice system expenses associated with street gangs—many hundreds of millions of dollars—directly attributable to the drug trade.

With regard to why youth become involved with gangs, I consider that there are both "push" and "pull" factors at play. For many gang-involved youth, a combination of socio-economic conditions and dismal family circumstances is often responsible for their push towards a gang. At the same time, the profits that might be made from the drug trade are a pull factor that entices them to become, and to stay, a gangster. The push and pull factors together conspire to create new Canadian street gangsters, so it makes sense to address both if we are to get a handle on this growing problem.

By and large, street gangs are not selling drugs to themselves. They are selling to Canadians who are not involved in gangs—millions of them (you know who you are!). Let's be clear about this: through drug purchases, Canadians are directly supporting the criminal underworld and contributing to the violence and degradation that the drug trade invariably produces. This is a statement of pure and simple economics—*if you buy dope from a gang, you prolong its existence.* So if you consume illicit drugs and you are concerned about street gangs in your community or worry that your son may someday join one or that your daughter may become one of its whores, the most important thing you can do is stop consuming. Today. Period. Don't contribute to their economic livelihood.

The problem is, we all know that this is not going to happen anytime soon, and more likely never will. All kinds of people around the world, hundreds of millions of them, have enjoyed and will continue to enjoy consuming illicit drugs. Despite million-dollar government prevention programs, stringent laws, parental admonitions, societal scorn, unsavoury gangster salesmen, dubiously doctored substances, hellhole prison sentences, the knowledge that we are supporting criminals, and the risk of debilitating addiction, this behaviour will never change. Humans have demonstrated from time immemorial a desire to escape from consciousness and slip into a mind-altered state by drinking, swallowing, snorting, injecting, smoking and inserting drugs. We also demonstrate a taste for the illicit, as is often the case with anything prohibited by the state.

With attention and interest growing on the issue of street gangs in Canada, I believe we need to engage in debate about our national drug policy, which I would say has failed miserably. Check out the disconnect between our country's drug policy and the prevalence of use. We have spent untold billions over the past two decades on attempts to control drugs and discourage their use—from the National Drug Policy to government prevention programs, the RCMP's DARE and police, court and corrections costs, among others—yet consumption has increased. The United States boasts one of the most punitive and expensive drug policies in the free world; its estimated cost is about $40 billion per year. America's much vaunted war on drugs, like a rerun of Prohibition, has failed too, filling its jails with more than two million people—half of them for drug crimes and most of them black and Hispanic Americans—and in the process creating more than 700,000 street gangsters. Yet per capita drug consumption remains high. Such is the futility of attempting to deal with drugs by focusing on the supply chain while ignoring the unstoppable momentum of demand.

Simply put, state-enforced prohibition of products that millions of people demonstrate a taste for does not work, and cannot work. We have proof of this from a perverse real-world experiment, but conveniently we choose not to remember it. Alcohol prohibition in the United States from 1920 to 1933 (and the temperance movement before it) was an utter failure. Not only did Prohibition fail to prevent the consumption of alcohol, it led to black-market production of dangerous unregulated and untaxed alcohol, the development of organized crime, massive political and police corruption, and constant violence.

Risking the scorn of my many police friends who work tirelessly to control drugs and educate young people about their dangers (sorry, Mark and Louise), I believe it is time we began the process of legalization for certain drugs. This notion is anathema to most people, I know. But as part of an effective approach to reducing gang activity and its associated violence (along with targeted suppression and prevention, among other things), we need to cut off the oxygen supply of gangs: the money they make, or try to make, from the drug trade. The push reasons why youth join gangs will continue into the foreseeable future, of course. But if we neutralize the most important pull factor by creating an environment of legalized drugs, the absence of potential riches from the drug trade will render the street-gang risk–reward balance unattractive for many at-risk youth.

I could write an entire book on this subject, but what I want to do in this brief chapter is seed the debate and provide my philosophic, scientific, economic and common-sense rationale for why we must look at the issue of drug reform if we are to keep our children safe from gangs.

SHOULD THE GOVERNMENT PROTECT US FROM HARM?

We can't engage in debate about drug legalization, of course, without addressing morality. The core question that vexes many of us is this: should the state protect its citizens from harming themselves? If you believe in drug prohibition, you will likely answer in the affirmative. However, the government is our servant, not our master, and it does not have the right to meddle in our private activities unless we are harming others. In this regard, words from John Stuart Mill's famous essay "On Liberty"(1859) have particular meaning:

> The only purpose for which power can be rightfully exercised over any member of a civilised community, against his will, is to prevent harm to others. His own good, either physical or moral, is not a sufficient warrant. He cannot rightfully be compelled to do or forbear because it will be better for him to do so, because it will make him happier, because, in the opinions of others, to do so would be wise, or even right. These are good reasons for remonstrating with him, or reasoning with him, or persuading him, or entreating him, but not for compelling him, or visiting him with any evil in case he do otherwise. Over himself, over his own body and mind, the individual is sovereign.

When it comes to drugs, our government simultaneously protects us from harm and throws us to the wolves, and we have become in a sense complacent about really hazardous substances. We are unfortunately—perhaps forever—stuck on a subjective plane of right versus wrong, and the facts get lost in the heat of the argument.

Consider the drug alcohol. According to the Canadian Addictions Survey, alcohol was consumed by 79.4 percent of Canadians over the age of fifteen in the previous year, and 44 percent reported weekly use. One in ten current drinkers reported that their drinking has caused harm to themselves or their social relationships, and almost a third of respondents reported that someone else's drinking had caused them harm. In 2002 Statistics Canada estimated that 641,000 Canadians had symptoms of alcohol dependence, but only 194,000 had symptoms of illicit drug dependence. In a 2001 Centre for Addiction and Mental Health study, researchers demonstrated that alcohol is a major contributor to mortality in Canada. Specifically, 6 percent of all deaths under the age of seventy, 4,010 deaths in total, were attributable to alcohol, representing a total of 144,143 years of life lost prematurely in 2001.

Consider another drug, nicotine. Health Canada says that forty-five thousand Canadians die each year of smoking, which is roughly *five times* the number of deaths caused by car accidents, suicides, drug abuse, murders and AIDS combined. What a ridiculous paradox it is that we ban substances that cause minimal harm (like cannabis), yet approve of those that produce such devastating consequences. Surely, if personal harm, death, destruction, ruined relationships and lost human potential were laudable things to avoid, we would immediately prohibit cigarettes and alcohol. Yet we let people consume these products, subject to certain controls, and we tax their consumption so we can afford to repair the consequences that inevitably arise.

Let's compare alcohol and marijuana on the basis of the harm the two substances cause. One way we can do this is by calculating toxicity profiles for the two substances. This will help us understand how a substance that is tolerated—or even beneficial in small quantities—can have harmful effects at higher levels. The amount of a substance that produces a beneficial effect in 50 percent of a group of animals is called the median effective dose, while the quantity that produces mortality in 50 percent of a group of animals is termed the median lethal dose. This relationship can be expressed as a ratio. For example, a healthy seventy-kilogram adult may start to feel a glow from approximately 33 grams of ethyl alcohol, which roughly translates into two 12-ounce beers, two 5-ounce glasses of wine or two 1.5-ounce shots of 80-proof spirit. The median lethal dose for such an adult is approximately 330 grams, or ten times the median effective dose, taken within less than an hour on an empty stomach (sadly, plenty of people have died this way, and many more have come dangerously close). So the effective dose–lethal dose ratio for alcohol is 1:10.

Contrast this with cannabis. Try as I have, I cannot find a single documented case of cannabis overdose in Canada or elsewhere, despite the fact that much of the marijuana smoked today contains about three times more THC (the chemical the produces the high) than it did a couple of decades ago. Estimates vary, but some suggest that the effective dose–lethal dose ratio for cannabis is a whopping 1:1,000! In an editorial in the March 2004 edition of Rhode Island's *Providence Journal,* Dr. Joycelyn Elders, a former U.S. Surgeon General, wrote, "Unlike many of the drugs we prescribe every day, marijuana has never been proven to cause a fatal overdose." A November 2002 *Time* magazine cover story stated, "No one has ever died of THC poisoning, mostly because a 160-lb. person would have to smoke roughly 900 joints in a sitting to reach a lethal dose." Surely, if alcohol were a new substance being introduced to the market today, it would quickly become—because of its toxicity, addictive characteristics and downstream damage (for instance, nasty drunks who drive)—a prohibited substance. Drinking in moderation is socially acceptable and broadly promoted, but through its consumption we allow many people to harm themselves and others.

When you engage in debate with your friends on this subject, you invariably get the same question: "So where do you draw the line? What drugs would you legalize?" It's a vexing question and we need to assess it carefully, using sound information, not just opinion. A drug's toxicity is an important factor. Heroin and GHB, at a ratio of less than 1:10, are more toxic than alcohol, while ecstasy (MDMA) and cocaine (1:20) and mescaline and Rohypnol (1:20 to 1:80) are not, so perhaps these should be considered as other drugs that could be legalized. Lethal dose ratios are but one consideration, however. A drug's capture ratio—the proportion of people who after their first exposure become physiologically or psychologically addicted—is another important factor. Heroin and methamphetamine purportedly top the list, followed by alcohol, nicotine and cocaine, then marijuana. So perhaps we need to fold these numbers into the mix along with other factors such as side effects, metabolization rates, pharmacological actions, extent of cognitive impairment, effects of routes of administration, effects of repetitive consumption and distribution of use.

In my opinion, many health professionals and government bureaucrats have pulled the wool over our eyes as far as the effects of drugs are concerned. You've heard the claims: marijuana reduces your intelligence; meth will drive you into a rage; cocaine will make your heart explode. Like alcohol and nicotine, these substances have harmful pharmacological effects, but some of what we hear may be the product of anecdote rather than good science. As important, the pharmacological effects described rarely take into consideration one of the most disastrous effects of prohibition: lack of purity. When you pour yourself a two-ounce "dose" of Johnnie Walker Black anywhere in the world, you know precisely what you are consuming: a consistently pure 80-proof Scotch. But the more restricted a drug is, the less pure it becomes on the street as dealers step on it more and more to make their desired return. When someone snorts some coke, all bets are off in terms of what's in it. At best it contains 20 to 30 percent cocaine, along with unknown quantities of lidocaine, procaine, talcum powder, dextrose and who knows what else. The same holds true for heroin: its street purity has ranged from 7 to 30 percent in the past two decades and it is sometimes cut with strychnine (yes, rat poison), making it impossible for the user to know whether or how much to consume. So what kills smack addicts? It could be the drug, the rat poison or their desire to get more bang for the buck from their illicit, artificially expensive drug purchase by injecting it, leading to HIV or hepatitis from a dirty syringe.

Back to the question I posed earlier: where do we draw the line regarding drug legalization? We can—and should—make policy decisions based on good science, rather than on speculation and puritanical morality. In my opinion, there is no logical reason why cannabis should be a prohibited substance. Its immediate legalization would help reduce gang rivalries and serve to productively reallocate the resources of the criminal justice system. Through the process of cannabis legalization, and the tax revenue derived from it, we could increase funding for drug-related health-care services and establish effective prevention and harm-reduction programs. Depending on the outcome of this policy shift, we could consider legalizing other drugs so that we could attain the financial benefits of the drug trade instead of just the costs. Through this process, and with the community-based street-gang prevention initiatives outlined in Chapter 8, we will see a decline in the prevalence and violence of street gangs.

DOES CANNABIS LEAD TO OTHER DRUGS?

The notion that consuming cannabis leads to use of other, harder drugs, such as cocaine and heroin, is known as the stepping-stone hypothesis. Drug prohibition supporters say that cannabis is a gateway to other, allegedly more dangerous drugs. It is difficult to answer this question, though, by looking at Canadian consumption data, which predominantly reflects cannabis use and offers no reliable indicators as to whether use of one drug leads to another.

In the absence of a controlled experiment, we can look to the example set by the city of Amsterdam. Decriminalization of cannabis started in the early seventies, when youth clubs were allowed to have their own house dealers. According to a 1996 report from the Centre for Drug Research at the University of Amsterdam, cannabis use increased from 23 percent of the survey population from their first study in 1987 to about 29 percent by 1990, then stabilized at that level through to 1995. While cannabis use was generally associated with other drug use (largely cocaine and ecstasy, not meth or heroin), the majority of cannabis users (more than 75 percent) did not report other drug use. Researchers tested the stepping-stone hypothesis several different ways and concluded that "the use of cannabis satisfies almost all curiosity [about drugs]."[37] While many of us think of drug users as "junkies" devastated by their habit, if that were the case, we would have millions of Canadian addicts. But we don't, and most illicit drug users, particularly those who occasionally use drugs recreationally, are employed, productive and not significantly impaired. These drug users are no more addicts than all drinkers are alcoholics.

THE BENEFITS OF DRUG REFORM

Health arguments aside, the biggest problem with drug prohibition is that we as a society incur massive financial costs associated with drug use. This includes addiction, disease and deaths resulting from overdoses or impure products. In addition we also pay the costs related to prevention, policing and corrections. However, we reap none of the massive financial benefits—the money made from the sale of drugs; they are reserved for the drug cartels, organized crime syndicates and street gangs. Rather than pay these costs from the taxpayers' pockets, why not impose a "sin tax" to be paid by the people who choose to consume legal, controlled drugs?

In 2005 the largest alcohol retailer in the world, the Liquor Control Board of Ontario (LCBO), remitted almost $3 billion to the federal and provincial governments in the form of realty, excise, licensing and sales taxes, in addition to more than $1 billion in dividends from its highly profitable business. A "Drug Control Board of Ontario" would likely do the same, producing untold financial dividends that could be used to pay for education, prevention, harm reduction, enforcement of laws prohibiting sales to minors, and negative health impacts—money that today goes into the hands of criminals.

In his Fraser Institute paper, "Marijuana Growth in British Columbia," Professor Stephen T. Easton of Simon Fraser University attempted to compute the value of the illegal B.C. marijuana grow-op industry, which he pegged at around $2 billion per year, or upwards of 2.8 percent of the provincial GDP of $130 billion. According to Easton, we could institute a tax on marijuana cigarettes equal to the difference between the prevailing production cost and the current street price (which he computed at the time to be $1.60 and $8.60 respectively). In other words, if we transferred the revenue from current producers and marketers (criminals) to the government, we could generate revenue of approximately $7 per joint, giving the government some $2 billion a year in new revenue just from existing domestic consumption, and more if we included possible export taxes and savings in the criminal justice system. Two billion dollars is significant tax revenue, and it would go a long way towards addressing the problems associated with drugs, problems that we would incur anyway, given our present robust consumption.

Repealing drug prohibition would achieve this and more. Product quality could be assured, with concentrations clearly indicated, reducing chances of accidental overdose and poisoning. Police resources could be redeployed to more productive activities (such as community policing programs) and gang-related violence would be considerably reduced, as would the promise of wealth that fuels gangs of every description.

Moreover, the incentive for young, at-risk people to hustle black-market drugs would disappear, perhaps encouraging them to pursue legitimate employment. Ask yourself this simple question. How would street gangs survive if their primary economic engine—the drug trade—largely disappeared? What would they do with their time? Of course, with a legal market for certain drugs, criminals would pursue other illegal ventures (the market for illicit drugs, after all, grew after Prohibition). And if the government taxed drugs too aggressively a black market would be created, as we see from time to time with cigarettes. But I can think of no other product or economic opportunity on Earth that could possibly produce as much in the way of crime proceeds as the present drug trade.

The only sensible way to deal with drugs is to create, through legalization of certain drugs, social conditions that allow for their safe, controlled, informed and moderate consumption, free from the rapacious influence of criminal organizations. I have argued, both philosophically and pragmatically, that drug prohibition violates our civil liberties and has been a costly failure. I challenge the advocates of prohibition to present hard evidence that it does more good than harm. I don't think for a minute that legalization will eliminate the drug problem any more than prohibition has. But legalization can go a long way to solving what Dr. Helen Nowlis, former director of the U.S. Alcohol and Drug Abuse Program, termed the "drug problem problem"—to me that means gangsterism and its associated street crime—and puncturing the belief that we can combat drug use through our strained criminal justice system. By eliminating the powerful pull influence of the drug trade and addressing the root causes of street gangsterism, Canada can become an international leader in gang prevention, and future generations of children will be safe from criminals looking to recruit them as street-level drug sales reps.

10: IT BEGINS AT HOME

Keeping Children Safe from Street Gangs

Street gangs and their members are here to stay. They will remain an ever-present feature of Canadian life despite the best efforts of police to suppress them, of courts to punish them and of communities to prevent them. The many forces that have conspired to create a street-gang problem in Canada over the past two decades or so continue unabated, and current trends in public policy suggest that the problem will only be exacerbated. I can project a doubling or tripling of street-gang membership in the next ten to twenty years, with a disproportionate amount of growth coming from the young Aboriginal community. Street gangs will become more broadly distributed across the country and they will become increasingly violent. In their constant quest for power and prestige, which is perhaps achieved most readily through sheer numbers, they will expand their recruitment efforts towards young people of all description, including those whom we would not now consider at risk of gang involvement. Since neither poor inner-city youth from immigrant families nor undereducated youth from Native reserves hold a monopoly on street gangsterism, all youth are to varying degrees at risk of being pulled into the thug life in some manner, and that could include members of your own family.

It may come as a surprise to some parents, but many young people today have been exposed to gangsters or the gangster lifestyle in some way. Ask a group of Grade 5 or 6 students in an urban public school whether they know a gangster, have seen a handgun, have been offered drugs for sale or have witnessed some form of gang violence, and you may be shocked to hear a majority answer in the affirmative. For many youth the presence of gangs or gang members in schools, malls and other public places is commonplace, a regrettable part of being young in the early twenty-first century. This fact should give parents cause for concern.

I contend that the gulf between awareness of gangsters and their activities and actually participating in those activities is not all that wide, and is becoming easier for youth to reconcile and justify.

I believe parents are the first and most important line of defence in preventing their child's participation in a street gang. No child is born a gangster; rather, he or she is shaped into one through a confluence of many factors to which they are exposed over a dozen-plus years. Street gangs and their breed of violence are indeed a major societal issue, and they are not just someone else's problem. The police, the courts, the education system, the business community, the government and the social service sector all have a role to play in preventing and suppressing street-gang activity. However, parents—or, more properly, families—hold the key as far as stemming the growth of street gangs.

It would be neither prudent nor practical to scare parents into taking drastic action insofar as their children and street gangs are concerned. Your chances of serious injury or death are far higher from driving a car, for instance, than from daily life in the possible presence of gangs. But that doesn't mean we should become complacent, throwing caution to the wind as if gangs did not exist. Maintaining a state of vigilance is important, and you, as a family, must critically assess the threat posed by street gangs and take common-sense action that suits the possible (or actual) risk. This chapter is specifically for parents who want to do whatever is humanly possible to keep their children safe from the dangers inherent in the street gang.

I must admit that I enter this territory with uncharacteristic trepidation. I am not, never have been and never intend to become a certified parent educator (yes, there is such a designation). There are plenty of bright lights, including Barbara Coloroso, Samantha Wilson, Dr. Karyn Gordon and Beverley Cathcart-Ross, among many others in North America, whose sage counsel can help you navigate the countless pitfalls of parenting. However, I take comfort in my deeply held belief that you need not be a certified parenting expert to be an effective parent. So much about parenting, after all, is common sense. I believe that my value in this discussion is rooted in my strong understanding of street gangs, including the underlying psychology of what leads a young person to join a street gang, and in a practical approach culled from other experts who have gone before me.

A FOCUS ON MORAL EDUCATION

As I indicated in the previous chapter, numerous risk factors contribute to and influence anti-social youth behaviour, including their participation in street gangs. Some of these risk factors are within your and your child's control, while others—the state of the economy, societal permissiveness of gang activity, the presence of gangs in your community, the extent of police presence in your neighbourhood—are not. It seems reasonable, then, that if you desire to ensure your child's safety and well-being, you should focus on mitigating the risk factors that are within your sphere of influence and on enhancing the countervailing protective factors that create a strong character to help steer your child away from gang participation.

First, and foremost, your behaviour, attitudes and demonstrated moral values as a parent are both crucial risk and protective factors as far as future gang involvement is concerned. Few would dispute that children learn morality mainly from people to whom they are emotionally attached, mostly by relying on their parents as role models. Parents who are gang-involved or otherwise engaged in criminal activity that is known to their children, or who express tolerance for criminal activities or the gangster lifestyle, are sending a powerful message of acceptance, if not permission, to their children. Especially for the first four or five years of your child's life, when you are the principal and sometimes the sole socializing influence, what you do, what you say and how you act are crucial in steering your child down the right path in life.

Children pay more attention to what an adult does than to what he or she merely says. As noted child psychologist Nancy Eisenberg wrote in *The Caring Child,* "socializers who preach . . . but do not model . . . may have little positive effect on children's prosocial development." In this respect, Ralph Waldo Emerson's "Who you are speaks so loudly I cannot hear what you say" has particular relevance. It helps explain the phenomenon of intergenerational gang involvement that is a growing problem in some countries such as the United States, and in the Hispanic community in particular, where the adoption of the *cholo* lifestyle means two and sometimes three generations of gangsters from the same family are actively represented in a gang set. Your actions and attitudes as a father, especially if you have a son, are extremely important, since so much of male adolescent development consists less of talking and more of modelling actions and behaviours. Like father, like son, as they say.

The odds are that the vast majority of you are not involved in criminal activity, so this parental behaviour risk factor is not really an issue. However, the absence of a risk factor does not mean that your job is done. You can help insulate your child from danger by building resilience and prosocial attitudes in your child—in other words, focusing on protective factors—especially through a strong system of values and morals. Frankly, we are not doing a particularly good job of this in many respects. Everywhere I go across the country discussing gangs and the reasons for their formation, I hear a diversity of opinions, many of which I have already summarized. My take on the root causes of gang activity is that it is socio-economics combined with ineffective parenting—specifically, a lack of emphasis on fundamental values.

The family, being our society's most basic and important building block, possesses what I believe are the two fundamental ingredients for children to learn morality and character: caring emotional attachments and prosocial behavioural counsel. With emotional attachment to their parents or caregivers, especially bonds formed in the crucial first five or six years of their lives, children readily learn right from wrong. As noted child development expert Willard W. Hartup has concluded, "A child's effectiveness in dealing with the social world emerges largely from experience in close relationships."[38] But, of course, attachment is not enough to ensure moral development. Prosocial attitudes must purposely be taught, modelled, reinforced and continually demonstrated through the actions of loving parents and caregivers. Honesty, empathy, co-operation, self-reliance, hard work, discipline, respect for racial diversity, self-responsibility, persistence, patience, forgiveness, dignity, humility, and respect for authority and social order are first learned within the sphere of the family. If taught, modelled and reinforced by engaged, moral and physically present parents and other family members, these traits will be transferred beyond the family to the child's future dealings with society at large.

In a perfect world all children would live in a two-parent family that engaged in regular activities, shared routines and traditions, and spent lots of time together. This nuclear family would be supported by members of the extended family, who would share the joys of family life and provide support to Mom and Dad. Absent the threat of marital breakup, and having achieved financial stability, such a family would create the ideal conditions for children to thrive and develop as morally robust human beings and one day go on to share this family legacy with their own children.

You could, rightfully, criticize me for describing the make-believe family life of the Cleavers of *Leave It to Beaver* fame, but I certainly don't underestimate either the challenge of raising moral children or the massive changes that have taken place in the structure of the family over the past four or five decades. Approximately 45 percent of Canadian marriages end in divorce. According to 2001 Statistics Canada data, there are more than 1.3 million lone-parent families in Canada, 80 percent of which are headed by women. Together those families are home to more than two million children. The effects of societal changes with respect to same-sex marriage and adoption (long overdue, I might add) are also challenging our notion of what defines a family. And there is a growing income disparity in Canada; the economic pressures are such that many parents, overburdened with debt and the financial responsibilities of raising a family in our culture of "affluenza," are working longer and longer hours, depriving their children of the emotional attachment and availability that is so essential in rooting moral values.

Sorry to be a contrarian, but the above excuses are baloney. Moral children are raised in both rich and poor families; they are raised in single-parent and dual-parent families; they are raised in families with heterosexual and with homosexual parents; they are raised in both visible minority and white families. They are raised in *all* families: the specific characteristics of a family are secondary to the attitudes within it. Some of the most respected gang experts I know will say that the decline in the traditional nuclear family is the source of gang growth, pointing especially to the absence of prosocial fathers. While I don't deny that this may be a risk factor that explains why many young men (and it is mostly men) choose the gang path, I believe this rationale misses the point. Differences in family conditions abound, but the common thread among families that produce moral children is a commitment to family, whatever its composition, and a clear commitment to teaching and modelling moral values.

Here are my questions to you, then, and to all parents: How much time do you actually spend on your child's moral education, and do you—*always and without fail*—model these behaviours in your own actions? I think that if parents seriously reflected on these questions and answered them honestly, most would say, "Not enough, I guess." We are in some respects purveyors of the "do as I say, not as I do" ethic. Brand me a heretic if you wish, but we adults are failing our children, and we adults are equally as responsible for the growth of gangs as the misguided youth who join them.

Having been a co-head of both, I am struck by the parallels between a successful corporation and a successful family. I surmise that most of you have been in the working world for at least ten or fifteen years. Many of you will have at some point participated in a corporate retreat, where executives rally the troops, engage in contrived team-building exercises and define compelling mission statements and ambitious codes of ethics. Once defined, the mission statement and ethics code are focus-tested among the rank and file and even outsiders, are massaged repeatedly and, once a consensus is reached, promulgated to all by the CEO, with the message that these are the behaviours to which all must subscribe. While I cringe at the thought of participating in another retreat, they do serve a purpose in helping define a moral compass of sorts for corporations and the people who work for them.

But how many families do the same? Does your family have a mission statement or other defining purpose, a unifying theme other than to just get by in this world? Have you defined a code of ethics, a set of moral absolutes that the family must follow? If so, are these morals discussed frequently and acted upon to model appropriate behaviour? Are there defined consequences for when the moral code is not honoured, even by the parents, and are the consequences enforced? Whether these moral codes are written down or are family oral tradition, do you and your young charges have a clear definition of the "rules of the family"? If you ask your children, "What does our family fundamentally stand for?" will you get blank stares and a "C'mon, Mom, this is stupid" response, or a concise answer rooted in morality? If you were to ask these questions privately of a hundred parents, you would get maybe one or two answering in the affirmative. This is shocking to me. We spend lots of time helping write down corporate mission statements, the weekly grocery shopping list and even family vacation itineraries, but we give little time and attention to defining, modelling and reinforcing the bedrock moral values that are, without a doubt, most crucial in protecting our children from the disaster that is the street gang.

As a resource guide on moral education, I recommend a book by billionaire philanthropist and "dean of global investing" Sir John Templeton, who in 1997 wrote *Worldwide Laws of Life,* which changed the way I view the teaching of morality. I had the pleasure of interviewing Sir John in September 2000 in his office in the Bahamas. I was struck by the easy grace, charm, honesty and humility of the man, then eighty-nine years old, who had sold his company in 1982 for more than $900 million, most of which he later gave away to his foundation. His book is a compilation of two hundred laws of life: wisdom drawn from the major sacred scriptures of the world and various schools of philosophical thought, as well as from scientists, artists, historians and other leading minds. Simply written at a high-school level, the book is divided into forty sections of five chapters each, approximately matching the average number of school days in a year. Each chapter contains a law written in the form of a quotation and includes both the source of the law and a one- or two-page discussion. Templeton's idea is bold but logical: *Worldwide Laws of Life* can be used by educators (or parents) to teach young people one universal law of life each day of their school year, so that their moral foundation can be assured.

What I learned from Sir John, and what we all would be wise to heed, is the notion that morality should be taught and discussed every day, especially when children are young, just as we do for other skills such as reading and arithmetic. If offered the choice between a prosocial role model teaching my child principle-centred morals and differential calculus or French, I would take the morality education every time, because that will equip her with the skills she needs to navigate an increasingly challenging world.

PRACTICE MAKES PERFECT

Moral education, however, is not enough to protect your child. There are gang-involved youth out there who were weaned on the Golden Rule by well-meaning parents, but they still could not withstand the pull of the street gang. Once a solid moral compass (knowledge) has been instilled, you must help your child test this new tool with actual practice (experience). This will result in a genuine sense of confidence that your child is capable of meeting life's challenges and enjoying happiness (belief, or self-esteem).

Knowledge, experience and belief will inevitably coalesce to develop competency in any human endeavour. I am a golf nut, so let me draw upon this fine sport for an example. You can read detailed instructions in *Golf Digest* about how to drive a perfect Tiger Woods two-iron "stinger" off the tee, but until you hit the range and practise the shot thousands and thousands of times, stimulating your body's adaptation process and building muscle memory, your competency will be all in your head, that is, knowledge only. But even a successful adaptation process gained through extensive practice is not enough to produce good results. If you step up to the first tee block with your buddies watching, and you have no confidence that you can hit the shot or not enough self-esteem to withstand your pals' trash talk if you spray it into the trees, you are probably destined for failure. The same thing applies to morality and the prosocial behaviours that we deem right and good for success in life: knowledge + experience + belief = success.

Let's discuss the experience element first. Perhaps the best way you can exercise your child's moral muscles is through active life-skills development, sometimes referred to in child development circles as "Skillstreaming." Its leading practitioners are Dr. Arnold P. Goldstein and Dr. Ellen McGinnis of the United States, who co-authored the book *Skillstreaming the Elementary School Child: New Strategies and Perspectives for Teaching Prosocial Skills* (add it to your reading list). Skillstreaming has its roots in both psychology and education. Its processes focus on four direct principles of instruction—modelling, role-playing, feedback and transfer—and have been used to teach a variety of behaviours ranging from academic competencies to sports, daily living skills, vocational skills and prosocial behaviours. The Skillstreaming model makes the assumption that the learner lacks or is weak in a behavioural skill, and the goal is to teach desirable skills by engaging youth in active learning through role-playing, practice and discussion.

Let me give you an example. One of the most important skills you can teach a child is how to deal with group pressure, which has particular significance in the street-gang dynamic, where individual wishes are subjugated to the goals of the collective. Young people seeking acceptance sometimes have difficulty distinguishing between true acceptance and being used, and they must learn how to protect themselves by short-circuiting situations that involve group pressure to participate in an anti-social activity (a gang crime, joyriding or shoplifting, for example). According to the Skillstreaming method, the facilitator (you, the parent) should address this important skill by using the following process.

1. Define the skill and its importance in a brief discussion with your child.
2. Model the skill, perhaps with another child or your spouse or significant other.
3. Establish the need for the skill by asking your child where/how/why he or she thinks the skill might come in handy in the future.
4. Role-play the skill with your child. For instance, set up a scenario in which you, as the leader of a group, ask your child to participate in a joyride.
5. Provide performance feedback in regard to the role play, and repeat if necessary.
6. Finally, discuss what was learned and even assign "homework," which for young children could be as simple as telling them to report back to you when they encounter a group pressure situation (at school, for example) and how they successfully dealt with it.

Most parents are unaccustomed to teaching their children life skills in this manner, and the Skillstreaming process at first glance seems artificial and contrived. Well, get over it. Most learning situations are contrived and are designed to manipulate (in a good way) people towards skills mastery. Hitting a thousand golf balls at the driving range is contrived; reciting the seven times table is contrived; practising guitar chords until your fingertips are calloused is contrived. But if you want to ensure the greatest protection for your children as they grow older, you need to begin thinking about formalizing the process of their life-skills development rather than simply relying on others to do it, for example, schoolteachers who are already burdened by the responsibility of teaching the government curriculum.

I have witnessed—and actually measured—the power of this approach in my professional life. Back in 1999 several leading crime-prevention specialists from the Ottawa Police Service and the acclaimed Ottawa Police Youth Centre created a crime-prevention demonstration program and sought funding for it from the National Crime Prevention

Centre. Louise Logue, Mark Houldsworth, Claude Turgeon, Tom Patrick and others employed by the Ottawa police conceived Project Early Intervention. It proposed a comprehensive curriculum of life-skills development initiatives (using the Skillstreaming approach) in addition to supportive sports and recreation programs that would, in part, provide scope for using the new skills. It was to be offered to youth aged six through twelve in the troubled Ottawa community of Banff–Ledbury. The community was chosen for its low income, high proportion of social housing units, history of frequent calls for police service and predominant population of large, at-risk families, many of whom were immigrants and refugees from countries such as Ethiopia, Afghanistan, Iraq and Somalia. After several months of negotiation the group obtained a $900,000 three-year grant to operate this experiment in crime prevention through social development. The goal was to demonstrate whether the proposed solution actually reduced crime and improved the social functioning of youth, and whether it could be readily exported to other communities across the country as a means of reducing youth crime and victimization.

Back then the NCPC, chaired by former Toronto mayor Barbara Hall, made significant and meaningful crime-prevention investments, and it had the foresight to tie the grant to a rigorous evaluation protocol that had to be conducted by an independent third party. That's where I came in. Having previously evaluated the Police Youth Centre and authored a guidebook for other Ontario police agencies on how to establish similar youth programs, I was selected by the Ottawa police to act as program evaluator. I created an evaluation protocol that included process, outcome and cost-effectiveness components. Since the NCPC wanted proof, not just anecdotes, that the life-skills development program actually improved the social functioning of youth (they already had ample evidence that sports and recreation programs help youth), the outcome evaluation component was particularly rigorous. It included internationally recognized standardized instruments, which program facilitators, schoolteachers and parents would complete at regular intervals (before, during and after the program), that measured the behavioural characteristics of the children participating. We even incorporated a random control group by placing half the participants on a waiting list, where they had access only to sports and recreation programs, until they could be admitted several months later to the life-skills program. By measuring their social functioning during each phase we could determine which programs produced the greatest gains in terms of attitude and behaviours.

I won't bore you with all the arcane details, but the results were quite impressive. Starved for attention and lacking community programs and positive role models, the group of 250-plus young people showed strong improvements in their social functioning and behaviours from participating in all aspects of the program (the life-skills components plus the sports and recreation programs). The data demonstrated that for many youth these improvements continued well after the program ended, as if the lessons learned had taken root and really blossomed. The younger segment of children (aged six to nine) made materially greater gains relative to their ten-through-twelve-year-old counterparts, with no demonstrable differences between boys and girls. Of special note, the control group strategy allowed us to determine that the life-skills component, relative to the sports and recreation programs, was responsible for the largest share of the gains.

School performance improved, police calls for service declined and parents and teachers alike offered anecdotal evidence that the children in the program were simply better behaved. My experience with Project Early Intervention is dear to me because it confirmed what I and others who have worked with at-risk youth knew all along: life-skills education, supported by sports and recreation programs that provide a positive outlet for youthful energies and a "proving ground" for the skills they have learned (honesty, fair play, humility, respect for the rules and for one another), builds resilience to the many pressures of life.

CONFIDENCE IS KEY

A third ingredient—belief, or self-esteem—must also be instilled in your children to give them the confidence to believe they can succeed and be happy in life. Genuine self-esteem is characterized by tolerance and respect for others, self-responsibility, integrity, self-respect, self-motivation, self-pride, the ability to be loving and lovable and the ability to assume risks and deal constructively with failure, among other things. We have all met people with low self-esteem, which manifests itself in different ways. For some it is low confidence and an openly dim view of their abilities, worth and social acceptability ("I can't do it"; "I'm worthless"; "No one likes me"). For others, low self-esteem is more sinisterly expressed in arrogance, aggressiveness, contempt for others and using people for their own gain. For still others, low self-esteem is expressed somewhere in the middle, by being defensive, impressing others with possessions, exaggerated accomplishments or name-dropping, or through blaming others or external circumstances for personal difficulties or shortcomings. While it is difficult to prove statistically through traditional experimental methods, researchers have documented a connection between low self-esteem and bullying (both physical and verbal), truancy, substance abuse, suicide, violence and poor academic performance. I should note also that authentic self-esteem must not be confused with arrogance, an air of superiority, conceit, narcissism or egotism—so-called pseudo self-esteem characteristics that research shows are linked to violence and juvenile delinquency.

As you can see by the characteristics of self-esteem, a solid grounding in morality and life-skills education are inextricably bound to its development. In some respects self-esteem can be thought of as the natural by-product of these two childhood development strategies, but you can give your children the protection of self-esteem by being a loving, positive, involved, sensitive and mature parent, especially by demonstrating high self-esteem yourself (again, modelling is key).

Here is a list of just a few of the many things you can do to raise children with high self-esteem who are capable of withstanding the many pressures that will be placed upon them as they grow up.

- Tell your children they are loved and appreciated for who they are.
- Celebrate their genuine achievements and successes and keep mementoes of their successes and life milestones.
- Show love and respect by spending time with your children in activities they enjoy.
- Demonstrate and encourage your children to have a healthy respect for failure. Rather than allow them to perceive failure as a setback or the result of personal deficiency, show them how failure is perhaps life's best teacher.
- Teach your children to set and manage goals.
- Reward your children when they demonstrate mastery of the values you have instilled in them.
- Give your children opportunities to contribute meaningfully to the work of the family, such as regular chores that earn them an allowance.

- Teach your children how to engage honestly in self-appraisal, which they can employ when they perform any task.
- Become involved in their school and social life.
- Children, especially young children, thrive when the family has special rituals.
- Help develop your children's problem-solving abilities by encouraging them to deal with adversity with your support.
- Tell your children that you believe in them, even when they make mistakes, and that they have the ability to accomplish anything they set their minds to.
- Encourage your children to offer their advice and opinions on family matters.

Once established when your child is young, self-esteem generally remains stable over time, but it can vary during different life phases, especially adolescence, when one leaves childhood and begins the journey into adulthood. You may need to be particularly supportive of your child and his or her self-esteem at this time, which you can do by applying some of the tips listed above. You should also be aware of other influences in your child's life and whether they augment or detract from self-esteem. Unfortunately, many people outside the family—teachers, other youth, coaches—don't "get" how to cultivate great self-esteem in young people. You can do everything possible to create strong self-esteem in your children, but all those lessons can be nullified by, for example, amateur sports coaches who believe in using criticism, belittlement and embarrassment to stimulate performance.

MANAGING THE EARLY ADOLESCENT YEARS

Much of what has been written for parents about youth and street gangs is overly simplified and won't help you much if your child has not been properly prepared through morals and life-skills education and practice. Search the Web for tips about gangs for parents and you'll come across many bullet-point lists that essentially read like this:

- Spend time with your child.
- Preach good study habits.
- Prohibit your child from wearing gang-related clothing.

- Review the lyrics of the music your child listens to.
- Take a parenting class.
- Listen to your child.
- Get your children involved in prosocial sports and recreation programs.
- Know where your child is going when he or she is out.
- Introduce your child to a police officer.
- Set rules and enforce consequences.
- Lecture your children on the dangers of gangs and prisons.
- Meet your child's friends.

I would never suggest that any item on the above list is inappropriate parenting practice, but without the protection of morals and prosocial life skills, many of these parenting tips will achieve little. Take the issue of your child's friends. As far as gang involvement and other risky behaviours are concerned, including alcohol consumption, drug use and early sexual activity, your children's friends really do matter. It is a popular misconception that, as children grow into adolescence, the influence of parents greatly diminishes while the influence of peers takes pre-eminence. In my opinion, parental influence can remain essentially the same, but peer influence does indeed increase, introducing complications into the parent–child relationship.

A consistent finding from research on gangs, as well as on delinquency in general, is the significant influence of peers on adolescent behaviour. Studies that have compared stable youth to gang-involved youth show that the strongest predictors or risk factors associated with sustained gang affiliation were a high level of interaction with anti-social peers and a low level of interaction with prosocial peers. A national research project in the United States that involved almost two thousand adolescents and was funded by several major research institutes showed that, for most risky adolescent behaviours, young people were about twice as likely to engage in a risk behaviour if a friend participated in the activity at the same time or had at some time in the past.[39] Perhaps as important, the same study indicated that peer influence was both harmful and protective for many risk behaviours—that is, youth will go along with those who do *not* engage in risky behaviours as readily as they will with youth who do partake in risky behaviours (of which street-gang participation is most assuredly one).

So what happens when you discover that your child has fallen in with the wrong crowd, say, gang-involved youth? What do you do? You can lecture him about the dangers of gangs. You can use the stick approach and ground him so he'll smarten up, or you can use the carrot and motivate him to change his behaviour through positive reinforcement. You can remove him from the situation by transferring him to a different school, hoping that will provide the necessary distance from the negative peer influence. You can issue a blanket prohibition, although it is debatable how well prohibitions of any sort really work. You can do a host of other things, such as speak to a trouble-making friend's parents, confront the friend, consult the local police or even report your child to them—or throw the kitchen sink at the problem and employ all of these strategies.

What works in this situation will undoubtedly depend on your circumstances and the type of child you have. For some families nothing will work and the child will progress through the gang ranks until he (or she) dies, is incarcerated or leaves of his own volition. However, I contend that if your child is grounded by good morals and life skills, ones that you have taught, modelled, reinforced, practised and tested since his early years, you have a much better chance of effecting a successful turnaround than if you have not done those things. When you are confronted with this situation, the discussion you have with your child need not be a judgmental rant about the quality of his friends or his decision-making—a tack that is sure to raise the ire of your child because he will surely feel obliged to defend his peers and himself, even at the expense of family harmony. Rather, it will be a discussion based on the morals and life skills that you have instilled in him and that your family has embraced since his birth. It will be a discussion about right and wrong, honesty and discipline, integrity and pride, self-reliance and personal control, empathy and respect for social order. Keeping the discussion on this foundational plane helps keep the temperature down, because the emotional issues of specific people and personalities never enter the fray.

I also think strident lectures about the dangers of gangs are an utter waste of time, especially those based on an underlying "scared straight" message. Young people don't like being preached to any more than you or I do, and since it is unlikely that you were ever involved in a gang, they will naturally consider you a biased and uninformed source of information about the topic (even after reading this book). Regrettably, the idea persists that youth can be deterred from crime by scaring them early and often. In a triumph of public relations over sound science, the scared-straight approach stems from a 1970s program of the same name that originated in a New Jersey maximum-security prison, Rahway. Featuring confrontational, in-your-face and often brutal presentations by inmates known as "the lifers" depicting a life behind bars of rape, murder, gang violence and constant brutality, the program brought seventeen delinquent youth into the prison in an attempt to deter them from crime—to scare them straight. An award-winning documentary called *Scared Straight!* came out in 1979, and over the next two decades advocates of the program offered bountiful anecdotes about how effective the program was in keeping youth on the straight and narrow. After the documentary aired, so enamoured were people with the program that it spread to dozens of cities around the United States and elsewhere, resulting in many thousands of at-risk youth (delinquent and otherwise) ending up face-to-face with tattooed convicts educating them on life behind bars.

There is little proof that the scared-straight approach works. A 1999 documentary, *Scared Straight!: Twenty Years Later,* presented no data on a comparison or control group, so we have no basis on which to judge the differential impact of the program. Indeed, various randomized tests of scared-straight programs (in which a random selection of youth take the program and a random sample do not) have shown these approaches to have very little statistically significant effect on their participants. Some of these studies even demonstrated that program participants were more likely to be arrested! Having reviewed dozens of similar studies over the years, my conclusion is that youth-focused deterrence-oriented programs produce few results, except what many adults crave and cling to: a cheap, short-term and deceptively elegant fix to an extremely difficult social problem. So if youth can't be intimidated by hardcore convicts inside a prison hellhole, your lectures about the dangers of gang life will surely fall on deaf ears.

In contrast to strident lectures delivered when it is often too late, I advocate an early "social marketing" approach to child education about serious issues such as gangs. Author Philip Kotler, in his book *Social Marketing: Improving the Quality of Life,* defines social marketing as the use of marketing principles and techniques to influence a target audience to voluntarily accept, reject, modify or abandon a behaviour for the benefit of individuals, groups or society as a whole. Examples of social marketing include the anti-smoking, safe-sex and drunk-driving campaigns organized by government and social service agencies across the country. While some are much more successful than others, they can have a tremendous impact in shaping young people's behaviours. Most of us don't think twice about warning our children about the dangers of smoking, drugs, alcohol, sexual predators, unsafe sex and dropping out of school, but we don't talk much about the dangers of gangs—in fairness, maybe because they have only recently entered the broader collective consciousness. We will likely have to wait a long time before government or social service agency street-gang prevention programs hit the airwaves, but when children are young, parents can play a part in laying down a realistic, fact-based picture of the dangers of gang life, hopefully using some of the information presented in this book.

Although some believe that awareness of gangs at an early age will only make young people more interested in them (a criticism of the GREAT program), I think that kids as young as six can understand the rudiments of this issue, if you use age-appropriate language and context, and can be taught to view street gangs and their participants with the suspicion and scorn they deserve. Just as my daughter believes that smoking cigarettes will threaten her life (which she values because she has high self-esteem), so too does she believe that street gangs can do the same. I am no more equipped to educate her in this than you are, despite my professional background. It is just common-sense information, grounded in a parent's belief that even very young children are capable of distinguishing right from wrong.

ASSESSING ATTITUDES ABOUT GANGS

I am not so naive as to believe that if you do all these things well, you and your family will somehow be immunized from the impact of street gangs. While you may do everything in your power to build your child's resistance to gangs, you cannot control all the other risk factors that are acting upon him or her outside your family. Street gangs are an elusive enemy, lurking in the shadows like ninjas, and they represent a constant threat to the welfare of your child. This is why you must regularly assess the risk posed by street gangs so that corrective actions can be employed.

A good place to begin this assessment is by having frank, non-judgmental discussions with your children from time to time. Chances are that even the average ten- or twelve-year-old has had some exposure to gangs, their members and their direct or peripheral activities, perhaps at school, the mall or social functions such as parties. Wherever young people congregate, gangsters will troll for possible members, drug sales and, indeed, the opportunity to create a nuisance (their version of sport). Engaging your kids in a discussion about gangs could be fruitful in assessing the danger and, of course, their attitude to gangs. Don't be surprised if your children are remarkably casual about gangs. A "no big deal" attitude should not be construed as acceptance of or support for gangs; it could reflect that they are becoming desensitized to them because of their regular presence in their lives.

Ask them if they know any gangsters. Have they been courted by gangsters to join the gang? Have they ever been to a party organized by a gang? What is their perception of gangs and the gangster lifestyle? Do they understand why other youth join gangs? Have they ever been threatened by gangsters? Have they ever considered actually joining a gang, and why—for money, for protection, for friendship, for other reasons?

I think the biggest mistake parents make when discussing the pitfalls of adolescence generally, and the impact of gangs specifically, is that they don't listen very well. We have heard it all before and we know what our kids think, right? We all make assumptions about how young people feel and what they know, but we often fail to remember that as kids grow up they develop their own ideas and opinions, which may have merit, even if they are contrary to our own. A meaningful dialogue demands that you listen to what your kids say and don't let your feelings block out what you are hearing. Often when we are faced with a difficult and potentially dangerous situation such as gangs, our protective streak kicks in and we begin to lecture and cajole. This only serves to alienate your children and shut them up, because they no longer feel that you value what they are saying or are considering their point of view.

More information about the possibility of gangs affecting your child can be gleaned from their school setting. Public schools are no longer a bastion of safety. Teachers are very much on the front lines of the war against gangs, and many no doubt have taught gang-involved youth. Speak to your kids' teachers to get an assessment of what is really going on. If your school has one, consult with the school resource officer, a member of your local police service whose job it is to counsel youth, defuse school tensions and otherwise help establish productive relationships between youth and the police service.

HOW DO YOU KNOW IF YOUR CHILD IS IN A GANG?

You must simply watch for signs of gang involvement. As a parent you may have done everything possible to protect your child from gangs, but they may elect to join one anyway, for a host of reasons such as economics, protection or camaraderie. Remaining vigilant to the signs of gang involvement is important, as early detection may help you embark on some corrective actions to convince your child he is headed down the wrong path. In this regard, I offer a few general guiding principles.

As noted earlier, for the vast majority of new gangsters their entrance to the gang rarely occurs suddenly or overnight—it's evolutionary rather than revolutionary. Thus you need to watch for warning signs of possible gang involvement early and often, as children may be exposed to the pull of gangs at a very young age. Evidence is growing that some street gangs are targeting children, including girls, as young as eight or nine for membership or other forms of participation (acting as sentries during crimes or holding drugs, for instance). By the time your child is a teenager—the typical age when a youth becomes involved in a gang—it may simply be too late, as the precursor influences are likely exercised well before then.

The following are some commonly reported warning signs of gang involvement by a young person. They are neither all-encompassing nor actual proof of gang involvement, so I caution parents to be extremely careful when judging on the basis of this list. Parents are urged to look for multiple signs indicating possible gang involvement, because some of these indicators taken alone, or even in small combinations, may mean very little.

- Change in type of friends, from whom your child may wish to keep you at a distance. Also look for situations in which your child begins to ignore long-standing previous friendships.
- Drawing gang symbols and using gang handwriting (usually graffiti-like, hard to decipher and characterized by crossed out and upside-down letters and gang symbols). Check school notebooks for evidence of such.

- Wearing jewellery with distinctive designs on the right or left side of the body only.
- Practising obscure hand signs or using hand signs to communicate with friends in public settings.
- Using strange language or slang.
- Changes of behaviour, including excessive secretiveness, defiance, aggressiveness and social withdrawal. Also look for out-of-the-ordinary defiance of authority figures, including parents and teachers.
- Behaviour, performance and truancy problems in school.
- Sudden interest in gangster-influenced culture such as gangsta rap, gangster movies and websites.
- Adopting the gangster style of dress, sometimes referred to as "sagging and bagging" (drooping oversized pants, bandanas, certain sports logos). Pay attention to use of a dominant colour in clothing (for example, youth associated with a Crip set will dress predominantly in blue, while Bloods wear red).
- Drug and alcohol abuse as well as possession of large quantities of marijuana, cocaine or ecstasy pills.
- Possession of unexplained cash or goods (stereo equipment, jewellery, automobiles), which may be the proceeds of theft or drug dealing.
- Physical injuries that your child is unwilling to explain to you or report to the police.
- Withdrawal from or change in attitude to favourite sports, recreation or social activities.
- Association with other youth who display some or all of these warning signs.
- New tattoos or brand marks of nicknames, gang signs, gang symbols or initials.
- Negative contacts with the police, which could include arrests or warnings/diversion referrals under the Youth Criminal Justice Act.
- Unusual fear of police, such as avoiding them in public settings.
- Possession of fake or real weapons, including guns, knives, extendos (telescoping metal batons) and homemade armaments.
- Staying out late beyond normal curfew.
- Change of hairstyle.

- Disclosure of gang membership.
- Confirmation of gang affiliation by friends, family members, educators or other witnesses.
- Missing valuable personal effects, perhaps sold to raise money for the gang or buy drugs or firearms.
- Use or possession of gang codes and ciphers, languages unto themselves that gangs use to protect sensitive information.
- Unusually territorial or protective attitude towards community, school or bedroom.
- Reluctance to go to school, perhaps indicating rival gang tensions or unpaid drug debts.
- Excessive use of codes and seemingly nonsensical acronyms in MSN or BlackBerry messages.
- Heavy use of cell phone and/or pager.
- Adoption of a new nickname: look out for names that are either very menacing or imply violence ("Crazy," "Psycho," "Shooter") or that contradict some attribute of your child (for example, "Shorty" to describe a tall young man).
- Brief late-night visits or phone calls to your home from other youth or adults, which may indicate drug dealing and possible gang involvement.

WHAT TO DO IF YOUR CHILD IS IN A GANG

All this leads to one question: What do you do if you suspect your child is involved in a gang? First, prepare for a challenge, because once they have been exposed to that combination of power, prestige, economic potential, protection and camaraderie, it can be quite magnetic. Even so, all is not lost. If you suspect that your child is involved with a gang, you must have a frank discussion with him or her. Present your concerns, listen to what he has to say, and make it clear that you love and support him. Ask good questions about why and listen—really listen—also watching his body language. You must, however, make it clear that the behaviour is unacceptable, that it is likely illegal and that it must stop. You'll have to convince your child that gang behaviour is unacceptable, as he or she will tend to minimize the potential danger or rationalize why the gang formed in the first place.

The most precarious part of this process is determining consequences for your child. If you elect to go the severe sanction route (loss of privileges, grounding, curfew), it may exacerbate the situation and drive your child deeper into the gang culture, especially since the gang may have become to him or her a new, less restrictive "family." I recommend a balanced approach consisting of some form of sanction that is meaningful to your child, combined with other strategies such as counselling and perhaps even peer support from a former gang-involved youth (your local police service, high school or probation office may be able to help with this). I would also present the facts—the "business case" against gangs, as it were—stressing such things as death rates and the fact that for many youth, leaving a gang comes with very few consequences, which is probably contrary to your child's "blood in, blood out" belief.

As with any confirmed anti-social or risky behaviour—illicit drug use, alcoholism, bullying—addressing these issues with children who are trying to find their way is never an easy task. I think that patience is key for a parent. Yes, your child is at some risk of injury, death or incarceration as a result of gang membership. Her decision to join a gang was likely formed over a period of time, so it is not reasonable to think that you can solve this problem with one big fire-and-brimstone conversation. Rather, you need to look to the issues that drove her decision to join, and address each of them in turn. If it was the need for camaraderie, help her find a prosocial group that can provide her with that; if it was money, help her find a prosocial business mentor or get the job skills she needs to succeed; if she is struggling at school, find an alternative school program that may better serve her needs; if it was for protection, work with the police, the schools, local politicians and other parents to reduce the overall level of violence in the community that is driving youth to gangs. The point is, gang membership is most always symptomatic of other problems that need to be addressed before a cure can possibly take hold.

Parents must be realistic and recognize that most kids screw up at some point, despite the love and counsel that have been bestowed upon them over the years. Think back over your own life. Perhaps you made stupid mistakes when you were growing up, and now you just want to shake your head, and ask yourself, "What the hell was I thinking?" Most of you probably didn't belong to a gang, but the odds are you did something that was contrary to your parents' wishes or to accepted societal norms, perhaps because you wanted to experience what it was like or because you allowed peer pressure or other factors to distort your otherwise sound reasoning.

I was brought up in a rather strict household and was taught right from wrong, but I made my share of stupid mistakes. At the age of twelve I beat up a kid on a dare from my schoolmates who were tired of his incessant practical jokes. At the age of fourteen, at a Friday night party, I got drunk as a skunk on rye whiskey in less than an hour and spent the rest of the evening throwing up, which my dad thought was punishment enough for my stupidity. At age seventeen, after a Major Junior A hockey game at Toronto's Maple Leaf Gardens, I drove two teammates home to Ottawa for our Christmas break while we consumed a case of beer in the car. I slid off the highway during a sleet storm while trying to insert a cassette in the tape player, crashing my ugly brown Buick into a rock cut. Thankfully, no one was injured and I didn't blow over 0.08 on the roadside Breathalyzer. My parents had never preached or modelled physical violence, had never advocated underage drinking and had never suggested it was okay to drink and drive, but—silly me—I just had to find out through experience that my actions, which seemed reasonable at the time, were just plain stupid. Marva Collins once wrote, "If you can't make a mistake, you can't make anything," and those youthful indiscretions ultimately made me a better, more responsible person.

Behaviourally speaking, perhaps it is simply part of the human condition to make the same mistakes over and over again, despite the often painful lessons learned by our forebears. When we review the great arc of technological and scientific progress over the past five hundred or so years, its scale and scope are breathtaking and sometimes overwhelming. Gutenberg's press, X-ray technology, genetics, Newton's laws of motion, the discovery of micro-organisms, nuclear fission, space travel, the microcomputer, modern medicine, electricity, the internal combustion engine—the list goes on and on. Such progress is very much cumulative in nature: each innovator stands on the shoulders of giants, informed by previous mistakes made and lessons learned, and advancements are therefore assured. But progress in human behaviour displays a much less dramatic progression, one that is at best incremental in nature. Sure, we have progressed as a species in the past five hundred years, but many of the challenges we faced five hundred years ago—war, poverty, racial strife, hunger, disease, violent crime—we still face today, despite the massive advances humans have made in other domains.

On a smaller scale, you no doubt see this in your family. You probably made the same mistakes as your father or mother did, and now you may be seeing the same mistakes being repeated by your child, despite your sage counsel informed by actual experience. Try as you might to change their path, young people, like their parents, are experiential creatures, and that may drive them to dip a toe in the waters of the street gang. All you can do is your best—teach them good morals, insulate them with as much protective self-esteem as possible, equip them with the life skills they need to navigate through an ever more tumultuous world, and work with others in the broader community to implement intelligent street-gang and youth-crime-prevention approaches. To you parents, and indeed to all Canadians, I wish you all the best in your own fight, whatever form it takes, against the scourge of street gangs.

ACKNOWLEDGEMENTS

Unquestionably, the journey of researching and writing *Young Thugs* has been wonderful. No author works in a vacuum, and I must pay homage to the many people who saw the merit of my ideas and helped make my passage from aspiring to published author a smooth one.

It has been my great honour to have as my editor Jim Gifford, whose keen interest in this subject and commitment to the expression of new ideas helped burnish my manuscript. I am grateful also to production editor Nita Pronovost and to copy editor Gillian Watts, who helped polish, trim and strengthen the text considerably. I am deeply indebted to HarperCollins Canada's fine leaders, David Kent and Iris Tupholme, who have always made me feel part of their family. Also thanks to other members of the HarperCollins team, including Rob Firing, Eric Jensen, Lindsey Lowy, Alan Jones and especially Barbara Bower, whose enthusiasm for telling others about *Young Thugs* knows no bounds.

From the moment he received my book proposal, my literary agent Rick Broadhead demonstrated great commitment to me and my project, and in a matter of weeks put me in front of the who's who in the Canadian book publishing industry. Thanks, Rick—your ability, creativity and discipline never cease to amaze me. For leading me to Rick in the first place and helping me avoid the often challenging process of gaining the ear of very busy literary agents, I must pay special thanks to Erica Ehm.

I must recognize the many people who took time from their hectic schedules to contribute their insights on our street-gang situation, especially: Louise Logue, Tony Moreno, Marc Pinault, Vince Bevan, John Medeiros, Patty Lowell, Jack Ewatski, Heinz Kuck, Keith McKasgill, Rick Dobban, Michelle Charette, Stu Auty, Dan Wiseman, Mike McIntyre, Jim Owen, Barry Ward and "Steve." Special thanks to Isora Van Dresser, who shared with me the heartbreaking story of the murder of her boyfriend, Philippe Haiart. *Meegwetch* to Larry Morrissette—thanks, Larry, for showing me your community and for doing all that you do, with great personal sacrifice, to turn around troubled young lives.

I would be remiss if I did not express my appreciation to the many people who allowed me into their world of at-risk youth, beginning more than ten years ago at the Ottawa Police Youth Centre. These people include Claude Turgeon, Tom Patrick, Mark Houldsworth and Shamus Hall. My personal gratitude also goes to my assistant Virginia McBride and to Dr. Leslie Landecker, one of our country's finest ophthalmologists; thanks, Doc, for keeping my eyes healthy and respecting my time by seeing me right away.

Last, but certainly not least, my greatest obligation is to my wife and soulmate, Robin, who inspired me to finally become the author I knew I was born to be. Robin has been a partner in the book in every respect; she stayed up late into many nights and arose early many mornings to read and edit my work with great dedication; she challenged my thinking with many "what if's" and well-timed newspaper clippings. She took care of our lives, and our daughter's as well, when my mind and body were elsewhere. For the sake of *Young Thugs*, she gave me the freedom to be totally consumed by this most important journey—a gift for which I will always be indebted.

NOTES

Statistics about street gangs in Canada are derived from the *2002 Canadian Police Survey on Youth Gangs*, published by the Government of Canada. Unless otherwise noted, Canadian statistics related to the economy, immigration and personal income are derived from Statistics Canada. Statistics about the incidence of crime in the United States are drawn from the Federal Bureau of Investigation's *Uniform Crime Reports* and the United States Census Bureau, while data on American street gangs is derived from the U.S. Department of Justice's National Youth Gang Center and from interviews with American street-gang experts.

1: INNOCENCE LOST

1. R. Sheldon, S. Tracy and W. Brown, *Youth Gangs in American Society*, 3rd Edition, Belmont, CA: Thomson Wadsworth, 2003.
2. Soon after the completion of the survey, a member of the Winnipeg Police Service retracted this original estimate, which was issued in error, and provided a new estimate of 2,000 youth-gang members. This new estimate, therefore, made Winnipeg in 2002 the city with the largest number of youth-gang members and the highest per capita concentration at 2.98.
3. Frederic Thrasher, *The Gang: A Study of 1,313 Gangs in Chicago*, University of Chicago Press, 1927, p. 268.
4. Ibid, p. 230.
5. Citizenship and Immigration Canada, *Facts and Figures 2005.*
6. Statistics Canada, 2001 Census Analysis Series, *Shaping the Nation's Workforce.*
7. Ibid, pp. 30–31.

8. Canadian Council of Social Development, *Who Gets In*, April 2004.
9. Statistics Canada, *Income Inequality and Low Income in Canada: An International Perspective.*
10. Standing Senate Committee on Aboriginal People, *Urban Aboriginal Youth.*
11. Statistics Canada, 1999 Survey of Financial Security.

2: GANGSTA GIRLS

12. The names of Sylvain Leduc's female cousins have been changed to protect their identities. Because of the threat of retaliation by Ace Crew gang members if they testified in court, the two girls were placed under a witness protection program. This was the first time in Canadian history that young offenders were placed under such protection.
13. This unnamed gang member was under the age of eighteen. She was also placed under a witness protection program to secure her testimony and therefore cannot be named.
14. CPIC (Canadian Police Information Centre) is a computerized information system that provides all Canadian law-enforcement agencies with information on crimes and criminals. CPIC is operated by the RCMP under the stewardship of National Police Services, on behalf of the Canadian law-enforcement community.
15. A popular slang term for a police officer, derived from the 1968 to 1980 television police drama *Hawaii Five-O. Hawaii Five-O* revolves around a fictional state police force of the same name, in honour of Hawaii's status as the fiftieth U.S. state.
16. Statistics Canada, *Family Violence in Canada: A Statistical Profile*, 2005.
17. D. Pepler and F. Sedighdeilami, *Aggressive Girls in Canada*, Human Resources Development Canada, 1998.
18. Statistics Canada, 2001 census.
19. The Pareto principle, named after economist Vilfredo Pareto, states that, for many phenomena, 80 percent of the consequences stem from 20 percent of the causes.

3: UNCLE SAM

20. Of all U.S. street gangs, Mara Salvatrucha, or MS-13, is considered one of the best organized and most violent. My police sources

suggest that MS-13 members, with connections to other MS-13 members in California, Mexico and their homeland, El Salvador, are establishing MS-13 gang sets in Canada. By late 2006, MS-13 gang sets were thought to exist in Toronto and Vancouver.

21. Commissioner of Firearms, 2004 Report, Canada Firearms Centre.
22. Intratec subsequently redesigned the basic design slightly, dropping some "assault" features, like the threaded barrel, barrel shroud and forward pistol grip. In this post-ban version the pistol was manufactured and sold as AB-10 (AB stands for "After Ban"). The AB-10 pistols were sold with ten-round magazines, but still could accept both factory and after-market high-capacity magazines from its predecessors, TEC-9 and DC-9.

5: SHOW ME THE MONEY

23. According to the 2003 RCMP report, *Vancouver Drug Use Epidemiology*, a chemical analysis conducted of drugs seized at raves between September 2001 and June 2002 showed that what most people purchased as ecstasy was actually a combination of all sorts of chemicals. Only 24 percent of tablets and 11 percent of capsules contained pure ecstasy. The most common ingredients mixed in were methamphetamine, caffeine, codeine, Dextromethorphan, ephedrine and the cat tranquilizer ketamine.
24. This estimate is from the United Nations Office of Drug Control and Crime Prevention.
25. United Nations Drug Control Programme, *Amphetamine-Type Stimulants: A Global Review.*

6: ON THE FRONT LINES

26. George L. Kelling and James Q. Wilson, "Broken Windows," *The Atlantic Monthly*, 1982.
27. George Kelling and Catherine M. Coles, *Fixing Broken Windows: Restoring Order and Reducing Crimes in Our Cities*, Touchstone, 1996.
28. Bob Herbert, "A Winning Strategy," *New York Times*, March 7, 2002.
29. According to the *2002 Canadian Police Survey on Youth Gangs*, approximately 35 percent of Canadian police agencies have a dedicated gang unit.
30. While estimates vary, there are anywhere between 40,000 and 150,000

gangsters in the Los Angeles County area, which boasts a population of approximately 10 million.

7: GLADIATOR SCHOOL

31. "Steve" is a pseudonym, used to protect the identity of this gang member.
32. Today, if a prisoner refuses their sanction, guards are not permitted to do cell extractions. Rather, they must contact an Emergency Response Team, composed of several anonymous officers dressed entirely in black and specially trained to do extractions.
33. Estimates, from a number of sources, peg the rate of HIV infection within Canadian prisons to be ten times the rate in society.

8: STEMMING THE TIDE

34. Irvin Waller and Daniel Sansfaçon, *Investing Wisely in Crime Prevention: International Experiences*, September 2000, International Centre for the Prevention of Crime.
35. I evaluated this program in 1997 on behalf of Health Canada. Developed by Manifest Communications of Toronto, the program was successful in getting major corporate commitments in the fight against HIV/AIDS, including from such firms as Molson Breweries, Aldo Shoes and Glaxo Wellcome.
36. G. Robinson, J. Conry and R. Conry, "Clinical Profile and Prevalence of Fetal Alcohol Syndrome in an Isolated Community in British Columbia," 1987, *Canadian Medical Association Journal*, 1987.

9: HOW TO STARVE GANGS OF OXYGEN

37. Peter Cohen and Arjan Sas, *Cannabis Use, A Stepping Stone to Other Drugs?: The Case of Amsterdam*, Amsterdam: University of Amsterdam, 1997.

10: IT BEGINS AT HOME

38. Willard W. Hartup, "Social Relationships and their Developmental Significance." *American Psychologist*, 1989.
39. The ADD Health Project, National Institute of Child Health and Human Development.

INDEX

Page numbers in **boldface** refer to illustrations and material discussed in charts and maps.